Atlas of Travel and Tourism Development

Atlas of Travel and Tourism Development

Myra Shackley

AMSTERDAM • BOSTON • HEIDELBERG • LONDON • NEW YORK • OXFORD
PARIS • SAN DIEGO • SAN FRANCISCO • SINGAPORE • SYDNEY • TOKYO
Butterworth-Heinemann is an imprint of Elsevier

Butterworth-Heinemann is an imprint of Elsevier
Linacre House, Jordan Hill, Oxford OX2 8DP, UK
30 Corporate Drive, Suite 400, Burlington, MA 01803, USA

First edition 2006

British Library Cataloguing in Publication Data
A catalogue record for this book is available from the British Library

Library of Congress Cataloging-in-Publication Data
A catalog record for this book is available from the Library of Congress

ISBN–13: 978-0-7506-6348-9
ISBN–10: 0-7506-6348-0

For information on all Elsevier Butterworth-Heinemann Publications
visit our website at http://www.books.elsevier.com

Printed and bound in The Netherlands
06 07 08 09 10 10 9 8 7 6 5 4 3 2 1

Working together to grow
libraries in developing countries

www.elsevier.com | www.bookaid.org | www.sabre.org

ELSEVIER   BOOK AID International   Sabre Foundation

Contents

Plates

Maps

The geography of travel and tourism as it is taught today is destination-focused, with students able to avail themselves of excellent textbooks which examine the geography of demand and present a balanced view of destination development. However, in the writer's view insufficient attention is paid to the historical factors that underpin destination development. With a very few exceptions, little has been published that explores tourism's history. Indeed, this is usually consigned to a small portion of the introductory chapter in tourism textbooks, and even there the development of travel and tourism in the ancient world is skimmed over in favour of more detailed analysis of the period following the development of the jumbo jet and the package holiday in the 1970s. And yet the early history of tourism is fascinating; all the elements of the modern package tour were in place in the Bay of Naples by 50 BC, for example. The history of tourism as a leisure activity goes back well before the classical civilizations of Greece and Rome. Egyptians participated in voyages of exploration and discovery in the fourth millennium BC. By the time that powerful Old Kingdom pharaohs such as Rameses II (probably the pharaoh of the biblical Exodus) reigned, the pyramids at Giza (p. 27) had been visitor attractions for a thousand years. The first tourist-related graffiti date back to 1244 BC (p. 26), the ancestor of modern Michelin guides was available to Roman tourists in Europe (p. 12), and merchant shipping crossing the Mediterranean carried passengers 2000 years earlier. There are few trends in modern tourism that cannot be paralleled several thousand years in the past.

The history of travel is, of course, as ancient as the history of humanity, but it would be reasonable to say that few significant developments in travel technology took place before the invention of the wheel around 3000 BC, although initially its benefits were geographically limited to the Near East. And yet entire complex societies, such as the Incas, managed without the wheel or the domesticated horse, as indeed many societies do today. Contemporary travel in parts of Asia and Africa, for example, is almost exclusively carried out on foot, just as travel in the Amazon Basin is carried out by water. Innovations in travel technology are only useful if the environment in which a culture is living is suitable for their use. Early sea-borne travel involved simple dug-out boats, and it is easy to chart their evolution through to the great clinker-built sailing boats of the Vikings, and indeed to the vast ocean liners of today. As with land-based travel, the need to travel was initially restricted to war, politics, economics and religion, and only in the modern world is it related to the pursuit of leisure.

The book has been divided on a regional basis, but the conventional global divisions of the World Tourism Organization have been massaged slightly, the better to fit in with the historical emphasis of the text. For example, since for most of recorded history the Middle East and North Africa were under the political control of a single sequence of empires, it made sense to consider them together. Most modern tours to Antarctica leave from ports in South America, making it logical to consider Antarctica in that chapter. The huge potential scope of the book has made it necessary to be selective, or else the result would have been an encyclopaedia. The reader may thus find that entire countries have been omitted, or only mentioned in passing. Nor has it been possible to allocate the same word length to all sub-regions. The work attempts to identify major trends, rather than to produce a blow-by-blow analysis of the historical geography of each country. Inevitably, this has meant that discussion of many topics is far more superficial than the writer would have wished. Many highly controversial issues are also treated far more briefly than they deserve, and in some cases it has been necessary to cut Gordian knots and suggest an opinion that not all readers will agree with. Where possible, this is supported by notes and references found in the back of the book and referenced in the text by superscript numbers. Such notes also refer the reader to the many general works which have been utilized as basic sources of facts for the book. A similarly cavalier approach has needed to be taken with some spellings, both of people and place-names. Consistency has been the aim here (even if not always achieved).

One of the book's underlying premises is that the development of tourism destinations is related to their history. In the post-colonial history of Africa, for example, there is a clear relationship between the nature of the colonial past and the tourism development of the present (and future). Travellers form destination images in a number of ways, including (very powerfully) from the mass media. The image that many travellers have of contemporary New Zealand is partly derived from the perception of high environmental quality, which has been visually shaped by the use of the spectacular New Zealand landscapes as the backdrop for some very successful films. Until recently, many visitors to the United States arrived with an image of place derived more from Hollywood than from preliminary reading. The book tries, where possible, to relate such factors to the historical development of different regions and destinations, and to knit these together within a framework of transport and travel history. This has sometimes involved value judgements, for which the writer would like to apologize in advance. But if this overview, albeit brief and superficial, gives its readers (and especially students of tourism) a better feeling for the chronological development of travel and tourism, to complement other works which examine its spatial distribution, its purpose will be achieved.

Myra Shackley

Acknowledgements

I am greatly indebted to Linda Dawes of Belvoir Cartographics and Design, who drew all the maps for this book, showing an almost uncanny ability to translate complex scribbles into cartographic reality. Thanks are also due to Francesca Ford of Butterworth-Heinemann, both for her patience and for her consistently helpful advice during the compilation process. All illustrations in the text are my own photographs.

Setting the scene

A glance at any textbook of travel and tourism will produce a summary of factors which affect individuals' propensity to travel and influence their destination awareness. Such a list would undoubtedly include available travel technology and support infrastructure, and the individual's disposable income, leisure time, level of educational achievement, and motivation. Many different methods and perspectives have been utilized to describe the components of tourism attractions/resources, including models and frameworks of tourism attraction systems which are often utilized by tourism planners and marketers to increase destination market values and competitiveness.[1] Such resources have commonly been evaluated in three ways: first, from an ideographic perspective related to the supply component of tourism products which lists those elements contributing most to destination attractiveness; secondly, from an organizational perspective which looks at their spatial and temporal linkages; and thirdly, from a cognitive perspective which examines issues of tourism demand. A full analysis of destination attractiveness and competitiveness requires a combination of such methods, considering those components of the tourism origin-destination system from both demand and supply sides. The environment of tourism destinations contains dynamic and static components which are interdependent, and also dependent upon the characteristics of the market, and which control overall destination attractiveness. Basic models of travel patterns[2] often distinguish 'push' factors (such as cultural, social and environmental pressures in the traveller's home country), which contribute to the desire and ability to travel, from 'pull' factors in the destination country, which determine the level of attractiveness to visitors. Destination awareness is created in the contemporary world by a number of factors, including the mass media, but is also conditioned by an individual's previous travel experiences and by the experiences recounted by family and friends.[3]

This book takes a historical perspective on destination awareness, looking at how that awareness has changed over time. Today's potential traveller has a virtually unlimited choice of destinations, with hardly anywhere in the world off limits. Even a basic Internet search can produce immense amounts of helpful information about potential travel destinations. But it is easy to forget that in the spectrum of human activity this is a VERY recent phenomenon indeed. Even ten years ago the Internet was only just coming commercially on line; twenty years ago the very idea was hardly conceivable. Fifty years ago the first computers were just being devised, while 500 years ago only a tiny fraction of the population would have been able to read, let alone to travel, with the very existence of the Americas and Africa only just being known to a favoured few Europeans and huge areas of the world still to be explored. The concept of travel-related literature as an aid to developing destination awareness is also very ancient. From at least the fourth century BC guidebooks to individual places and monuments existed, and between AD 160 and 180 Pausanias published his *Guidebook of Greece*,[4] intended as preparatory reading to assist travellers in planning their journey. Ancient books were handwritten on leather sheets or papyrus, and thus were too bulky and valuable to be carried around, but from such simple beginnings have developed the sophisticated and topical guidebooks of today – from which will undoubtedly develop travel guides in increasingly portable formats (easily downloaded onto iPod, PDA or laptop computer). Future travellers can envisage a world where new satellite technology and better geo-referencing enables them to be guided every step of their journey and provided with constantly updated information *en route*.[5]

Map 1.1 shows the immense variations in contemporary travel patterns on a global scale, emphasizing the dominance of Europe by measuring the percentage of global travel market share of incoming international travellers held by the different regions of the world which have been utilized in this book. To a certain extent, this is related to destination awareness and attractiveness. An individual's propensity to travel can be high, but it must be shaped by destination awareness and facilitated by the existence of appropriate technology. Historically, such awareness has been created by voyages of exploration and discovery, by the establishment of new trade routes to exotic areas of the world, and by encounters with new cultures and people in the context of pilgrimage or military activity. In prosaic terms, such

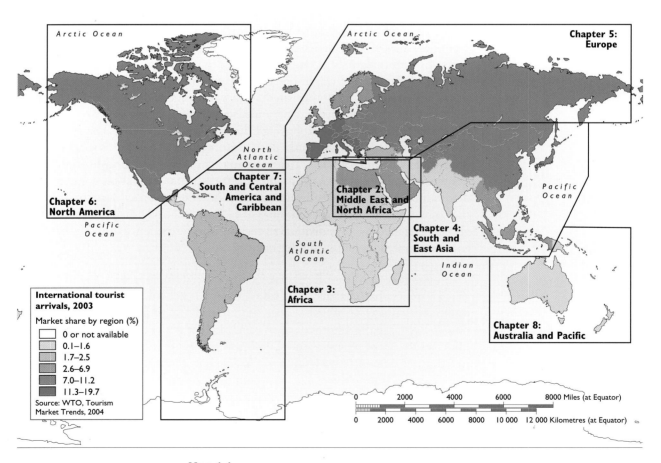

Map 1.1
International tourist arrivals 2003

contacts are reflected in new trade routes and colonialism. Such activities long pre-dated leisure travel and the idea of taking a holiday from one's daily work as a right, not a privilege. But leisure travel is not necessarily a prosaic business, and destination awareness is also created by the romantic myths and images derived from 500 years of European-driven travel and exploration, as well as by the visible remains of ancient cultures and empires, promising the adventurous traveller glimpses of ancient worlds. It is easy for us to forget in this information age the effect that 'traveller's tales' once had on those back home. A returning Crusader brought back to thirteenth century Europe stories of exotic people and places which shaped destination image for centuries to come. Two hundred years later, the Venetian merchant Marco Polo's tales of Kublai Khan's court in Cathay (China) were received with incredulity by Europeans' unaware of events happening elsewhere in the world. And in the ancient world it was often difficult for the recipients of traveller's tales to distinguish myth from fact. Travellers often embroidered their factual accounts with mythical lands containing strange people and stranger beasts. Even the Greek historian Herodotus, writing his classic fifth-century BC history of the Greek wars against the Persian Empire, elaborates his serious history with miscellaneous and sometimes fictitious travel information about Asia Minor, the Black Sea and Mediterranean islands.[6] But his work remains our best source for understanding the realities of early travel. Herodotus travelled as far as Egypt, sailing up the Nile to Thebes and the First Cataract, and giving us some idea of what the Egyptian, Greek and circum-Mediterranean world looked like in his time, yet he mixed scientific observation with tales and fables. But mankind has always had a fascination with the exotic, things outside our personal experience.

Travel history has created myths of its own; romantic and exotic destinations that appeal to the potential traveller, yet whose appeal may be based more on historic significance than contemporary visitor facilities. Sometime in the third century BC, an unknown scholar in Alexandria devised the concept of 'The Seven Wonders of the World' to give his successors an idea of what were the most significant (and frequently visited) tourist attractions of his time.[7] It is interesting to note that, in contrast to its equivalent today (the World Heritage List),[8] all the original canonically-accepted Wonders of the World were man-made, including the Pyramids, the Hanging Gardens of Babylon, Phidias' statue of Zeus at Olympia, the Temple of Artemis at Ephesus, the Mausoleum, the Colossus of Rhodes and the Lighthouse at Alexandria. Tourists in the classical world often wanted to see their country's traditional glories, but made no distinction between historical and mythical past. Nor do we necessarily do so today – legends such as the outlaw Robin Hood in Nottingham have generated entire tourism industries with no definite factual basis.[9] Tourists in the classical world of Greece and Rome went to see the graves of mythical heroes and heroines, including those of Achilles and Ajax at Troy, or visited the supposed house of the philosopher Socrates in Athens and the palace in Babylon where Alexander the Great died. Today's visitors go to the same kind of places, such as the memorials of great battles (including the two World Wars and the Vietnam War), just as classical visitors to Athens took excursions to the battlefield at Marathon, some twenty-two miles south of the city, where the Greeks won a spectacular victory over the Persians in the first Persian War. But today's visitors have a far wider choice, and their travels are facilitated by considerably better technology and the existence of a supporting travel infrastructure.

Travellers have always created destination myths. The city of Timbuktu (Mali) is a classic example – an icon of remoteness seen as a destination at the end of the known and explored world. Yet travellers who visit Timbuktu today (p. 51) are almost invariably disappointed by the crumbling mud buildings and dilapidation which are all that remain of a city that was once the heart of the medieval Islamic world. Similarly romantic images of place abound – such as Port of Spain in Trinidad, whose very name evokes pirates, rum and treasure ships. The mythical 'road to Mandalay' evokes the mystic East rather than the moral dilemmas involved in travel to modern Myanmar (p. 86), and Outer Mongolia has become an icon of remoteness rather than a central Asian backwater mainly attractive to ecotourists (p. 80). Sometimes these romantic images have been utilized in destination marketing – the WTO Silk Road project (p. 77) is a classic example, where the romance of the ancient trade route is being used to stimulate travel to central Asian countries, such as Uzbekistan, struggling to survive after the disintegration of the USSR (p. 76). The romance of ancient 'lost' cultures attracts visitors to remote areas from Machu Pichu (Peru) to Lhasa (Tibet) (p. 78), but relatively recent and current events also have their place in creating destination awareness. The Falkland Islands, for example, were virtually unknown as a travel destination until the UK–Argentina Falklands War of 1982, but now have a growing tourism industry. And one of the most fashionable contemporary travel motivators is nostalgia, whether for the remains of lost empires (both prehistoric and colonial) or the utilization of outmoded means of travel which contribute to the spirit of place, be they *feluccas* on the Nile (p. 28) or the Trans-Siberian Railway (p. 103). Destinations (such as spas) sometimes reinvent themselves to conform more closely to a historically conditioned image of place.

Destination awareness is also created by sport (an example here is the possibilities offered to any city that hosts the Olympic Games). Indeed, in ancient Greece, travel mobility began to increase when the first Olympic Games were held in 776 BC and it is recorded that visitors came to Mount Olympus from all over Europe and the Middle East.[10] Part of the ancestry of modern tourism can thus be traced back to ancient Greece, including problems resulting from the need to deal with large numbers of visitors in small spaces, such as the crowds at the Olympic Games, or even the beginnings of state support for the development of an Olympic accommodation industry. But recent events shape destination awareness too; an entire generation got to know the geography of South-East Asia after the Vietnam and Korean Wars in the 1960s and 1970s – knowledge later capitalized on by today's destination marketers. Some destinations have images derived from appearances in films, ranging from the media-created 'antebellum' plantation life of the USA southern states (as seen in *Gone with the Wind*),[11] to the spectacular landscapes of New Zealand utilized in the filming of Tolkien's *Lord of the Rings* trilogy.[12] Images can also be generated by the history of music, such as the relationships between jazz and New Orleans, Elvis and Memphis, Mozart and Salzburg. The first performances specifically for tourists were noted in Egypt by Herodotus, who commented on the fact that men from the nearby village of Busiris climbed the Pyramids of Giza to entertain visitors, and that tourists visiting the crocodiles at the temple of the god Suchus were expected to come armed with food for them.

The history of travel is inextricably related to the developing technology of travel, as well as to a host of political, cultural and social factors. Today's 'soft adventure' travellers,[13] who imagine that they are discovering brave new worlds, are the lineal descendants of the Victorian explorers who really were. And yet the achievements of the Victorian explorers in Africa, for example, pale into insignificance before those of the early Polynesians voyaging across the vastness of the Pacific with nothing except a large outrigger canoe and considerable expertise in navigation using natural phenomena (p. 164). Moreover, exploration is only useful in creating destination awareness if records are kept and shared; the first prehistoric explorations of Europe left no such records, with the result that the first European encounters with sophisticated cultures of southern and south-eastern Asia came as a considerable shock, since Europeans have always thought themselves at the forefront of 'civilization'. The idea that Europeans 'discovered' America is now realized to be ludicrous; exploratory migrations of people from Asia into parts of the North American continent took place 40 000 years ago, and were followed even in the post-Christian era by Viking voyagers, who unfortunately left only ambiguous records. The great technological advances which opened up the world to international travel include not only the wonders of the post-industrial revolution, such as the jet engine, but, far earlier and much more significantly, the domestication of the horse (and its eventual use as a draught animal), the domestication of the camel (permitting travel over previously inaccessible desert regions throughout the Middle East and North Africa), and the discovery of the wheel.[14]

Creating destination awareness

Accurate perception of the shape of our world is a very recent phenomenon. The Roman Empire marked the furthest extent of European knowledge of global geography until the sixteenth century, but despite its excellent internal communications network of roads it did not extend far into central Asia, or much beyond the Atlas Mountains in North Africa (p. 42). In the succeeding early medieval period, European awareness of even the boundaries that had been achieved by Rome had been lost. Alexander the Great, in the fourth century BC, was better informed about the geography of Asia than the average medieval European, meaning that the emergence of the Mongols from central Asia in the early thirteenth century came as a surprise. The narrowness of European experience meant that knowledge of Middle-Eastern and Islamic civilizations was rudimentary, until the Moorish conquest of southern Europe (p. 96). Europeans liked to think that their great voyages of exploration made from the fifteenth century onwards[15] were innovative when in practice they were travelling to places explored hundreds and sometimes thousands of years before (although without leaving documentary evidence). During the great Age of Exploration in the late nineteenth century, European culture was spread throughout the world, but its travellers were technically recorders, not explorers, because someone else actually got there first. The European explorers of the sixteenth century were generally motivated by the need to expand royal dominions, exploit new commodities or conquer new people rather than by any academic or scientific enquiry. That came later, with the scientists of the seventeenth century onwards gradually increasing the world's stock of knowledge about natural phenomena, later to be supplemented by the results of expeditions to Asia, Africa and the Americas which brought back new forms of life, generated the development of the sciences of botany and zoology and set the scene for modern science.[16] The propensity of European nations to acquire colonial possessions also generated curiosity and a desire to visit these new areas, and set the scene for many contemporary travel trends. In England, the Great Exhibition of 1851 presented to an astonished public an extraordinary collection of objects from the furthest reach of Britain's colonial empire, and stimulated unprecedented levels of public awareness of the shape and structure of the world.[17]

Today's special-interest travellers are merely continuing a process begun by the Egyptians who participated in the first known voyage of exploration in 3200 BC, and recorded it in hieroglyphic inscriptions.[18] A thousand years later we have a record of a named explorer, Harkhuf, who travelled up the Nile to Yam (in southern Nubia) around 2300 BC and left a record of his journey on his tomb at Aswan together with an account of the commodities he retrieved (a dancing dwarf, panthers, ebony and ivory), and which were presumably the economic motivation for his travels. Indeed, trade, military conquest and religion remained the principal motivators of travel until the sixteenth century, although some early accounts of leisure travel are available from the empire of Greece and Rome. With the Renaissance, Europeans established a dominance over other parts of the world that was to last for centuries, derived from the extraordinary voyages of exploration and discovery undertaken from the mid-fifteenth to the mid-sixteenth centuries, especially by the Spanish and Portuguese (p. 73). Portugal's search for direct access to the spices and luxury commodities of the East led to Vasco Da Gama's journey to India around the Cape of Good Hope (p. 48), and ultimately to the establishment of the boundaries of the world as we know it today. Although at least the northwestern and western fringes of Africa had been known from Roman times, only after the discovery of Americas were Europeans brought into contact with an entire continent that they had never known before, and whose very existence profoundly altered European consciousness. European royal courts and traders funded expeditions like those of Columbus (p. 140) or Cortés (p. 139) for commercial or political reasons, with their cultural and geographical discoveries often being incidental. In the history of exploration it is possible to discern a watershed between exploration motivated by greed and exploration motivated by scientific interest,[19] and this took place in the eighteenth century. Much later came the notion of travel as a way to appreciate natural beauty, which forms the boundary with the modern era of ecotourism, and a world full of professional travellers and travel writers whose voyages are prolifically documented. The Industrial Revolution of the nineteenth century had produced a prosperous middle class who had the time, intellectual inclination and money to travel, and who merely needed the travel infrastructure and destination awareness to be added to create modern mass tourism. However, in today's world many people travel to search for authenticity, seeking a 'pure' culture somehow untouched by mechanization, globalization or commoditization,[20] whose location has become the tourism equivalent of the Holy Grail and whose existence is equally improbable. Some people travel to find other people and others to find themselves, some for breaks from routine, others for educational reasons or to make the world a better place. But it was the early travellers who opened up the world for modern tourists, albeit for an entirely different set of motives. Today's travellers touch the remains of worlds that were 'discovered' (in the sense of being brought to European awareness) by *conquistadores*, missionaries, mountaineers, traders and empire builders. The great events of history set scenes in our mind and condition our tourist gaze,[21] whether these are the handshake between David Livingstone and Stanley, or Scott's doomed polar expedition.

As we have already seen, in the ancient world the main motivations for travel were mainly commercial, religious, political or military, although limited amounts of travel for pleasure had been evidenced from at least Greek times. There is no sharp junction between the periods dominated by travel and that dominated by 'tourism'. Indeed, the word 'tourism' did not actually appear in the English language until the early nineteenth century, when the idea of a 'tour' still implied a circular journey being made away from home, rather than its more contemporary meaning of any form of travel for leisure purposes. Most writers[22] on the history of tourism (as opposed to travel) distinguish three separate periods in its development. The first goes from its roots in early leisure travel, which we have already considered, right through the medieval and Renaissance world to a conventionally agreed date of 1840 (in Britain), which marks the start of the railway age – although of course this happened a lot later elsewhere in the world. A second period of tourism history (in Europe) involves the age of railways and the years between the two World Wars, which witnessed the development of the private motor car, bus and coach. After the Second World War, the private car became the dominant mode of transport in tourism and continuous advances in travel technology gave us increasingly sophisticated means of travel including jet aeroplanes, Concorde, high-speed electric trains, hovercraft, etc. One could also argue that the 1970s should be taken as a watershed in tourism history since they marked the development of the Boeing 747 jumbo jet, which ushered in an era of mass tourism based on all-inclusive package holidays and charter flights, initially to Mediterranean destinations and eventually throughout the world. But this chronology is only really applicable to western Europe and North America. Remote destinations in Asia, Africa and South America are still reached today on foot, by camel, cart or canoe, in exactly the same way that they have been for millennia, and only a very small proportion of the world's population has any form of access to international travel or its technology and infrastructure.

Travel in the ancient world

The earliest evidence for the history of travel (and tourism) is to be found in the Near East, with the focus moving towards the Greek world around 500 BC and to the Roman world between 300 BC and AD 300.[23] In the ancient and classical worlds short-distance travel was by foot (or using pack animals) whereas long-distance travel was, wherever possible, by sea, and it therefore follows that early travel had a pronounced focus on Mediterranean shipping routes and on the rivers of Mesopotamia and Egypt. The first boats were made from hollowed logs, rafts and skins, with early log-boats found in Europe dating back to 7000 BC. More advanced boats involved sewn or stitched planks, later replaced by pegged or riveted planks. The first sailing ships probably appeared in Egypt or Mesopotamia around 3500 BC, but were still relatively small with square sails, later replaced by triangular (lanteen) sails. It was not until the classical period that large merchant ships were constructed (there are Roman examples capable of taking 1000 tons of cargo), with ships of a similar size also evolving in China, but not until around AD 1000. The great ocean voyages of the Vikings used clinker-built boats (p. 96) up to thirty metres long. In the Nordic countries, the UK and North America, commercial wooden shipbuilding developed early and still continues today for recreational use. However, shipping changed for ever with the development of the first steam-driven ship in 1807, albeit with a wooden hull and paddles, and over the succeeding 150 years ships with steam or combustion engines would compete with sail, the last great sailing ships being in service in South America in the 1950s. During the nineteenth century iron and steel ships gradually took over from wooden ships, initially built using riveted steel but then with the welded steel hulls still in use today, as well as modern materials such as fibreglass.

The earliest beginnings of travel, tourism and exploration were confined to a relatively small geographical area on a global scale, and are related to cultural and political history and to the development of transport technology – a pattern that has set the model for all future developments up to the present day. Despite the sophisticated travel patterns of much of the developed world, and innovative travel technologies in global terms, the vast majority of the world's people still walk.

Within early farming cultures most people travelled only short distances, to reach market towns, local festivals and events. It was only after the rise of the urban-based Near-Eastern civilizations in the Tigris, Euphrates and Nile valleys that any systematic longer-distance travel patterns evolved at all, and these were related to business travel and the expanding and increasingly complex requirements of government and empire in these two regions.[24] Early trade routes were very local affairs, involving local or at the most sub-regional movement of goods, and before 3000 BC travel was limited to these three great rivers and the areas around the hills, valleys and coastal plains of Syria and Palestine. Around the Mediterranean considerable volumes of passenger traffic were carried in season by shipping, although during the winter passengers reverted to roads. For the next 5000 years, right up until 200 years ago, the most useful form of transport was the horse, and historically the one-man one-vehicle principle predominates. The multi-passenger vehicle is one of the ways in which the modern world differs structurally from its predecessors, although the development of the motor car has enabled us to return to the historical norm of individual transport. After 3000 BC shipwrights were able to design vessels that would go over open water, and thus establish a cargo trade across the eastern Mediterranean and the coastline of the Near East, up and down the Red Sea, and over the Persian Gulf and Indian Ocean between Mesopotamia and the north-west shores of India (Map 1.2). It is not yet known who developed the first seagoing craft, but sea-going travel developed early – by 2200 BC there was a flotilla of forty ships crossing from the Lebanese coast to the mouth of the Nile. River travel also developed especially quickly on the Nile and its tributaries, including the marshes of the Delta, and Egyptians were even able to sail upstream since the prevailing wind in Egypt blows from the north. By the first half of the fourth millennium BC Egyptians were travelling in substantial rafts made of the papyrus reed that grew along the banks of the Nile, and by 2700 BC they were using wooden river craft with sails, similar to the *feluccas* which can be seen on the Nile today.[25] Both the rivers of Mesopotamia were navigable but not so convenient as the Nile, although by the third millennium BC small wooden river boats were in constant use there, as well as light rafts carried on inflated skins. Where water transport was not possible (such as in the interior of what is today Syria, Israel and Lebanon), those who needed to travel had to walk, or ride a donkey over short distances.

Trade is older than the beginning of settled urban life; even early farming cultures had traded in particularly desirable types of greenstone and obsidian and flint (commodities later to be joined by copper, salt and tin) over considerable distances by sea. However, longer and better established trade routes developed with settled agricultural life, for the exchange of surplus and eventually to support new urban economies. Land trade routes developed very early and in the Middle East involved considerable distances on foot, such as the early Neolithic people in Jericho importing stone from Anatolia. Early dynastic Egyptians imported turquoise from Sinai, coral from the Red Sea and (eventually) gold from East Africa. The opening up of such trade routes was followed by merchants, and eventually by armies, as control of

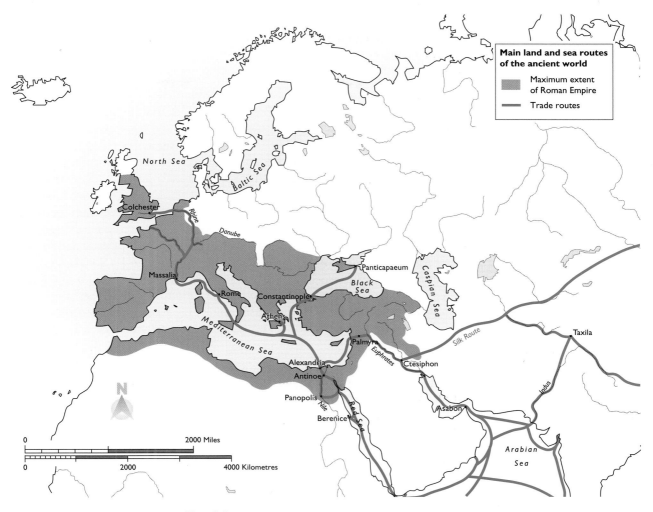

Map 1.2
Main land and sea routes in the ancient world

the resource became significant. But the formation of the kind of extensive trading network throughout the European and Asian continents really only developed with the rise of the first civilizations and empires, which became capable of maintaining a system of roads and harbours. The most significant of all early trade routes is the Silk Road (p. 76), which linked China with the Middle East by 600 BC via Central Asia, and had extended to Europe by Roman times. By the sixth century BC, trade throughout Asia utilized the 1400-mile 'Royal Road' of the Achaemenid Persian Kings from Sardis to Susa, and with the rise of the Roman Empire in the west and the Han Empire in China in the third century BC the whole Mediterranean littoral became a network of well-established trading routes, utilizing highly organized market and trading networks. Some port cities became extremely powerful. Troy, for example, strategically located at the mouth of the Dardanelles, was able to control all trade between the Aegean and the Black Sea. International trade (and international travel) was a luxury in the ancient world, but it had a significant impact on the exchange of ideas, the spread of religion and (unfortunately) on the spread of disease. International trade often developed where a culture was lacking in a significant resource; Egypt needed timber, for example, and thus needed to trade with what is now Lebanon and Syria. The need to ensure regular supplies of essential commodities (especially timber and metallic ores) was also a significant motivator for the military campaigns which so often followed the establishment of trade routes, and which brought their own travellers in the way of military apparatus and subsequent civilian bureaucracies and religious hierarchies.

Coastal trade routes around the coasts of the Mediterranean and across the Black Sea had certainly developed by the early Bronze Age, as they had through the Red Sea and the Persian Gulf, and around the coasts of Indo-China and India (Map 1.2). The first European civilization, that of Minoan Crete, had trading links throughout the Aegean islands and Egypt, exporting timber, pottery and metalwork even before 1500 BC, and importing silver, shells from the Aegean, copper from Sardinia, amber from as far away as the Baltic and lapis lazuli from Afghanistan. This coastal trade was expanded to allow long-distance shipping across the Indian Ocean after around 100 BC, which utilized the monsoon winds (p. 68). Greek vessels were able to trade across the Red Sea and directly to Indian ports such as Barbaricum, Barygaza and Muziris, where they connected with other coastal shipping bringing goods from Indo-China, thus establishing a sub-global network of sea-borne trade routes connecting China with the Mediterranean even before the Roman Empire was firmly established. The ports which functioned as nodes on the sea routes were also connected to a land trans-port network, initially on foot and later using pack animals and wheeled vehicles.

Tourism has always been a seasonal business. Travel across the Mediterranean, and later across the Indian Ocean, was determined by weather and prevailing winds. Land travel in circum-Mediterranean Europe and Asia would also generally take place in summer. But by the end of the fourth century BC travel was still neither easy nor pleasant. Those who went by sea were dependent on merchant shipping without proper guest cabins, and with constant worries about pirate attacks. Those who went by road found poor roads, bad inns and bandits. However, in the ancient world, as today, life for travellers was much easier if they had money and could afford either to charter a ship or to stay with friends at private houses. Little has changed – today far more prestige is attached to people travelling with individual itineraries permit-ting flexibility and comfort, than to mass travel where the passenger is travelling on a collective timetable. Although the era of short-haul cargo boats around the Mediterranean has long been replaced for leisure travel by the cruise ship, substantial numbers of travellers in the Middle East do still go by sea across the Mediterranean using scheduled ferry services – the only place in the world where coastal shipping services are still important. The shipping routes are still those of several thousand years ago, such as ferry services linking Venice with ports such as Antalya, Izmir or Marmaris in Turkey, or ferry connections between Bari (in southern Italy), Venice and Alexandria. Those taking the scheduled ferry services between Cyprus and Beirut (Lebanon) or around the Black Sea and the coasts of Georgia, Turkey and Romania are following exactly the same routes that have been used for 4000 years.

The classical world

On land, simple wheeled vehicles had been invented in Mesopotamia by around 3000 BC, including heavy wagons with a boxlike body drawn by oxen or *onagers* (a type of wild ass). Covered wagons date from at least 2500 BC, and were fitted with an arched canopy closely resembling those in use by *voortrekkers* in nine-teenth century southern Africa (p. 62) or by pioneer families in the American West (p. 117). Two-wheeled carts were developed slightly later, and around 2300 BC the horse was introduced into the Near East as a draught animal. Within a few centuries a lighter kind of horse- or mule-drawn cart had been developed, which around 1600 BC evolved into the horse-drawn chariot.[26] Perhaps the best example of such a chariot is that found in the tomb of Pharaoh Tutankhamun (1334–1325 BC), with a lightweight floor of interlaced leather thongs – several examples of which are to be seen today in the Egyptian museum in Cairo.[27] This new invention spread rapidly, and within two or three hundred years chariots could be found throughout Greece, Crete, northern Europe and eastwards into India and China. However, wheeled transport was the exception rather than the rule, and throughout the ancient and classical world the majority of travellers went on foot or donkeyback. Not everyone had access to carts and wagons, and in any case their use was limited without an adequate road network; pack animals and pedestrians only needed simple tracks. In the ancient world few roads were capable of taking wheeled traffic, although there is a suggestion that at least an adequate road system had been developed within the Sumerian kingdom of Ur from about 2100 to 2050 BC. But even the finest of these early highways were unpaved, with the development of the paved road attributed to the Hittites whose domination of Asia Minor from 1800 to 1200 BC was closely related to their extensive use of chariots.[28] Even so, the Hittites only paved the distance of slightly over a mile around their capital city to carry the weight of heavily loaded wagons on festival days, with the rest of their war chariots bumping over dirt roads. In addition to the lack of paved roads in the Near East there was also a lack of bridges, such being practically non-existent in Egypt and Mesopotamia since the great width of the rivers and extensive seasonal flooding provided great difficulties for contemporary engineers. Early vehicles therefore needed to be folded or dismantled to be carried on ferries. There were exceptions to this lack of early interest in road-building, including in the island of Crete, where the impressive civilization of the Minoans flourished between 2000 and 1500 BC, and in the mainland Greek Mycenean kingdom (1600–1200 BC). Both Minoans and Myceneans went in for extensive road-building; Cretan archaeologists have traced the remains of a highway that ran from a port on the south coast of Crete north to the Minoan capital at Knossos, which was thirteen feet wide, strengthened when necessary by terracing walls, and included a great viaduct. Mycenean roads were generally single-lane width and included bridges and culverts to keep them open during the rainy season. At the approaches to towns they were often paved, as in the famous stretch leading up the Lion Gate at Mycenae. Greece in the thirteenth century BC probably had a better system of roads than it did in the third century BC, this being not unrelated to the Mycenean fondness for chariots which they used for general travel, whereas elsewhere in the ancient world chariots were used only for war or hunting.[29]

Medieval trade and travel

By the year 500 BC, the Near East, previously the focus of the early history of travel, gave precedence to developments in the Greek (and later the Roman) Empires and changed the focus from the Near East to the circum-Mediterranean world. But by this time the general structure of ancient travel had been fixed, involving merchant craft sailing between the major ports of the eastern Mediterranean, and a network of variable quality dirt roads and tracks on land – the best of which would have bridges, ferries, road signs and way stations. There were some paved roads, although these were rare, and travellers had their choice of wagons (mainly drawn by donkeys), horses or camels. The sheer size of the Roman Empire and problems of administering it efficiently made it necessary to construct a network of roads connecting the capital to outlying provinces for administrative and military purposes, but once built these also enabled ordinary people to travel around more freely – although few had the opportunity or the means to do so. By the first century AD, the Mediterranean had been virtually encircled by a Roman ring road with major roads and branches radiating from it deep into Europe, Asia and the coast of North Africa (p. 42). In each Roman province, two or three cities came to serve as nodal points for the new road network (e.g. Lyons in France, London in England, Pergamum and Ephesus in Asia Minor). The directness of Roman roads was remarkable even in areas like Britain; the network was usable at all times of year and in all weathers, was built on firm foundations and properly drained. Widths varied from comfortable two-lane roads wide enough for carriages (such as the Appian Way in Italy) to narrower provincial roads and lanes, all marked by *miliaria* milestones placed every Roman mile, which in Italy gave distances from Rome and in other provinces the distance from major cities. Although not as complex as the Roman system, on the other side of the world in Han Dynasty China (200 BC–AD 200) a comprehensive highway system had also been developed to connect a far-flung empire, but since it utilized unpaved gravel surfaces virtually nothing survives. Travelling in the Roman Empire was safe and convenient to a degree unknown until the beginning of the nineteenth century. Most relatively affluent travellers along Roman roads would be riding mules or slow-paced horses, although servants walked. Saddle horses were used for dispatch riders and the army, though without stirrups (which were unknown until the ninth century in Europe). Someone could leave Hadrian's Wall and travel 4500 miles to Ethiopia on first-class roads and by using relays of horses to cover long distances in short periods of time. Julius Caesar travelled from the Rhone to Rome in eight days, and relays of messengers could carry dispatches 150 miles per day, making the journey between Rome and Byzantium (Constantinople) in twenty-five days. The need to provide accommodation for travellers on the road network led to the development of posting houses on the main roads, where horses could be changed (the forerunner of today's garages) and where accommodation facilities were often available. Some post-houses could only be used by officials equipped with a document called a *tractatorium* carried by those on official business, and nicely paralleled in today's business class and frequent-flier VIP airline lounges only available to the holders of special tickets. Anyone using these public roads needed a list (*itineraria*) of where inns and hostels could be found, and details of stopping places along the road. Maps were designed to show specifically the location of such places and what they had to offer. One medieval copy which has survived is the Tabula Peutingeriana,[30] drawn on parchment but giving a recognizable although distorted view of the Roman Empire plus a schematic outline of the road system with distances and stopping places. Coloured picture symbols against many of the names give the map a strong resemblance to the *Guide Michelin*, since they indicate the kind of accommodation available. A little four-sided building with a courtyard indicates the presence of an inn, with a twin-peaked roof being a simple country inn and a single-peaked boxlike cottage offering bed and breakfast. Unfortunately, when the Roman Empire declined the road system disintegrated with it, since no nation had the necessary money or organization to maintain it. Roman roads were not really surpassed until the nineteenth century, with the introduction, by Mr J. L. McAdam, of a system of surfacing with a layer of small cut stones (tarmacadam)[31] which was essential for motorized transport.

Roots of modern travel and tourism

With the decline of the Roman Empire in the fifth century AD, the conditions under which European long-distance land travel was possible on any significant scale simply disappeared. The surfaces of the Roman road network began to deteriorate and the roads become infested with bandits. Long-distance travel on the scale of Rome did not effectively resume again until the middle of the eighteenth century, although travel for military and religious purposes (and sometimes both combined, such as the Crusades) still flourished. Since at this time 80 per cent of Europe north of the Alps was still covered in dense forest, the disintegration of the road network was very significant. There is very little evidence about the travel history of Europe in the Middle Ages, with the exception of information on pilgrimages and travel for political, diplomatic or military purposes. Individuals undertook only limited domestic travel, although pilgrimage (to Rome, Jerusalem and Compostela) was still significant. Long-distance land travel also declined during the early medieval period; the Silk Road linking the Mediterranean to China was cut, sea travel became difficult because of pirates, and land travel was troubled by brigands. International travellers who had previously utilized merchant ships found that this was no longer possible, and only after around AD 1000, with the restoration of relatively stable conditions, did international trade and travel begin to revive. The settled conditions in Asia which resulted under the Mongol Empire allowed a resumption of long-distance land-based travel, as is evidenced by the journeys of the Venetian merchant Marco Polo between 1271 and 1295 – but this was only temporary.[32] However, by the thirteenth century the trading centres of Europe re-established communications with the Near East, and the early medieval fairs held in northern Europe stimulated the development of new land-based trade routes connecting the cities of Italy with the emerging industrial centres of Flanders and northern Europe (Map 1.3). The Rhine Valley, Lombardy and the Champagne area began to host trade fairs where goods from the Near East were exchanged for cloth from the emerging northern European manufacturers. Major trade routes developed utilizing the river valleys of the Seine, Rhone and Rhine, and new passes over the Alps, including the St Gotthard Pass, helped the establishment of these trade routes and resulted in the growth of new commercial and financial centres in southern Germany during the fourteenth century, New coastal trading ports developed, including Lübeck, founded in 1158 at a strategic location controlling trade routes between the Baltic and the North Sea (Map 1.3). The Hanseatic League, an association of German merchants which developed in the thirteenth and fourteenth centuries, formed a network of linked trading cities including London and Bruges, as well as connections south to Venice and Genoa – which between them controlled sea-borne trade and travel in the eastern Mediterranean (and thus to Asia) until 1453. Venice controlled the spice trade with the Levant, and Genoa the silk trade with Asia, through their merchant colonies established at Constantinople and Trebizon. Venetian merchants imported spices from the Malay archipelago and the Moluccas, utilizing Arab and Indian middlemen and a network of sea routes centred on the port of Malacca (p. 85), crossing the Red Sea, Gulf of Arabia, and South China Seas. During the early fifteenth century the Chinese sent several expeditions through the Straits of Malacca to the Indian Ocean, and the Portuguese were beginning to explore the western coast of Africa. By the year 1500 the Portuguese had reached India and Christopher Columbus (backed by Spain) had reached America, inaugurating a New World and a shift in emphasis in international travel from a focus on the Mediterranean

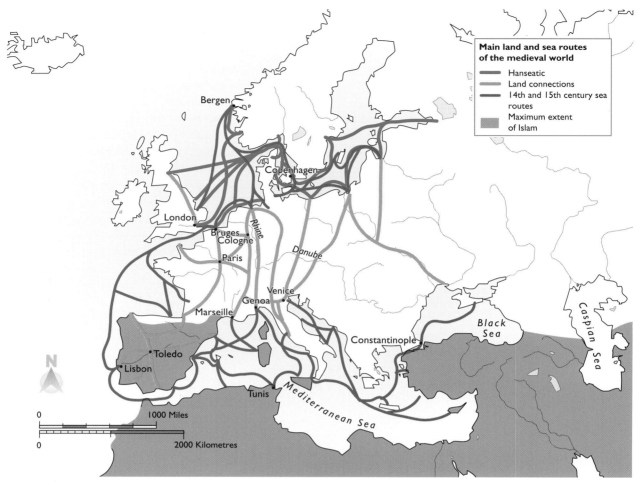

Map 1.3
Main land and sea routes in the medieval world

to a focus on the Atlantic. A hundred years later the shape of the world and the configurations of the continents as we know them today had been established. However, travel was still dominated by trade and exploration, with little known about leisure travel. In medieval Europe, the vast majority of the population (with the exception of merchants, pilgrims and crusaders) would seldom travel more than a day or two away from their homes, and then generally for markets or religious festivals. After the Dissolution of the Monasteries in 1539, travellers in England who had previously utilized the network of monastic guest houses were obliged to stay with relatives or friends (although this was not true in Europe until the eighteenth century), since public inns and hotels were a much later invention.[33] Nothing much was to change until the development of accommodation providers and destinations that were attractive in themselves to leisure travellers. The Renaissance, which originated in fourteenth century Italy and peaked in western Europe during the sixteenth century, continued with the pre-existing pattern of festivals, markets, fairs and events still acting as foci for domestic tourism. However, the rise of travelling theatres and increased patronage of the arts created more opportunities to travel. However, after the Reformation the ideas of Luther and Calvin stimulated the growth of what would come to be known as the

'Protestant work ethic',[34] often considered as a turning point in the history of leisure and tourism, since it questioned the value of leisure by portraying it as idleness.

Industrial revolution

In the sixteenth century travellers were forced to use whatever accommodation they could find – often taverns or ale houses along main highways, with no travel infrastructure at all existing away from the main lines of communication. Within the UK, until the middle of the seventeenth century the roads were maintained by local funds, but with the growth of increased trade and long-distance traffic great pressure was placed on the road system and the provision of better roads was left to the devices of the turnpike rather than to the creation of a national road authority.[35] European countries with land frontiers adopted a more centralized system, and this greatly helped military movements.

However, until the eighteenth century, travel in Europe (at least travel unrelated to commercial or religious activities) was only undertaken by a small, wealthy and mostly land-owning elite who travelled principally for educational and official purposes. The concept of leisure travel did not really exist until the eighteenth century, and even then was related to social class. An example of this can be seen in the eighteenth century concept of the 'Grand Tour', which involved travel through Europe by wealthy young men for educational purposes, to enable them to experience European art, architecture and manners.[36] Foreign travel became part of an aristocratic man's education, but domestic travel for pleasure began at the same time with the emergence of fashionable spas and seaside resorts (such as Bath or Brighton in the UK, p. 100). The practice of taking mineral waters (both internally and externally) for health and pleasure goes back to Roman times, with spas (*aquae*) distributed throughout Roman territories. These declined at the same time as the Empire, but their existence became the basis for the growth of fashionable spa resorts throughout Europe in the eighteenth century – including Aquae Sulis (Bath, UK), Aquae Calidae (Vichy, France), Aquae Mattiacae (Germany) and the hot spring resorts of the Bay of Naples, which had been a tourist resort in Roman times (p. 109). Nor was the development of spas confined to Europe; Philadelphia in the USA was served by several spa resorts, such as Bristol and Yellow Springs. The rapid growth of spas in England between 1660 and 1815 was related to royal patronage, an emerging affluent middle class and public sector partnerships with entrepreneurs. The population of Bath in England was under 2000 in the 1660s and 13 000 in the 1760s, but had risen to 33 000 in 1801 as a result of the town's investment in visitor facilities and accommodation.[37] In Scotland, late Victorian and Edwardian entrepreneurs created a range of successful 'hydro' hotels for health tourism, which had the added benefit of being located in areas of high scenic quality such as Pitlochry, Dunblane and Crieff. This also occurred in Canada and New Zealand, with the development of Radium Hot Springs in British Columbia in the 1920s and Rotorua in the North Island of New Zealand (p. 165).

The twentieth century

Many European countries in the late eighteenth century developed their coast-lines as a new form of tourism destination for the leisure classes at the same time as the expansion of spas and other inland resorts. In England and Wales no major population centre was more than seventy to eighty miles from the coast, although the populations of rural France and Germany had very much further to cover. Europe's social elite began the search for increasingly exclusive and undiscovered destinations – a process which led to the development of the French Riviera in the 1920s and to the promotion of several Bahamian islands in the post-war period. Such developments were also related to the new popularity of sunbathing. Although the Greeks had promoted sunbathing for health reasons, a white skin became popular in medieval Europe (partly since it differentiated aristocrats from those who worked outside and thus became tanned). Very little changed until the 1920s, when a new fashion was started by the French fashion designer Coco Chanel. The tanned, bronzed look achievable on a beach became fashionable in the 1940s and remained so for fifty years, even when the dangers of skin cancer began to be appreciated.

Although the idea of wealthy young men travelling to broaden their minds can be traced back to classical times, it reached its peak in the eighteenth century with the Grand Tour. This rise in culturally-motivated travel was initially related to Renaissance-inspired interest in classical antiques, art and education. Around the early 1800s, an interest in landscape and nature accounted for the increasing popularity of Switzerland as a destination, with such scenic tourism being facilitated by new modes of transport on land, inland waterways and rivers – such as the emergence of steamers on Swiss lakes in the 1820s. Entrepreneurs such as Henry Lunn organized the first packages to Switzerland for skiing in the 1880s, starting another new trend (p. 98). By the end of the eighteenth century the concept of modern leisure was beginning to appear, although its facilities were available only to the very small fragment of the population able to avail themselves of the newly-developing spas and seaside resorts. Very little overseas travel took place for leisure purposes right up until the middle of the nineteenth century, when travel still remained both expensive and dangerous. Local tolls and taxes and unreliable rates of exchange of foreign currency meant that travellers had to take with them enough money to cope with all eventualities (which might include a prolonged stay in hospital), and the gold they carried made them a source of prey for bandits or highwaymen.

However, this was all about to change. The Industrial Revolution, which began in England during the early nineteenth century, was also responsible for the greatest revolution in travel and tourism since the invention of the wheel – namely the development of the internal combustion engine. The effects of this new industrialization were felt first in England and in a few areas of Europe, with significant development occurring during the last quarter of the nineteenth century (though in France, Italy and Russia not until after 1890). But outside Europe (with the exception of the USA) the impact of industrialization was not immediately felt, and the industrial strength of the UK, rich in basic raw materials, without major civil unrest or the recent Napoleonic wars of continental Europe, enabled it to dominate world markets. This was facilitated by the expansion of its Atlantic ports, such as Liverpool, Glasgow and Bristol, as well as its network of canals and rivers which were of great importance in the movement of raw materials and finished goods before the industrial age (though insignificant in the movement of people). By 1816 the first crossing of the English Channel by steamboat took place, with a regular service beginning four years later, which was to lead to established passenger ferries, catamarans, hovercraft and, eventually, to the Eurostar and Channel Tunnel services of today. However, the most significant technical innovation of the Industrial Revolution relevant to travel was, of course, the development of a railway network which began in the 1830s; within thirty years the railway networks of Britain, Belgium and Germany were virtually complete, although those of Austria, Hungary and Russia were only just starting.[38] The dismantling of obstacles to trade and the emergence of new banking systems contributed to the rapid industrialization of Europe, and also revolutionized patterns of leisure travel. The invention of steam locomotion enabled people to travel at a price previously not dreamed of. In 1835, 417 miles of track were opened in Great Britain and Northern Ireland; 20 years later this had risen to 13 411 and by 1875 to 16 803 miles of track (Map 1.4). By 1870 a traveller could reach virtually any major region of western Europe by train, with the exception of much of Spain, Portugal and southern Italy. The export of railway technology to colonial possessions resulted in the rapid development of railway systems in India (p. 69) and southern Africa (p. 62), paralleled by an equally rapid growth in the independent USA (p. 120). Between 1880 and 1914 Europe added one-fifth of the land area of the globe to its colonial possessions. Shipping routes and railway lines were consolidated so that raw materials flowed back into Europe and finished goods could be exported. Major commercial sea routes developed, especially between Britain, the eastern seaboard of the USA, Brazil and Uruguay, with transit to the Pacific facilitated by the opening of the Panama Canal in 1914 and to the Indian Ocean via the Suez Canal after 1869. By 1900, only South America, mainly colonized during the sixteenth century by Spain and Portugal but largely independent by the nineteenth century (p. 143), was not under European rule, with the extent of the new colonial possessions most striking in Africa and South-East Asia (p. 86). By 1914, European colonial powers had absorbed 90 per cent of Africa and most of Asia, with the establishment of new colonial administrative centres, mines, ports, plantations and manufacturing enterprises, and the exchange of political, military and colonial personnel completely changing the cultural networks of the planet. The effect of this can be seen especially powerfully in India, for example, whose British legacy includes more than 50 000 miles of railway tracks, a language and an administrative system. Within the newly-industrialized countries of western Europe a new middle class developed, with wealth that for the first time in history was not derived from or committed to land, and this new middle class formed the market for new innovations in travel services, such as the development of the package tour by Thomas Cook (p. 101). During the Industrial Revolution the shift in population from the countryside to industrial towns led to a demand for periodic escape to quieter surroundings – the beginnings of recognizable holidays from monotonous factory routines. This eventually led (but not for 100 years in the UK) to the granting of annual holidays with pay, which enabled many people to take holidays for the first time. In the UK, the 1851 and 1875 Bank Holiday Acts provided for four statutory holidays per year, but middle-class workers had already begun to take more extensive holidays from the 1850s. There was still a distinction between those who could only afford an annual day trip and those who could afford a fortnight at a seaside resort, but eventually the middle classes joined the aristocracy at the seaside resorts which had been developed in the eighteenth century, just as the aristocracy graduated to holidays overseas where again they were pursued first by the middle and ultimately by the working classes. All this new leisure travel resulted in extensive hotel-building throughout Europe (especially in Switzerland) and in America.

At the same time, the influence of the North Atlantic foreign trade and the replacement of sail by steam were decisive in the development of transatlantic passenger

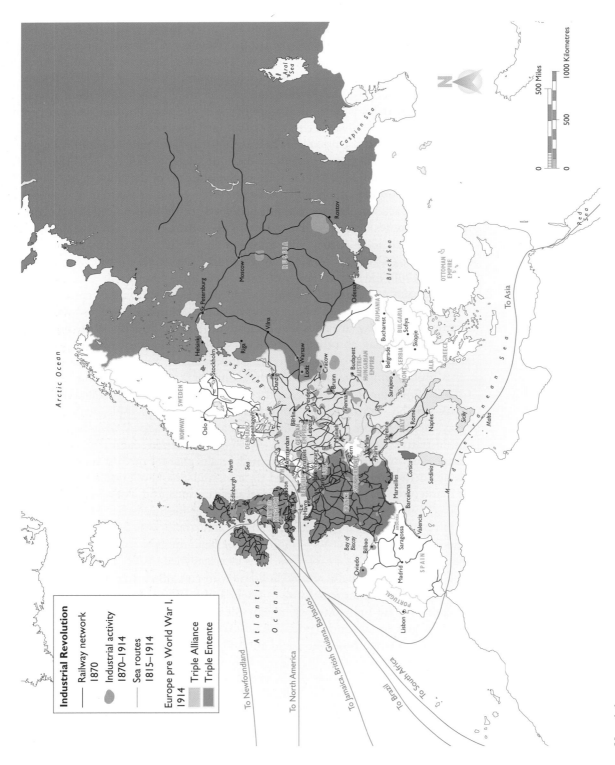

Map 1.4
Post-Industrial Revolution transport links

shipping, leading to the era of the great ocean liners. The application of steam power to the means of transport at the start of the nineteenth century that revolutionized travel is often known as the 'Golden Age of Travel', when luxury travel became possible for a wider variety of people than ever before. The era is epitomized by trains such as the *Orient Express* (p. 102) or the *Flying Scotsman*, luxury liners such as the *Lusitania* and *Titanic* and palace-style hotels such as the Ritz and the Waldorf-Astoria. The sinking of the *Titanic* on 14 April 1912 with the loss of 1500 lives was only one element that caused a loss of confidence in the future of ocean liners for transatlantic travel, which were soon to be replaced by the aeroplane. Orville Wright had already completed the first sustained flight in 1903, and in 1927 Charles Lindbergh was to cross the Atlantic in the *Spirit of St Louis*. Sentimentality for such lost steam trains and ocean liners, which date from a period when time was not necessarily money and when travel was accompanied by a high service quality, has generated the nostalgia travel industry of today. Today's nostalgia travellers utilize the re-vamped *Orient Express* or patronize those cruise ships such as Cunard's *Queen Mary II*, launched in 2004, which still maintain the traditions of formal clothing for dinner and a Captain's Table. But today's luxury travellers also have a far wider range of options and can, if they choose, take a customized safari holiday in Africa at vast cost (p. 63) or shun the cheaper but de-personalized travel of today, epitomized by budget airlines (p. 105).

Technological advances, which increased the speed of ships and aeroplanes and replaced luxury with efficiency, effectively ended the Golden Age – a process completed by the development of the jet engine after the Second World War, after which the majority of intercontinental travel was carried out by aeroplane, not by boat. By 1919, Thomas Cook had become the first travel agent to offer pleasure trips by aeroplane. The development of the motor car (following Henry Fords 'Model T' in 1908) was an equally significant travel milestone on land, meaning that journeys which previously could have only been possible by a combination of means (including horse power, foot and, later, railways) could start at the travellers' front door and end at their destination with a personalized itinerary and single means of transport which accomplished the journey in a fraction of the time. The growth of commercial aviation stimulated by the First World War resulted in peace-time dividends for leisure travel, such as the conversion of bombers for civilian use on routes linking Europe's major population centres such as London and Paris,[39] although these early flights did not offer anything like the luxury still obtainable on trains and boats and were generally unheated and with no inflight services. Air traffic control was virtually non-existent, pilots used landmarks such as mountain ranges and railway lines to assist navigation, and aeroplanes could not cope with bad weather conditions. Moreover, early air journeys were expensive compared with ferries or rail, but much faster. In the twenty-first century we see an interesting example of this phenomenon being reversed, whereby a journey from London to Paris is technically faster by air than rail, but only as long as the journey from central London and Paris to and from the airports, plus queuing at both ends, is not factored in. Hence the success of services such as Eurostar, which once again offer direct city-to-city services accompanied (at least in First Class) by adequate service quality. These compete with budget airlines only on price. Air travel developed rapidly, at least in Europe, and by 1922 more than 10 000 passengers per year were using the London–Paris routes, with airlines improving service quality by the introduction of new purpose-built aircraft (with upholstered seats, toilets and cabin service) in imitation of luxury trains. National airlines gradually came into existence, starting with KLM in 1919, Imperial Airways (which would evolve into BA) in 1924 and Pan American World Airways in 1928. Imperial Airways began its first regular service to India in 1926 (displacing the dominance of P&O shipping) and to South Africa six years later. By 1937 the world had around sixty major airlines, with Imperial even offering a twice-weekly departure for Brisbane (Australia) – a journey that took nearly a fortnight.[40]

Intercontinental travel expanded very rapidly. It is estimated that before the First World War 150 000 Americans crossed the Atlantic annually to Europe, where they spent lavishly, and these Americans were also partly responsible for the growth of the idea of the business conference (and thus for the start of the meetings and conference industry). The newly-established travel industry recognized, even at this stage, the importance of attracting high-spending international visitors – such as the Indian maharaja who reserved all thirty-seven suites, a whole floor of the Savoy hotel, for himself in 1925. At the opposite end of the scale, post-war European developments included the invention of the holiday camp (the first of which was started in 1936 by Billy Butlin at Skegness in the UK) to cater for the domestic market.[41] On the eve of the Second World War in 1939, less than 50 per cent of the British population spent more than one consecutive night away from home.

Wealthy Europeans were increasingly looking towards the Mediterranean coast, with the forty miles of the French Riviera having effectively been turned into one large resort by the end of the 1930s.[42] However, the Second World War effectively put an end to domestic and international tourism, with many hotels requisitioned and used for other purposes, and some being bombed. But the Second World War also accelerated the development of the aeroplane and the construction of airfields, and this was to prove more important in the long term than the loss of hotels. The War also increased destination awareness and levels of knowledge about global geography (p. 103), which added to travel motivations at the end of hostilities. Between 1950 and 1956, tourist traffic to and from member countries of the OECD (Organization for Economic Co-operation and Development) grew at levels of between 10 and 16 per cent per year. Incoming tourism to the UK (where records were now being kept) rose from 200 000 in 1946 to 1.7 million in 1960, and 7.2 million in 1971. Traffic to Spain rose from 4 million in 1959 to 24 million in 1970. During the twenty years after the War, air travel grew faster than sea travel, with the number of passengers crossing the Atlantic by air exceeding those travelling by sea for the first time in 1957. Car ownership had risen from 200 000 in 1920 to 2 million in 1939. The post-war period saw a phenomenal growth in international travel, although punctuated by drops and troughs in demand related to political activities and terrorism. By 1965 Spain had become Europe's leading tourism destination, with 14 million visitors a year, although that figure would later quadruple in size (largely as a result of the UK-driven package holiday market). By the 1990s, travellers had a very wide range of potential holiday options, their choice being facilitated by experience and increasingly sophisticated consumption.

However, the almost limitless availability of new travel products and destinations has not actually led to a major change in the proportion of people taking holidays, although today's consumers are taking holidays of shorter duration, and more of them. This trend has been amplified by the development of budget airlines in the 1990s, which have brought a wide range of destinations (principally cities) on line (p. 105) and developed tourism industries in places which people had hardly heard of but were prepared to travel to if a very low fare was available. Companies such as Ryanair and Easyjet dominate the European market. New travel patterns include the development of holiday products for the active (and highly lucrative) retired market, a boom in adventure and ecotourism holidays to the developing world, a current fashion for spa holidays and expensive lifestyle 'boutique' hotels (again, mainly in the developing world and in European cities),[43] a flourishing VFR (Visiting Friends and Relations) market for migrant groups and a resurgence of interest in cultural tourism.

Transportation improvements since the 1970s have included the introduction of jet aircraft (especially the wide-body jet, such as the DCE 10 and Boeing 747) and supersonic Concorde, as well as the rise of high-speed trains and new larger aircraft such as the new Airbus A380, currently being developed. An Airbus A380 weighs 560 tonnes and costs $285 million, has a range of 9000 miles and is able to take up to 800 passengers. However, airport modifications are needed to take the new aircraft, including wider runways and improved gangways and baggage handling. Heathrow will become the leading hub for this mega-jumbo, and is planning to invest over £400 million in associated facilities over the next decade. The A380 will be the latest in a development programme which started with the Douglas DC3 Dakota in 1935, the first modern airliner. This eventually led to the Boeing 707 aircraft with 200 seats from 1955, after which transatlantic travel by air was seen as more glamorous than the same journey by sea. In 1970, the Boeing 747, the first wide-bodied jumbo jet capable of carrying 400 passengers, was launched, allowing airlines to cut fares and opening international travel to the masses. Six years later, the supersonic Anglo-French Concorde halved transatlantic flying time for those who could afford to pay, and set a new standard in luxury travel. However, it was never a commercial success, and was eventually withdrawn from service in 2003.

During the 1970s, Europe and North America continued to dominate world tourism both as generators and as destinations – as they still do today – but probably three-quarters of all tourism in the world continues to be domestic. Even in international travel, probably 80 per cent of all international tourism involves short- or medium-haul flights (four to six hours in length) and only 20 per cent long-haul travel between the WTO regions (Map 1.1). Today's tourists are able to reach new geographical frontiers, such as the depths of the oceans, the South Pole and now outer space, and these 'trailblazers' will eventually be followed by mainstream or mass tourists in the future, as development occurs, infrastructure is set up and the frontier areas lose some of their unique qualities.[44] This phenomenon can already be seen in places such as Antarctica, which now attracts tourist cruise boats (p. 150), and this drive to seek out unique destinations can be characterized as a hallmark of our post-modernist society while the exodus towards 'distant places' is arguably one of the propensities of tourism.

And in the future?

It seems inevitable that the first few decades of the twenty-first century will see major developments in space tourism, capitalizing on interests and dreams first stimulated by Neil Armstrong's walk on the moon in 1969.[45] The subsequent thirty years kept the possibility of sending people to Mars in the public consciousness, and space travel is a part of popular culture. At the time of writing (end of 2005), the thirst for space travel is being satisfied in a number of secondary ways; by viewing exhibits in Air and Space Museums, attending space camp or following the exploits of the first two space tourists – the American millionaire Dennis Tito's controversial visit to the International Space Station (ISS) in April 2001, which allegedly cost him US$20 million, and Mark Shuttleworth, a South-African Internet millionaire in April 2002. Space Adventures Inc. has advertised a range of space-related travel programmes, including astronaut training, zero-gravity experience, sub-orbital and orbital flights. In the future, they also expect to offer stays at an orbital hotel and lunar flights,[46] although there is as yet little sign of the new low-cost technologies that might make tourist moon flights and orbiting hotels a reality. It has been suggested that converting the aging Mir space station into a hotel would cost approximately US$200 million, but the cost of maintenance and safety provision would be too great. While the level of growth in space tourism is hard to predict, it seems very likely that it will eventually become an important component of the tourism industry despite environmental concerns about atmospheric pollution, orbital debris and launch-site noise. Virgin Galactic (a company established by Richard Branson's Virgin Group to develop efficient, reusable space vehicles) may well be the future of space tourism, operating privately built spaceships modelled on the history-making SpaceShipOne craft, which flew successfully in 2005 using innovative technology to overcome the difficult issues of re-entry into the Earth's atmosphere. Virgin Galactic plans the first commercial flights for 2008, and is already taking reservations with a ticket price of US$200 000. Business is apparently brisk.

In the future there is also the possibility that cybertourism (an electronically simulated travel experience) may well become an alternative to physical travel, whether in Earth or in space.[47] It has been suggested that, possibly in the next two decades, new nanobot and computer technologies, still on the design board, will allow vastly enhanced electronic simulation reality programs to be developed that will give users an internalized computer-generated reality experience. This offers users immense scope for visiting remote and exotic places in this world, or for using externally projected stimuli in a manner fictionalized in the Star Trek 'Holodeck'.[48] Limitless possibilities would open up tourism frontiers, from responsible eco-tourism to future versions of sex tourism. While creating an illusion of place, the major limitation to this technology is the passivity of the participant and the external nature of the stimuli. When there is a convergence of these technologies at some time in the future, it will be possible to create a realistic virtual environment that will play out in the human brain in a form that seems entirely real. Cybertourism offers an exciting range of possibilities, including space travel, without the physical danger and at an affordable cost. It will be interesting for the travel historians of the future to see whether the future of travel and exploration lies in Earth or in space, outside the Earth or around it, or whether travel will go full circle with the cyber-traveller never needing to leave home at all. But for the moment travel is essentially an activity that moves people physically from one point on the globe to another, and a process which started 50 000 years ago and is explored regionally in the remainder of this book.

CHAPTER 2

Middle East and North Africa: ancient empires

The Middle East is rightly regarded as the cradle of civilization, and within this enormous and diverse region, which includes part of the Mediterranean littoral and most of Asia Minor, travel and transport systems developed very early but in quite similar ways. It would make no sense to consider the development of travel in Egypt, for example, separately from similar developments in the 'Fertile Crescent' of the valleys of the Tigris and Euphrates in modern-day Iraq. Moreover, for much of its history the entire region, together with parts of North Africa, has been under a single unified political control, and the whole area is here considered as one region – at least for the purpose of considering its travel history. Different writers use different geographical descriptions, so in order to avoid complications in trying to define the boundaries between the Near and Middle East, Asia Minor, the Levant, etc., the whole region is considered together here under the general heading of 'Middle East and North Africa' (Map 2.1).

The 'Fertile Crescent' of Mesopotamia in modern Iraq and the valley of the River Nile in Egypt were the locations for the development of some of the earliest known urbanized societies. The processes of urbanization required domestic trade and travel, and from this small beginning sprang a network of trade routes across the region and, slightly later, across the Mediterranean (Map 2.1). Broadly speaking, the history of travel in the Middle East can be divided into five major periods: the ancient world (from first beginnings until the defeat of the Persian Empire by Alexander the Great in 331–330 BC); the Hellenistic (Greek) and Roman world from 323 BC until the decline of the late Roman/Byzantine Empire in the fifth century AD; the Arab world from the seventh to the twelfth centuries AD (with interruptions such as the Crusades and culminating in the Mongol invasions); the Ottoman Empire (the thirteenth to the late nineteenth centuries); and the modern Middle East of the twentieth and twenty-first centuries. Unlike sub-Saharan Africa or South America, most of the area that we know today as the Middle East was under the control of a single political entity for much of that time (albeit under a succession of different empires), which lent a unity to the development of a transport infrastructure both by land and by water to service the complex communications requirements of extensive empires.

The Middle East itself is a rather vaguely defined area where the three continents of the 'Old World' meet. It encompasses South-West Asia, Turkey, Egypt (and its neighbours) and the shores of the Black, Caspian, Arabian and Red Seas, with the Caucasus and Atlas Mountains forming natural barriers. The core of the Middle East consists of the Arabian Peninsula and the Levant, with Iran (and sometimes Afghanistan) considered as providing its eastern border, although it is currently more common to include Afghanistan as part of Central Asia – even though it was conquered by Alexander the Great and included within his empire. The topography

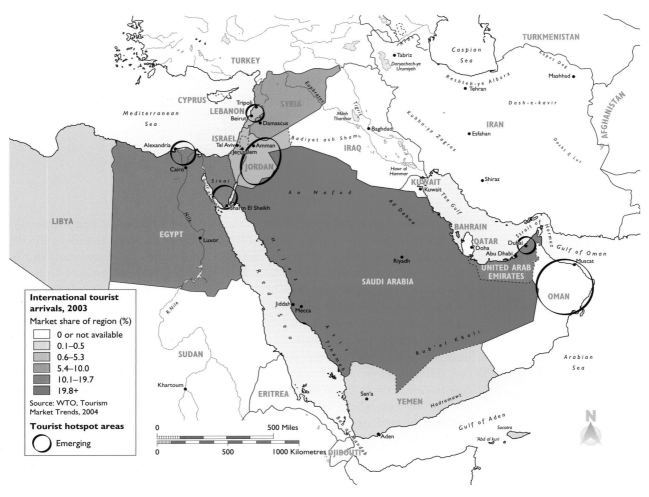

Map 2.1
Middle East and North Africa – international tourist arrivals 2003

of this vast area is immensely varied; sand deserts in Saudi Arabia and Egypt, and extensive mountain ranges and high plains in Turkey, Iraq and Yemen. The region's major rivers (the Nile, Tigris and Euphrates) were central to early development of river travel. Alexander's empire also included Egypt and part of North Africa, and Rome controlled the entire circum-Mediterranean area. There is a key sense in which the Mediterranean and its surrounding coast is the world's travel hub; many of the great developments in the history of travel and exploration were either devised here (like the metalled road or ocean-going ship-building) or resulted from the political systems that controlled the region. Climate, too, was an important influence on the travel history of the region, with the aridity of its northern Sahara and Arabian Peninsula requiring the development of specific means of transport, including the domestication of the camel and the first 'road trains' – the great camel caravans that crossed Arabia and the rest of the Middle East from at least the third millennium BC. The huge distances involved in travel across Asia stimulated the development of new transport types, such as the light, fast chariot, which was so helpful in covering the long, straight roads in arid outposts of the Persian Empire. The seasonality of winds in the Mediterranean affected trade and travel patterns right from early prehistoric times, as did the monsoon winds that were eventually to be utilized to develop transport links between the region and

India. The raw materials of travel were available here, too, such as the wood for ship-building, and animals for domestication.

Despite the fact that it was the hub of ancient empires, in the modern world the Middle East and North Africa region is synonymous with conflict, not unity. However, its history has contributed to an extraordinary diversity of tourism products, from cultural tourism in Syria, Jordan and Egypt to beach tourism in Morocco and Tunisia. For the latter three countries tourism is a major source of jobs and foreign currency, and throughout the region the growth of modern tourism not only gives governments an incentive to protect endangered species and historic monuments but also can provide foreign visitors with a deep appreciation of the region's history, which is often at odds with current political crises.[1]

The history of trade and travel within the region can be traced back several thousand years, but the tourism (in the sense of leisure travel) also has a long history here. As far back as the Roman occupation of Egypt, beginning around 30 BC, Roman tourists explored the ruins of Thebes and the tombs in the Valley of the Kings. For centuries, Arab, Asian and, later, European explorers trekked across portions of the region, keeping records of the sites and peoples they encountered. Map 2.1 emphasizes the dominance of Egypt as a tourism destination, both ancient and modern; modern Egypt receives a steady stream of tourists, most of whom come to see the sites of the Nile Valley but increasing numbers of whom visit the Sinai Peninsula, Alexandria and the western desert. In terms of tourism numbers Egypt is by far the most important country in this region, although its North-African neighbours (such as Tunisia) are also significant leisure tourism destinations – largely because, for European tourists, North Africa's proximity makes it a viable destination even for short trips. However, Map 2.1 also shows many areas where modern leisure travel is minimal or non-existent. Some (like Iraq and Iran) correspond to the heartlands of the great empires of the ancient world, while others (such as Yemen) mark regions whose immense tourism potential cannot be realized until greater political stability is achieved. The region includes countries that either virtually forbid tourism, such as Saudi Arabia (although this is now opening up a little). The map also emphasizes how deceptive statistics can be; Saudi Arabia appears as a major international tourism destination comparable to Spain and France in Europe. Numerically this is true, but the large numbers of visitors are all *haj* pilgrims going to just one site – Makkah (Mecca). Some Middle-Eastern locations (such as Alexandria and Tyre) have been centres of travel and trading empires for millennia, but some significant players in the contemporary tourism scene, such as Dubai, are relative newcomers. The contemporary Middle East is a place of great economic contrasts, between the affluence of the Gulf states (especially Kuwait and the United Arab Emirates) and extremely poor countries such as Yemen. The region's history as a trading centre is also reflected in today's economies, with major ports and shipping and the development of new airport hubs such as Dubai. Dubai has invested very heavily in airports, leisure facilities, hotels and shops to make it the Middle East's most popular transit and short-break destination.[2] Jebel Ali at Dubai is the largest artificial port in the world, and the Middle East's most active duty-free zone. Oil is the economic mainstay of Iran, Iraq and all the Gulf states, and is an important source of income for Egypt, Yemen and Syria, but tourism is the other major economic basis of the region. The Middle East is the birthplace of the world's three monotheistic religions (Christianity, Judaism and Islam) and has been the seat of or battleground for many of the great empires of antiquity, resulting in a surfeit of religious and archaeological treasures. And nowhere can this be seen more clearly than in Egypt.

Egypt

Even from pre-dynastic times, the communities of the Nile Valley utilized the river for domestic travel and network links, together with pack animals (initially donkeys or mules) to travel within their local area. But the start of more formal 'business travel' in Egypt can be set at around 3200 BC, when the whole country had been unified under a single ruler, necessitating the development of travel networks for administrators, agents and messengers up and down the river from the capital at Memphis.[3] We know that prospectors, miners and traders were also crossing the eastern desert to Sinai from a very early date, and that the first Egyptian copper mines had been established there from 3000 BC. Egypt sent its first diplomatic missions north into the Levant and south into the Sudan around this time, to be rapidly followed by trading links. It would appear that there was a major trading post located on the Nile between the second and third cataracts which was the terminus of a caravan trail running south to the highlands of Sudan and Ethiopia, allowing the import of gold and luxury trade goods from the south. However, by 2000 BC the Egyptians had bypassed these hazardous and slow land routes and sent ships down the Red Sea directly to the shores of Ethiopia and probably to Somalia to further develop trade in incense, ebony, oil, leopard skins and elephant tusks. Whether civilian explorers accompanied these trips we have no way of knowing, but the expeditions would certainly have included army detachments, clerks, merchants and their servants. We can assume that trade caravans and troop movements were a common sight on the roads of both Egypt and Mesopotamia at that time, and clay tablets found in the Iraqi city of Assur document the extent of this early caravan trade and its sophistication.[4]

However, government couriers, merchants, traders and soldiers were not the only travellers in early Egypt, since at certain times of year large numbers of people made pilgrimages to festivals held at sacred places. In Egypt, major festivals attracted huge numbers of people from outlying areas, and as early as 1500 BC we see the first emergence of travel motivated by curiosity or pleasure, the first tourists, and the gradual emergence of a tourism infrastructure similar (albeit less developed) to that of the tourism industry which we have today, based around its three pegs of transport, accommodation and visitor attractions. Major monumental building of temples had begun in Egypt by 2700 BC, and these were already attracting visitors and the curious, so that subsequent generations of Egyptians effectively lived in an open-air museum (and indeed are still doing so). By the time of the powerful Old Kingdom pharaohs such as Rameses II (1292–1225 BC), the construction of the Pyramids at Giza and other major complexes was already a thousand years in the past, and they had become visitor attractions as well as tombs and sacred sites. On their walls are left messages by people who have made a special trip to see them and whose prime motivation seems to have been curiosity or enjoyment, but not religion. They also contain the first graffiti, and thus the first recorded negative impacts of tourism.[5] One such message, scratched 1244 BC on the wall of the funerary chapel attached to Djoser's pyramid, says ' Hadnakhte, scribe of the treasury came to make an excursion and amuse himself on the west of Memphis, together with his brother Panakhti, scribe of the vizier'. The habit of leaving graffiti (a word literally meaning 'scratching with a sharp point') clearly developed very early, as did the habit of buying souvenirs; the first references to people bringing back objects from their travels as mementos also come from Egyptian sources, at nearly 2000 BC. But we can assume that visitation levels to the pyramids at Giza remained relatively low in the ancient world, although they had certainly become major tourist attractions in Greek and Roman times. They are still the largest, most important and best preserved ancient monuments in the world, and the only one of the original 'Seven Wonders of the World' to remain. The Greek historian Herodotus visited them in 450 BC, and claimed that the pyramid of Khufu (Cheops), built *c.* 2585 BC, was constructed by 100 000 slaves over a period of thirty years, although modern Egyptologists feel that it was far more likely to have been built by salaried local peasants during the time of the Nile flood (annually in July–November) when fields became unworkable.[6]

Despite the fact that very substantial crowds of people descended on popular tombs and temples at festival times, either using river transport or travelling on foot, the idea of hospitality as something that was bought and paid for had not yet arisen. Again we get further information from Herodotus, who commented in the fifth century BC on the large numbers of people on the move in Egypt to sites like Busiris without any facilities being available for food or accommodation. One presumes that such tourists must therefore have slept in the open if they were unable to find temporary lodgings or stay with families and friends. It would also be reasonable to assume that they left the locals to clean up after them, thus providing the model for many contemporary rock festivals. Those travelling on official business were, however, well provided for in the ancient world. Government officials in Egypt in the middle of a journey were allowed to take food from temples and storehouses, and in early Mesopotamia there was a system of sizeable government hostels serving official travellers. None of these have survived, but there is an example from Crete, dating to 1500 BC, near a highway on the south coast. The people of early Mesopotamia also developed the first public house in the first half of the third millennium BC, the core business of which was supplying both drinks and women – a service followed by other establishments for the next 6000 years.

Although Egypt's tombs and temples have been visitor attractions for millennia, the serious study of Egyptology (and the implications of this for the management of cultural resources) is less than 300 years old. In 1798, Napoleon Bonaparte invaded Egypt in what he thought was the first step in building a French empire in the Middle East.[7] In practice French control lasted only three years, but it left its linguistic and legal mark on the country. During Napoleon's campaign many of Egypt's great monuments were studied and recorded systematically for the first time, and the display of some of Egypt's treasures at the Louvre in Paris generated a great deal of interest from the world's archaeologists and started a programme of excavation and study which is still going strong 250 years later. Scientific interest was followed by cultural tourism, and in 1869 Thomas Cook took his first party of travellers to Egypt (for the opening of the Suez Canal).[8] Luxor, with its temples and access to the tombs of the Valley of the Kings, became the most popular tourist destination in upper Egypt and has remained so ever since, although tourism in the area has been fragile since the 1990s as a result of terrorist activities.[9] Today Luxor has more than thirty-five hotels, including the famous Winter Palace on its riverside Corniche, popular since Edwardian times with heads of state and famous people, including Noel Coward and the novelist Agatha Christie (herself married to an archaeologist). The Old Cataract hotel at Aswan is of a similar genre. Aswan, located at Egypt's southern frontier, lacks the commercialization of Luxor, and became internationally famous for its High Dam. This was started in 1960 but took more than a decade to complete. However, it resulted in the formation of the 6000 square kilometre Lake Nasser, now the world's largest reservoir and a strategic water reserve for Egypt, surrounded by extended cultivated land. From Edwardian times it was a fashionable winter resort for Europeans, partly because of the dry heat and partly for its cultural history. Today most visitors come to see the relocated Abu Simbel Sun Temple of Rameses II, moved to its present position by a UNESCO-financed and -organized project that cost some S$40 m between 1964 and 1968 and reassembled the monument 61 metres above and 210 metres behind the original site, which was destroyed by the rising waters of Lake Nasser.[10] However, the most famous find in Egypt was made by the archaeologist Howard Carter in 1922, after several years of excavation in the Valley of the Kings near Luxor under the patronage of Lord Carnarvon. Carter discovered the tomb of the obscure eighteenth dynasty boy pharaoh Tutankhamun, who ruled between 1325 and 1334 BC.[11] The small tomb was so crammed with objects that it took ten years to remove, catalogue and photograph all the pieces within its four unfinished chambers. Tutankhamun's tomb remains the only apparently previously untouched royal tomb found in Egypt, although even then there were signs that tomb robbers had been active soon after the tomb had been officially sealed. It is thought that Tutankhamun ruled for only nine years, and that the tomb was saved from the usual complete grave-robbing by its position low in the valley and by the construction of workmen's huts across the entrance. Fascination with the boy king and the remarkable objects from the tomb, including the gold coffins and a funeral mask, continues to be a major motivation for visitors to Egypt, stimulated by the exhibition of many of the objects in London in 1972 – an exhibition that marked the start of the 'blockbuster' exhibitions which are now commonplace throughout the developed world. Even now the contents of the tomb have not been completely studied, and it is a source of grief to Egyptologists that they included no manuscripts or parchments. The artifacts are kept in the Egyptian Museum in Cairo under tight security, where they remain the principal reason that visitors go to the capital. Today's visitors to the Valley of the Kings can see the tomb, complete with the mummy of its owner which has been returned to it, as well as a wealth of other tombs in the area – including the newly-opened tomb of Queen Nefertari, a wife of Rameses II, whose tomb is remarkable for the high quality of its wall paintings. However, archaeologists are becoming increasingly concerned at the environmental impact of visitation to these tombs, which continues to grow despite control measures which include timed ticketing and price rises (Plate 2.1).[12]

The Valley of the Kings is not, however, Egypt's sole tourism attraction. In 1869 the 167-kilometre Suez Canal opened, allowing, for the first time, passage from the Mediterranean to the Indian Ocean via the Red Sea without sailing round the tip of Africa. Previous (failed) attempts to create such a passage include those of a twenty-sixth dynasty pharaoh, and the Persian Emperor Darius. The ultimate phase of this great engineering project started in 1859 as a result of the vision of Ferdinand de Lesseps, with the Canal opening only ten years later.[13] The opening events was attended by tourists on Thomas Cook's tours, travelling in the wake of the European dignitaries who formed the invited guests. Initial financial problems resulted in a final transfer of 44 per cent of shares in Suez Canal Holdings from the bankrupt Egyptian ruler Kedive Issmail to the British Government under Disraeli, with the result that the opening of this main route, which short-circuited the passage between England and India, began to produce substantial profits for Britain rather than being ploughed back into Egypt. In the 1920s and 1930s the strategically vital Canal Zone of Suez was one of the world's largest military bases, and since 1945 the Suez Canal has been the subject of major political disputes. Britain reluctantly removed its troops in 1954, but Britain and France used the Israeli invasion of Sinai in October 1956 as an attempt to re-occupy the Zone although they were forced to withdraw. The Six-Day War with Israel in 1967 damaged newly built canal cities, and the Suez Canal was blocked by sunken ships. In the Yom Kippur War of 1973 Israel held the east bank of the canal against Egypt, but was forced out in 1982, when the canal was dredged and reopened.

Today, Egypt is investing substantially not only in the Canal Zone but also in new tourism infrastructure on both sides of the Gulf of Suez and in the southern Sinai. This is partly to diversify Egypt's tourism product from the attractions of Luxor and the Nile Valley (thought to be vulnerable to international terrorism), and partly to capitalize on the coral reefs of the Red Sea and create beach and dive-tourism resorts. Much of this investment has gone into the Sinai Peninsula (see Box 2.1), with the added advantage of increasing the Egyptian presence in Sinai and decreasing the likelihood of another Israeli invasion.[14]

Box 2.1: The Sinai Peninsula	The Sinai Peninsula, a sparsely populated 62 000 square kilometre desert peninsula, acts as a land bridge between Africa and the Middle East. It was the route by which in the Judao-Christian tradition the Israelites reached the Promised Land, and by which Islam arrived in Africa. Sinai contains spectacular landscapes, has an offshore coral reef and also contains the outstanding historical site of St Katherine's Monastery near Mount Sinai, where the Prophet Moses received the Ten Commandments.[15] Although part of Egyptian territory, it is divided from the rest of Egypt by the Suez Canal and the Gulf of Suez, and was subjected to several Israeli border disputes between 1948 and 1989. Virtually unvisited before 1960, today's millions of tourists can fly directly to Sharm El Sheikh international airport (Map 2.1), or travel overland from Cairo or Eilat (Israel's Gulf of Aquaba port), or come by ship from Hurghada or Aquaba in Jordan. Even after the opening of the Suez Canal in 1869, Sinai remained a sparsely-population desert region of great natural beauty which few travellers visited – its main cultural site, St Katherine's, probably had less than twenty visitors per year. Today, the coastline around southern Sinai is littered with major resort developments and protected areas, both designed to exploit the Red Sea's diving resources. The rapid development of the Egyptian Red Sea resorts (especially around Sharm), Aquaba and to a lesser extent Eilat (where little development is now taking place), gives great cause for environmental concern – particularly regarding the unplanned building of hotels and tourist infrastructure, inadequate arrangements for waste disposal, overuse of energy and water resources, and poorly supervised tourist activity of various kinds – so that the unique environment and biodiversity of the Gulf, the very basis for its tourist appeal, is increasingly threatened. By 2010 Egypt's Sinai coast resorts will offer at least 55 000 hotel rooms (compared with the 15 000 available in 1997), whereas the Jordanian Government plans similar increases in Aqaba from 700 to 5000 bedspaces in the same period. However, all these developments are progressing more slowly than planned, owing to the Gulf and Iraq Wars.

This rapid development of the Sinai Peninsula, with the justifiable concerns over its environmental impact, is the most significant series of resort developments in the Middle East. However, if we were to look for the single most rapidly-growing resort and the largest numbers of tourist arrivals, both would be found in the Arabian Peninsula, with the rapid expansion of Dubai as a travel hub and destination and with the continued growth in Muslim travellers making the *haj*[16] pilgrimage to Makkah (Mecca).

The Arabian Peninsula

The present political profile of the countries which comprise the Arabian Peninsula was shaped by the events of the First World War when, in 1914, the remains of the Ottoman Empire sided with Germany. In the closing years of the War the British occupied Palestine and Damascus and a secret deal to carve up the remains of the Ottoman Empire was implemented, by which France took control of Syria and Lebanon and Britain retained Egypt and was given control of what were then Palestine, Transjordan and Iraq. The events of the period have, of course, become forever immortalized by the writings of T. E. Lawrence and the David Lean film *Lawrence of Arabia*.[17] During the Second World War, Egypt became briefly the centre of desert fighting – notably the British victory at the battle of El Alamein in Egypt's desert west of Alexandria, which halted the German advance across North Africa. However, after the Second World War problems began to surface in the Middle East, beginning with tensions rising in Palestine and pressure on its British administration for unrestricted Jewish immigration, and eventually partition. The subsequent Arab–Israeli War, the overthrow of the Shah of Iran, the Suez crisis, continuing Arab–Israeli conflict, the Islamic Revolution in Iran, the Gulf War and later the Iraq War have all combined to create the political boundaries of the Middle East which we know today. The balance of power in the Middle East was further changed by the discovery of oil in the Gulf, with two oil booms in the 1970s, followed by the rise of powerful rulers in the previously poor and under-populated Gulf states, which became world powers in ways that were previously unimaginable.

The history of travel to and around the Arabian Peninsula is a long one, and is intrinsically related to shipping routes through the Red Sea, Arabian Gulf, Gulf of Aden and Arabian Sea. Until the opening of the Suez Canal, land trade routes were also of great significance – notably the camel caravan routes which connected the great port cities of Arabia (such as Aden, Jiddah, Muscat and Bahrain) by an overland network that also connected with the Nile Valley (and thus with Cairo and Alexandria) and with the Mediterranean coastal ports such as Tyre, Sidon and Beirut (Map 2.2). By such means it was possible to travel from India to Arabia using the monsoon winds, and connect by land routes to the Mediterranean and thus to Europe. The Middle East is one of the few areas of the world where passenger shipping is still an expanding market, with services in the Arabian Gulf showing particular levels of growth. Modern routes and hubs are often of very ancient foundation. Many of the Middle East's trading ports were already established by 3000 BC – such as Bahrain (Map 2.2), which grew because of its strategic position along the trade routes linking Mesopotamia to the Nile Valley in the era of the Dilmun Empire, and remained a significant port for the next 6000 years before oil was discovered there earlier than in the rest of the Gulf. During the 1970s and 1980s Bahrain experienced huge growth as a result of the skyrocketing price of oil but, like so many of the Gulf states, it has now begun to diversify and become less dependent on its fossil fuel resources and is looking to tourism for this

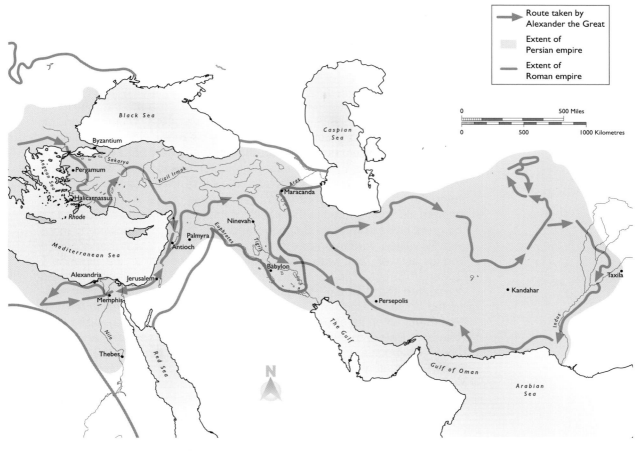

Map 2.2
Ancient empires

purpose. However, not all Arabian cities are of such ancient foundation; in contrast to Bahrain, the headland now occupied by Kuwait city was settled only 300 years ago but it grew rapidly. By 1760 Kuwait had a *dhow* fleet of 800 boats, which connected with the camel caravans based there and that travelled regularly overland to Baghdad and Damascus.

During the Middle Ages, much of what is now the United Arab Emirates (UAE) was part of the Kingdom of Hormuz and controlled the entrance to, and the trade within, the whole of the Gulf of Arabia. The Portuguese had occupied and built a custom's house near the site of present day Ras Al-Khaimah, through which they were able to generate tax revenue on the growing trade between India and the Far East.

The Sultanate of Oman is gradually becoming a major contemporary player in Middle-Eastern tourism (Map 2.1) by developing its natural tourism resources to appeal to the upper end of the cultural tourism market. The country presents a dramatic contrast to the vast deserts of Saudi Arabia and the small city-states of the Gulf, and has dramatic mountains and beautiful beaches, now accompanied by several World Heritage sites. Between the seventeenth and nineteenth centuries Oman was an imperial power, competing at first with Portugal and then with

Britain for influence in the Gulf, Indian Ocean and trade routes with eastern Africa. However, the region of Dhofar in southern Oman has been the epicentre of the world's trade in frankincense[18] (see Box 2.2, Plate 2.2) since 2000 BC, with caravans setting out from here eastwards through Yemen and north across what is now the Empty Quarter of Saudi Arabia.

Box 2.2: **Trade in frankincense**	Frankincense gum is produced by medium-sized thorny trees of the *Boswellia* sp. and extracted by incising the trunk, in a manner similar to tapping rubber. Frankincense was the most valuable commodity in the ancient world, being crucial to religious ritual in many different traditions. Frankincense caravans connected the southern part of Oman with the world of the Middle East and with the Mediterranean. Pliny, writing in the first century AD,[19] claimed that control of the frankincense trade had made the southern Arabians the richest people on earth. Trade in frankincense also contributed to the wealth of the Nabateans, as evidenced by the great cities of Medain Salah in Saudi and the better-known and more heavily visited Jordanian site of Petra. Frankincense was harvested in Yemen as well, and was responsible for the wealth of the legendary Queen of Sheba. The frankincense trade and the routes which it created dominated the Arabian Peninsula for millennia, and successfully supported powerful kingdoms such as that of Saba, mentioned in the Old Testament when its queen, Bilqis (the real Queen of Sheba), visits King Solomon. Before the eleventh century BC frankincense resin (and many other commodities) was carried on trade routes through the Arabian Peninsula by donkeys, but after this date trade and travel were facilitated by the introduction of the camel. Some caravans could include as many as 1500 camels, stretching out for miles and moving at around three miles per hour. There were well established land connections between the main Yemeni frankincense-growing area in Wadi Hadhramau, a 160-kilometre valley which stretched east–west from the coastal trade route between Yemen and Oman. However, even after the introduction of the camel it took two months for a caravan to travel from the Yemeni port of Quana (modern Bir Ali, near Aden) up the coast of the Arabian Sea to Gaza in Egypt. Such caravans carried other products as well as frankincense, including gold and other valuable items that had reached Quana from the sea routes to India.

The decline of the frankincense trade started in the third century AD and was related to both the decline of the Roman Empire and the discovery of how to utilize the monsoon winds on voyages from India, thus transferring cargo from camels to ships and utilizing ports such as Aden at the expense of the land routes. But frankincense is still a significant commodity today, and many sites associated with the ancient trade in Oman have been developed as tourist attractions.[20] The same is true (to a more limited extent) in Yemen, where the remains of the great cities made wealthy by the frankincense trade support limited amounts of incoming international tourism, although modern Yemen has a reputation for political instability and hostage-taking by guerrillas. The legacy of the trading links of Yemen may still be seen in the Indian and Javanese influence on the decoration of Yemen's unique six-storey plaster-covered mud-brick townhouses, the best examples of which are seen in the city of Shibam. Yemen later developed a second commodity, which was traded as far away as Europe in the 1500s, when the trade in coffee grown in Yemen's mountains started utilizing the port of Al Makha (hence 'mokha' coffee). Coffee became a fashionable European drink, and the first coffee factories were built in Yemen by the British and Dutch in the early 1600s. By the 1630s coffee houses could be found from Venice to Amsterdam, but Yemen was unable to meet the soaring demand and its monopoly was broken in the early 1700s when plants were smuggled out of the country and new plantations established in Ceylon.

Oman's current tourism success story is interesting and is related to the rise to power of Sultan Qaboos as the result of a coup in 1970 – an event followed by rapid modernization of the country. His wish to preserve Oman's traditional culture accounts for the focus on low-volume/high-cost cultural tourism, along with Oman's reputation for being the easiest country in the Gulf for non-Muslim tourists to visit, with a more relaxed approach to religion. Many eighteenth to early twentieth century travellers' accounts of Oman stimulated interest and awareness of the country, and a latent demand to visit. Of these, the most significant account is probably Wilfred Thesiger's in his book *Arabian Sands*,[21] which gives an account of his travels in and around Salalah, which he visited at the end of one of his journeys into the Rub' Al-Khali or the Empty Quarter – the world's largest sand desert. But Oman's success story in attracting cultural tourism is not matched by Saudi Arabia, with which it shares a border. Saudi Arabia is another country that has exerted a perennial fascination for travellers because of its vast emptiness, its significance as the cradle of Islam and the Arabic language, and because it is still virtually closed to visitors. Although opening up a little to modest numbers of cultural tourists travelling in small groups, in view of the many restrictions on travel it seems unlikely that Saudi Arabia will become a major player in the leisure tourism market – and nor would it wish to be. Yet, as we have already seen, Saudi Arabia is actually one of the most heavily visited countries of the Middle East because of the *haj* pilgrimage to Makkah, the *haj* being an obligation laid on able-bodied practising Muslims, who must make the pilgrimage to Makkah at least once in their lifetime, if they can afford to do so.

The immense wealth of the Saudi royal family is based on oil discovered in the 1960s, and the country has little need for economic diversification. However, during earlier political regimes it was visited by European travellers and explorers. Exploration of the Gulf and desert areas started with Sir Richard Burton, a remarkable man who spoke twenty-nine languages and worked as an army intelligence officer, often travelling in Arabia disguised as a Muslim (Map 2.3). It had always been his dream to travel to the sacred city of Mecca (forbidden to non-Muslims), and eventually he did so, travelling via Cairo, Suez and Medina disguised as an Afghani pilgrim. Burton sketched and measured the Ka-Bah (the most holy shrine of Islam) and then organized an expedition to the equally forbidding east-African city of Harar, becoming the first European to enter without being executed. Charles Doughty, travelling in the 1880s, became the first Westerner to see the Nabatean tombs of Madain Salah, and in later centuries the pilgrim road from Damascus to Mecca passed near the site. The Nabatean empire, based at Petra, dominated what is now Syria and Palestine after the break-up of the remains of Alexander the Great's empire at the hands of his successors, and eventually (like all the rest of the western Mediterranean, Near East and North Africa) fell under Roman domination. But the history of travel and trade in what was often called Asia Minor and the Levant (modern Iraq, Iran, Syria, Jordan, Palestine, Lebanon and Israel), and its legacy visible in modern tourism, goes back to prehistoric times.

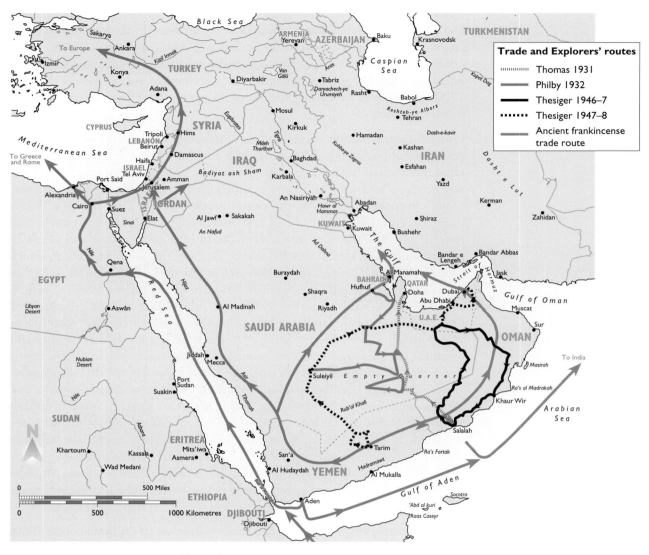

Map 2.3
Explorers' routes

The worlds of the Bible

We have already encountered the story of the visit of the Queen of Sheba to King Solomon in Jerusalem, which probably took place in the early tenth century BC, and indeed one could argue that she was the first international tourist in the modern sense – although most now think that her motivation was trade rather than romance. But she was undoubtedly travelling along the network of ancient camel caravan routes which honeycombed the Middle East at this time. The story of Solomon and Sheba is found in the Bible in I Kings 10, where it is used to illustrate Solomon's wealth and fame.[22] From biblical sources we know that Solomon's wealth was based on the strategic position of his kingdom, which enabled him to control the major north–south caravan routes. The two most important arteries through what is now Israel, Jordan and Lebanon were the Kings' Highway and the Via Maris (Way of the Sea). The latter ran from Memphis in Egypt through Gaza, north along the Mediterranean coast through Tyre and Sidon, then east to Aleppo in Syria where it joined a major road linking the valleys of the Tigris and Euphrates in the east with Asia Minor in the west. This, indeed, was the route that the Bible tells us[23] was taken by Mary and Joseph when they fled to Egypt with the infant Jesus. The Kings' Highway followed the east bank of the Dead Sea, winding east of the River Jordan and Sea of Galilee and branching south of the Dead Sea, with one fork going westwards to join Palestine with Egypt and another connecting to Petra and the Red Sea ports. Such major roads were connected by many lesser roads, which took travellers, soldiers, traders and pilgrims throughout the Middle East for several thousand years before the Roman network was created. The extent of such trading links is illustrated by Solomon's activities between 965 and 922 BC. He apparently had dealings with the King of Tyre (for Lebanese cedarwood for the building of the Temple in Jerusalem) and with Egypt (for the supply of horses and chariots), and operated a Red Sea fleet in partnership with Hiram of Tyre trading in gold, hardwood, silver, ivory and jewels along the east coast of Africa. The Bible is, indeed, a rich source of information on early trade routes and activities, such as the military campaigns in Chapters 26 and 27 of the Book of Ezekiel, which describe trade and commerce in ancient Tyre (in modern-day Lebanon) and recount the travels made by the merchants.[24] Travel at this time was hazardous, though necessary to carry on trade, escape war and famine, find work, maintain family ties and make religious pilgrimages. However, until the Romans built extensive roads the travellers would be well advised to join a caravan, for protection from brigands, if nothing else. The establishment of the vast Roman Empire, united by a single language, enabled the reinforcement of existing travel and trade networks and the creation of new ones. The Romans built, over five centuries, 53 000 miles of highways and 200 000 miles of secondary roads. They also made sea travel easier by subduing the pirates of the Mediterranean.

Although in Egypt travel and transport systems remained essentially unchanged until classical times, in the eastern Mediterranean the travel patterns changed around 1200 BC after the break-up of the great Minoan–Mycenaean civilization of Greece, which created conditions of great uncertainty for travellers that were only paralleled in the declining years of the Roman Empire. In this unsettled world, travel by sea was the easiest way of getting around – at least for trading purposes. The Phoenicians became the next great maritime power and, from about 1100 BC, were to monopolize the Mediterranean for around 400 years until the Greeks learnt ship-building well enough to challenge them successfully. King Solomon himself had used Phoenician traders to carry on trading with India, reopening routes that had existed 1000 years before, and a little over a century later Phoenician seamen founded a colony at Carthage in modern-day Tunisia and eventually passed through the streets of Gibraltar into the Atlantic to found a new colony at Cadiz in Spain. By 600 BC, Phoenician traders had possibly circum-navigated Africa.

After the division of the Roman Empire into two halves in AD 395, the eastern half, centred on Byzantium (Constantinople, now modern Istanbul), benefited from the transition, partly because it was in control of the Silk Road as well as the maritime trade routes of the eastern Mediterranean. The slow decline of Byzantium (and constant conflict with the Persian Sassanian Empire) took place at the same time as the rapid expansion of Islam throughout the Middle East. Within twenty years of the death of the Prophet Mohammed in AD 632, Arab armies had occupied Syria, Palestine, Egypt, Persia and parts of what is now Afghanistan. Within a century of the Prophet's death, they occupied an empire stretching from Spain to India and Uzbekistan. This had the effect of making it difficult to visit the traditional Christian pilgrimage locations in the Holy Land, which included not only the sites of Christ's birth (Bethlehem), death and burial (Jerusalem) and public ministry (Galilee) but also sites associated with the development of the early church and the missionary journeys of early apostles such as Paul through much of Asia Minor (now Turkey). Pilgrimage to the Holy Land had been, from a very early date, a significant travel link between Europe and the Middle East (p. 94) that was only minimally related to trade or politics. Even before the establishment of Christianity as the official religion of the Roman Empire by the Emperor Constantine in AD 314, Christians had already begun to travel long distances to visit martyrs' tombs. A turning point occurred when Helena, Constantine's mother, travelled on pilgrimage to Jerusalem in the early fourth century and discovered a number of Christian relics, including the cross on which Christ had been crucified. Upon her return to Europe (accompanied by many sacred objects in a way that might uncharitably be described as looting), Constantine began erecting churches and basilicas throughout all Christendom – including Bethlehem, the Mount of Olives in Jerusalem and the Vatican Hill in Rome. Pilgrims living in Europe travelled to the tombs of Peter and Paul in Rome, whilst those living in the eastern half of the empire visited biblical sites and locations associated with well-known monks such as St Simeon Stylites (who lived on a pillar in the north of what is now Lebanon), the monasteries of St Anthony in Egypt (near the present new Egyptian Red Sea resort of Hurghada), and St Katherine's monastery in Sinai.[25] Some, but very few, European pilgrims travelled from Europe to the Holy Land, including the so-called Bordeaux Pilgrim who made the long journey in AD 333, leaving behind a travelogue. This itinerary (also known as *Itinerarium Burdigalense*) is the earliest description left by a Christian traveller in the Holy Land; it is written in Latin and consists mostly of a list of localities and distances.[26] The localities are subdivided into cities, halts and changes; in these places travellers could remain for a while, rest, have dinner, or just change their horses and keep going. It is, in fact, one of the earliest published examples of a tourist guidebook, and is especially interesting because the anonymous pilgrim is travelling in the time of Constantine and is thus an eyewitness to the establishment of the first imperial basilicas in Palestine. A far more detailed record was made, perhaps surprisingly, by a female traveller usually known as Egeria, who was possibly a member of a religious order making a leisurely pilgrimage to the Holy Land (p. 95).

In 1095, Pope Urban II called for a Christian military expedition to liberate the holy places of Jerusalem from Islamic control. Thus was born the first of the Crusades – ultimately ineffective in their aims, but whose influence on destination awareness of Europeans should not be underestimated. People from relatively remote areas of northern Europe not only travelled to the Middle East for the first time, but (sometimes) also returned with stories of a different environment, climate and culture that must have seemed fantastic at the time. The Crusades were deeply influential in early medieval European life, in everything from medicine to music. Until then, the only long-distance leisure travel had been undertaken by pilgrims. A further obstacle to pilgrims reaching the Holy Land was the rise of the Mongol Empire, initially under Genghis Khan and later under Timur Lang (Tamerlane), who added Persia, Syria and part of Iraq to the Empire of Genghis.

The dying remnants of the Byzantine Empire were poorly controlled from Constantinople, and by the fifteenth century the Ottoman Empire had taken over, reaching its peak under Suleiman the Magnificent (1520–1566), when it controlled the entire Middle East, North Africa and eastern Europe.

Greeks and Persians

On land, a major innovation in the history of transport came under the rule of the Assyrian Empire, which dominated the Fertile Crescent and Levant from the Persian Gulf to Egypt, and lasted almost 300 years between 900 and 612 BC. The Assyrians were an organized military force, and Assyrian rulers laid down a network of roads, complete with road signs, suitable for heavy Assyrian chariots and military equipment. Every six miles or so there was a guard post, and on long roads through deserts there were wells and small forts at appropriate intervals. Assyrian roads were used by the king's messengers as well as the army, and were in many ways forerunners of the great roads of the Roman Empire. The horse was first used as a draught animal around 1600 BC (probably by the nomads of the steppe country of southern Russia, Asia Minor and Iran), but it was not until the Assyrian Empire that people first learnt to ride them.[27] By 875 BC the Assyrians had cavalry in the army, but despite this throughout the ancient and classical world horses were of minimal importance in leisure transport, being expensive to buy and maintain, with the majority of ancient travellers preferring to go by donkey or in a cart pulled by mules.

This efficient network of roads and government posts that the Assyrians had built up was greatly refined by the later Persian Empire into a system which included their so-called 'Royal Road' (primarily maintained for government officials), which ran from Sardis near the east coast of the Mediterranean some 1600 miles to Susa near the head of the Persian Gulf. Rest houses and inns for royalty and notables were located at intervals of ten to fifteen miles, together with forts at strategic points. It was recorded that ordinary wayfarers could average eighteen miles a day on it, taking three months for the whole route, although the Persian dispatch service, efficiently organized into stages, did it in one-fifth of that time. However, goods were still transported on cross-desert camel caravans which carried goods across the Near East, and these were responsible for the camel's key role in the trade of the Near East. The Persian Empire, under the great kings Darius I and Xerxes, had expanded throughout Asia by the late fourth century BC, stretching from India to Egypt and the Aegean Sea. Its capital, Persepolis, was burnt by the invading Alexander the Great in 323 BC.[28] Alexander, the son of Philip II, King of Macedon, demolished the Persian armies, liberated Greek cities on the Asian mainland (in the south of what is now Turkey), and occupied Syria, Palestine and Egypt before marching westwards to include the whole of the former Persian Empire under his control, together with some parts of India beyond the then Persian frontier. Unfortunately this vast empire disintegrated after his death, having been carved up by his chief generals who became kings – the best known of whom being Ptolemy, who founded a dynastic line in Egypt. Today's Persia (Iran) is only gradually opening up to modern tourism, with visitors being attracted not only to the ruins of Persepolis but also to cities such as Esfahan (Isfahan), with its magnificent sixteenth century Islamic architecture, and Shiraz, one of the leading cities of the medieval Islamic world. Modern Iraq, which occupies the region of Mesopotamia, also has no tourism industry because of the Gulf and Iraq Wars and subsequent civil unrest. There is great concern about the preservation of its stunning archaeological sites, including Ninevah and Babylon, which include relics of all the great historical empires of Assyria, Babylonia, Persia and Greece (under Alexander). Wilfred Thesiger also travelled in southern Iraq, with his book *The Marsh Arabs*[29] describing the world of the tribal people of that area, where he lived for five years in the 1950s. The marshes were drained under the regime of Sadam Hussein but are now being revitalized, which is more than can be said for Iraq's virtually non-existent tourism industry.

If we were to look at the Middle East at around the year 500 BC, we would see it unified under the Persian Empire (ruled by Darius the Great), which then dominated the world, having combined the great nations of the Near East – including Assyria, Babylonia and Egypt – into one enormous empire stretching out as far as the Greek cities on the western coast of Asia Minor. The power of this vast empire was challenged by some Greek city-states, notably Athens, in the Persian Wars fought between 490 and 480–79 BC, in which the Greeks were victorious. Despite this, there was never a unified nation called 'Greece' but instead a series of separate city-states such as Athens, Sparta, Corinth, Thebes, etc. Athens reached its zenith in the second half of the fifth century BC by establishing control of a federation of these city-states that paid it tribute. This Greek-controlled world stretched from the eastern shores of the Black Sea to Marseilles, but then ran up against the Phoenician colony at Carthage, which had established control over the western Mediterranean, the gates of Gibraltar and the coasts of Spain and Morocco. But east of the Phoenician territory sea routes operating from Marseilles were open to sea traffic across the Mediterreanean, linking with land trade routes using the fine roads maintained by Persia.

One of the most important sources of our knowledge of the Persian Empire is the Greek historian Herodotus, whose *History of the Persian Wars* documents the attack on Athens by Darius, the Persian king, in 490 BC. Herodotus's significance is not only in his record of historical sites, but that his history begins with an extended survey of the vast Persian Empire and its neighbours, drawing upon information from his own travels as well as stories held. He thus becomes the world's first travel writer as well as historian. Herodotus was born in Halicarnassus, a Greek city-state on the south-west corner of Asia Minor, in the early fifth century BC, and died somewhere between 430 and 425 BC after a lifetime spent exploring the Greek and Persian world. He was a man of endless curiosity; nothing escaped his attention in the course of a number of individual voyages all over Greece and the Aegean Islands, part of North Africa, southern Italy, Sicily, the west coast of Asia Minor, the Black Sea, Syria, Palestine and Babylon. His work includes records of religions, customs and physical geography, but he was also a cultural tourist. In Egypt he went to the pyramids, visited the Greek battlefields at Marathon and Thermopylae, and travelled by ship whenever he could.

By the fifth century, educated or well-travelled Greeks knew the geography of the whole of the Mediterranean and the Black Sea and were also aware (although unable to travel there because of the dominance of Carthage as a sea power) of the existence of a vast ocean beyond the pillars of Hercules, and of the island of Britain far to the north. Their geography was, however, essentially coastal; they knew the coasts of Arabia and lands as far east as the Indus Valley, and knew that Africa was surrounded by water, but were hazy about the situation inland. Although there is a possibility that Phoenician traders had circumnavigated Africa around 600 BC (although this was only a story picked up by Herodotus in Egypt), it is certain that by *c.* 500 BC large Phoenician expeditions travelled through the Straits of Gibraltar, intending to set up colonies on the west coast of Africa. One, led by Hanno of Carthage (from which a 650-word report survives[30]), numbered some 50 vessels, but we are still unsure how far he got. Most scholars think that it was no further than Sierra Leone and into the Gulf of Guinea, although some interpret the text references as referring to Cameroon or even Gabon. The expedition, although interesting, had no lasting impact on contemporary people's knowledge of their world, and did not colonize West Africa. Indeed, geographical errors in the mapping of the African coast were not to be corrected until the days of Henry the Navigator (p. 53).

Bridges to Europe

The core of the Roman, Persian, Egyptian and Babylonian Empires finally ended up as part of Ottoman Turkey, which declined steadily but very slowly from its peak under Suleiman the Magnificent[31] until its final handover to France after the First World War in 1920. If it were necessary to pick a critical moment in that decline, it would probably be the destruction of Ottoman naval power at the Battle of Lepanto in the Aegean Sea by the Spanish/Venetian navy in 1571, which marked the point at which the unity of great empires in the region was finally lost. Europe began colonial expansion into the Middle East in 1498, when the Portuguese explorer Vasco da Gama visited the northern coast of Oman, the Strait of Hormuz and what are now some of the Gulf states. Portugal kept control of what is modern Bahrain until 1602 and a presence in Oman until 1650, but only as way-stations on the route to India, with little attempt to penetrate the interior of Arabia.

Today's Middle East has an interesting and complex relationship with Europe in terms of tourism, which has been episodic, affected by events such as the ongoing Arab–Israeli conflict, the Gulf War of 1990–1991 and the US invasion of Iraq. Since the 1980s much of the region has opened up to cultural tourism, with innovative and unexpected new developments taking place (such as short shopping-and-culture breaks in Damascus), the increased popularity of Nile cruises, continued interest in pilgrimage to sites in Israel and Palestine (despite political tensions and interruptions), and the growth of Jordan as a cultural tourism destination. Until the Gulf War it had looked as though an increasingly political liberal Syria might become a major cultural tourism player, but although there is still interest in visiting the great cities and *suqs* of the ancient world, such as Aleppo and Damascus, and Silk Road link cities like Palmyra,[32] confidence has diminished since the invasion of Iraq. Oases like Palmyra (Map 2.3) used to serve as way-stations for the caravans that connected the Mediterranean and Mesopotamia. Nowhere is the influence of political crises seen more clearly than in Lebanon. Before its disastrous seventeen years of fighting between 1976 and 1992, Lebanon was one of the most popular countries in the Middle East as a leisure tourism destination.[33] In antiquity, as we have seen (p. 35), the cedars of Lebanon built Solomon's Temple and supplied the raw material for the ships of the Phoenician trading empire based at the Lebanese ports of Tyre and Sidon. Modern Lebanon emerged from the break-up of the Ottoman Empire after the First World War, and between the two World Wars had a French mandate – still very evident to its contemporary visitors, who frequently remark that Lebanon is essentially a Mediterranean country which happens to be located in the Middle East. Its unique geography famously makes it possible to ski in the morning in the mountains of the Mount Lebanon and swim in the Mediterranean in the afternoon. Despite the horrific social and environmental effects of the 1976–1992 war, the creative rebuilding of Beirut, and World Heritage designation for the early monastic and pilgrimage sites of the Quadisha Valley (Plate 2.3), are once again attracting European visitors. Still, Lebanon's main tourist revenues come from incoming Arab visitors (mainly from the Gulf states, some of whom maintain summer houses in Lebanon) and others attracted by Lebanon's socially unconstricted society. However, continuing Arab– Israeli tension and the apparently unresolvable dispute between Israel and Palestine in the West Bank and Gaza strip still continues to affect the possibility of cross-border tourism throughout the region. Israel itself remains a significant Christian pilgrimage destination, and has substantial volumes of incoming tourism from non-Israeli visitors from Jewish communities scattered throughout the world as a result of the diaspora (migration of Jews from the Roman period throughout the Middle Ages, initially to the western and northern shores of the Mediterranean and eventually, from the early Middle Ages, from there to central and eastern Europe and North Africa).

Many Sephardic Jews who were expelled from Spain and Portugal in the thirteenth century settled in the Ottoman Empire, with its capital at Constantinople (Istanbul) in modern Turkey. Turkey, ruled by Ottoman sultans from the fifteenth century, is the bridge between Europe and the Middle East, both physically and culturally. By the nineteenth century, Ottoman decline had made Turkey the 'sick man of Europe' and the country entered a period of turbulence from which it emerged in the 1920s under Kemal Ataturk, who embarked on a rapid modernization programme, setting the scene for modern Turkey. Today's Turkey is partly looking towards the West (and aiming for EU membership) and partly looking towards a deeper relationship with the Islamic world. Turkey is the only country of the Middle East that can really be said to have experienced a tourist boom during the 1980s, which brought even more European influences – from rock music to topless beaches. Cruise-ship ports like Kusadasi and the so-called 'Turquoise Coast' east of Marmaris have become inexpensive and popular alternatives to the beach tourism destinations of the western Mediterranean coast, but Turkey's market share of circum-Mediterranean tourism has varied with factors such as the exchange rate of the Euro, and the Gulf and Iraq Wars. Turkey's road network is still largely based on the routes established by the Silk Road network, but its capital (Istanbul) dominated the sea trade routes of the Mediterranean until the fifteenth century, having been the strategic centre of the transport and political networks of the Byzantine Empire for the previous thousand years, keeping Roman culture alive throughout early Middle Ages.

Turkey has always been a significant maritime power because of its ability to dominate trade into the Black Sea through the Dardanelles, Sea of Marmara and the Bosphorus. Today this trading legacy is reflected in Istanbul's reputation as a major shopping location (now popular as a European short-break destination), and its long, complex cultural history has provided major attractions such as the Topkapi Palace, Hagia Sophia and the Blue Mosque. Tourism marketing for Turkey has also aimed to turn the prehistory of the country to its advantage, particularly interest in the site of ancient Troy (Map 2.3), and there is an increasing volume of pilgrim traffic to its ancient Christian sites, including the early Christian rock-cut churches and entire underground cities at Kaymakli and Derinkuyu in

Cappadocia. Ephesus was the capital of Asia in Roman times, and later a centre of early Christianity famously visited by St Paul, and can claim to be the best preserved classical city on the Mediterranean. The Basilica of St John is said to be built over his tomb, and there is a completely unsubstantiated legend that the Virgin Mary lived the last years of her life on a nearby mountain top at Meryemana. Some of the most significant sea routes of the ancient world are still perpetuated by well-used ferries connecting Istanbul, Venice, Cyprus and the Greek islands.

The relationship between Greece and Turkey in Mycenaean times has always been a source of great interest since the story of the Bronze Age 'Trojan War' was first recounted by the Greek poet Homer. Indeed, Homer himself was born at nearby Izmir around 700 BC. His epic poem *The Iliad*[34] is considered one of the landmark works of Western literature. Composed over 2700 years ago, it depicts the war of the Greeks against the Trojans, theoretically precipitated by the beautiful Helen, who was married to the Greek King Menelaus and eloped with Paris, son of Priam King of Troy. In fact it seems more likely that this was a dispute concerning trade routes between the Black Sea and Mediterranean; Troy's legendary wealth was built from its strategic position covering sea-borne trade through the Bosporus and land routes to the east. The legend of Troy re-entered public consciousness after the excavations, starting in 1871, by the archaeologist Heinrich Schliemann, who found the remains of a succession of cities at the uninspiring hill of Hissarlik, each one built on the ruins of the earlier settlements.[35] Schliemann thought that the second Troy, Troy 2, was the city featured in Homer's tale, although modern archaeologists consider that it was more likely to have been Troy 6. Visitors to the city in ancient times included Alexander the Great, who identified with the hero Achilles. More recently awareness of Troy (Ilium) has been created by a film version of the story (starring the American actor Brad Pitt as the hero Achilles),[36] but apparently many visitors to the site are disappointed not to see Homer's 'topless towers of Ilium' as they were recreated for the film, and find the lack of visible monuments on the site rather disappointing.

The legendary city of Troy was not the only significant visitor attraction on the Turkish coast during ancient times. The city of Bergama (Pergamum) was especially significant in the ancient world for its *Asclepion* medical school, whose library rivalled its more famous contemporary in Alexandria in Egypt and drew visitors from all over world between the third century BC and the third century AD. Other visitors came to Bodrum on the Aegean coast, which was formerly called Halicarnassus and was the site of the Mausoleum, the monumental tomb of the eponymous King Mausolus and one of the Seven Wonders of the World. It was completed around 350 BC, three years after the king's death. It remained visible and a tourist attraction for sixteen centuries, until an earthquake caused some damage to the roof and colonnade. In the early fifteenth century, the Knights of St John of Malta invaded the region and built a massive Crusader castle. When they decided to fortify it in 1494, they used the stones of the Mausoleum. By 1522, almost every block of the Mausoleum had been disassembled and used for construction. Some visitors today are drawn to see the remains of more recent conflicts. In the First World War the Dardanelles were the site of a famous battle at Gallipoli, where Turkish forces opposed stronger British–Anzac troops, leading to much loss of life. Visits to the battleground and war graves form a specific kind of cultural tourism.

North Africa

Part of the justification for including North Africa with the Middle East is the indisputable fact that for much of recorded history it was a region that mainly came under the same political control, most recently under the Ottoman Empire but more significantly under Rome. Map 1.2 shows the greatest extent of Roman domination in Africa in the middle of the third century AD, when Roman Africa was divisible into nine major provinces. Indeed, in the Roman world 'Africa' usually meant North Africa (with the exception of Egypt), with the territory south of Roman control often referred to as 'Ethiopia'. Roman settlement was densest in the provinces of Africa and Numidia. To the west of Numidia, the Roman controlled area was about the same as that previously controlled by Carthaginian trading posts initially founded centuries earlier by Phoenician traders. In the south of the Nile Valley the province of Dodekaschinus formed a buffer zone against tribes called the Nobatae, to whom the province was lost in the third century. In the fourth century, the fertile plains of Tunisia and eastern Algeria were intensively colonized by, and eventually lost to, the Vandals (though later reclaimed by Byzantine emperors). The introduction of Islam into northern Africa was synonymous with the Arab

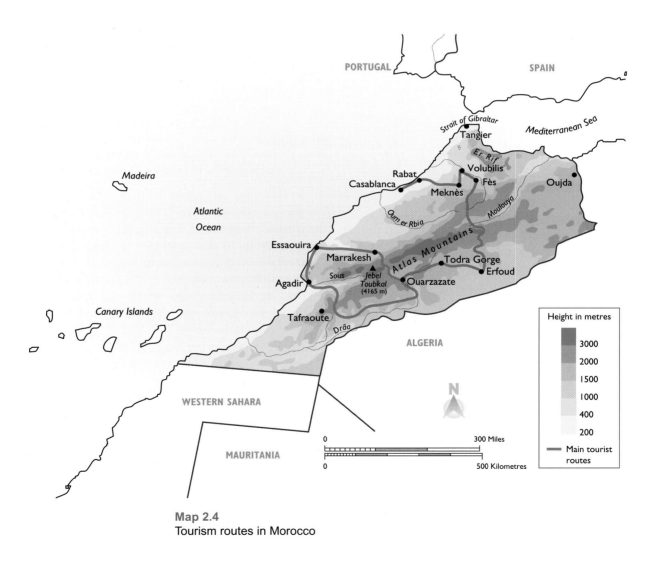

Map 2.4
Tourism routes in Morocco

conquest starting in the seventh century, but the Arab world had little knowledge of anything south of the Congo River, with the exception of coastal ports in the east. Until the fourth century AD, movement of goods and people around North Africa took place either by sea or by draught and pack animals utilizing the network of Roman roads. The Romans had little knowledge of much to the west of the Pillars of Hercules (the coast south-west of the modern Straits of Gibraltar) or south of the Atlas Mountains. However, by the fourth century the camel had been fully adopted as a pack animal in North Africa, which led to the development of trans-Saharan trade, and by the tenth century the Sahara was covered by a network of trade routes with commodities carried including gold, salt, gum and cola-nuts.

Box 2.3: Contemporary tourism in North Africa

If we look at the distribution of contemporary tourism in North Africa (Map 3.1), the clear market leader is Tunisia, with its well-developed beach tourism products. There are, however, also substantial areas (Mauritania, Western Sahara) with no tourism development at all (largely for reasons of political instability), and one country, Libya, where a fledgling cultural tourism industry is emerging quite rapidly and whose core products are based around major Roman sites such as the city of Leptis Magna and caravan cities associated with the trans-Saharan caravan routes. The fastest-growing destination, however, is Morocco, which is investing heavily in tourism development. Tourism now accounts for 7 per cent of GDP, and the country attracts 2.2 million international tourists (mainly French and Spanish). Morocco's tourism product originated in urban tourism focused around the Mediterranean cities of Tangiers and Casablanca (Map 2.4), while the country was still a French Protectorate (from 1912–1956). In the early 1900s Tangiers was a very popular resort with the smart set, and it also attracted many writers, such as Jack Kerouac and William Burroughs. After a phase of beach resort development at locations such as Agadir on the Atlantic coast in the 1970s and 1980s, Morocco's contemporary product is increasingly focused on the cultural tourism possibilities of its ancient cities, and 60 per cent of its visitors are motivated by cultural and heritage tourism. Although French influence is still strong, a new era for Moroccan tourism started in 1999 with the accession of King Mohammed VI, and the development of a new tourism strategy, Vision 2010. Plans are now being formulated for an ambitious new series of beach resorts to assist in achieving Morocco's target of 7.5 million international visitors by 2010, by which stage it is hoped that tourism will have risen to 20 per cent of GDP. Currently, the fastest growth area in Morocco is activity and adventure tourism in the Atlas and Rif Mountains, which offer superb walking and trekking opportunities from late March to mid-November. In the 1980s there was increased awareness of Morocco's cultural heritage (which includes seven World Heritage sites), especially the so-called Imperial cities of Fes, Meknes, Rabat and Marrakech.[37] Marrakech dominates Morocco's international tourism industry, with increased interest in short breaks and winter sun holidays. A significant trend has been the conversion (by private investors) of traditional *riads* (urban courtyard houses) into small luxury hotels, especially in Marrakech and Fes, although it appears that there is now over-capacity in the *riad* market following an explosion of investment. One of the most significant trends in Moroccan tourism, set for expansion in the future, is the development of trekking tourism within the High Atlas, particularly around Mount Toubkal (Map 2.4). Visitors stay in Berber villages or in spectacularly-located converted *kasbahs* (fortified houses) such as Kasbah du Toubkal. In order to capitalize on this trend, the Moroccan government is investing in trekking circuits, with renovated shelters and better infrastructure. A pilot project in Azilal province refurbished 800 lodges. Other popular trekking areas include Djebel Saghro, between the Atlas Mountains and the desert, with dramatic, volcanic landscapes. At the southern edge of the Atlas, the Todra and Dades Gorges are popular for hiking and mountain biking. Morocco is also developing desert tourism to compete with Tunisia, although the Sahara gateways such as Ouarzazate in southern Morocco, which is the main point from which to visit locations such as the Skoura Oasis and the *kasbahs* of Ait Benhaddou, now a World Heritage site but used as a film set for many epics such as *Jesus of Nazareth* and *Gladiator*.[38]

In many ways we can see Morocco as illustrating many of the issues in the tourism history of the Middle East and North Africa (Box 2.3). Its modern tourism industry not only capitalizes on its ancient sites, both Roman and Islamic, but also on its landscape and cultural history. The routes of its land transport networks were laid during the Roman period, but much of the flavour of the country as a modern destination comes from its much more recent colonial history as a French Protectorate. But Morocco, as with the rest of North Africa, has little in common in terms of tourism history with the rest of the continent south of the Sahara. Near its southern border town of Zagora, some three hours from Ouarzazate, there is a sign saying that it is fifty-two days by camel to Timbuktu, utilizing trans-Saharan trade routes which have been in use for thousands of years. And it is here that our exploration of the tourism development of sub-Saharan Africa must start.

Africa: slavery and safari

If it were desirable to list the factors which account for the contemporary shape of tourism in the vast continent that is Africa, the most significant would undoubtedly be its geographical diversity. Even a cursory glance at a map of Africa (Map 3.1) shows that it can be readily divided into five major regions on the basis of topography, environment and cultural history. The first of these would include the ten million square miles of the Sahara desert (together with the sub-Saharan Sahel region), and the second would be the west coast (south and west of the River Niger). An eastern region is focused on the countries surrounding the Rift Valley, and there is a southern region south of the Kalahari Desert. This leaves a central area which today includes countries such as the democratic Republic of Congo (once Zaire), with very low levels of tourism activity. Each region has a distinct political history, with its natural and cultural history and its environment shaping its current tourism geography. Other highly significant factors include the different legacies of colonial rule, the legacy of the slave trade (in western and to a lesser extent in North Africa) and the political uncertainties of post-colonial Africa, which persist right into the present day and create extensive no-go areas for visitors. These can sometimes be temporary and reversed by a change of power, but there are some countries in all five regions that seem almost permanently out of bounds for that reason (such as Liberia, Congo and Sudan). The geography of Africa also means that certain areas are richer in tourism resources than others. East Africa, for example, is famous for its mammalian biodiversity which (when combined with the legacy of British colonial rule) accounted for the early development of the safari industry (now sanitized into wildlife-watching holidays).

Although the cultural and travel histories of the emerging nations of sub-Saharan Africa are markedly different from those of the Arab states of the north (p. 42), in earlier times there was considerable travel across the great barrier presented by the Sahara and the high mountain ranges (such as the Rif of Morocco) which separate the Sahara desert from the coastal plains of North Africa. The rich cultural legacy of the great African empires (particularly that of Mali) has left western Africa full of cultural interest while virtually devoid of significant wildlife attractions. But the most significant historical factor shaping contemporary African politics, and indeed the nature, orientation and significance of contemporary travel and tourism within the African continent, remains the different encounters with imperial rule. Colonialism defined the boundaries of the contemporary political units; dominant political forces and leaders in many countries began as movements of nationalist resistance. The social map was changed beyond recognition, with new kinds of class divisions and the transformation of racial, ethnic and religious boundaries. Economic infrastructure and production patterns were shaped by the interests and needs of the colonial powers. The colonial experience in Africa was distinctive in

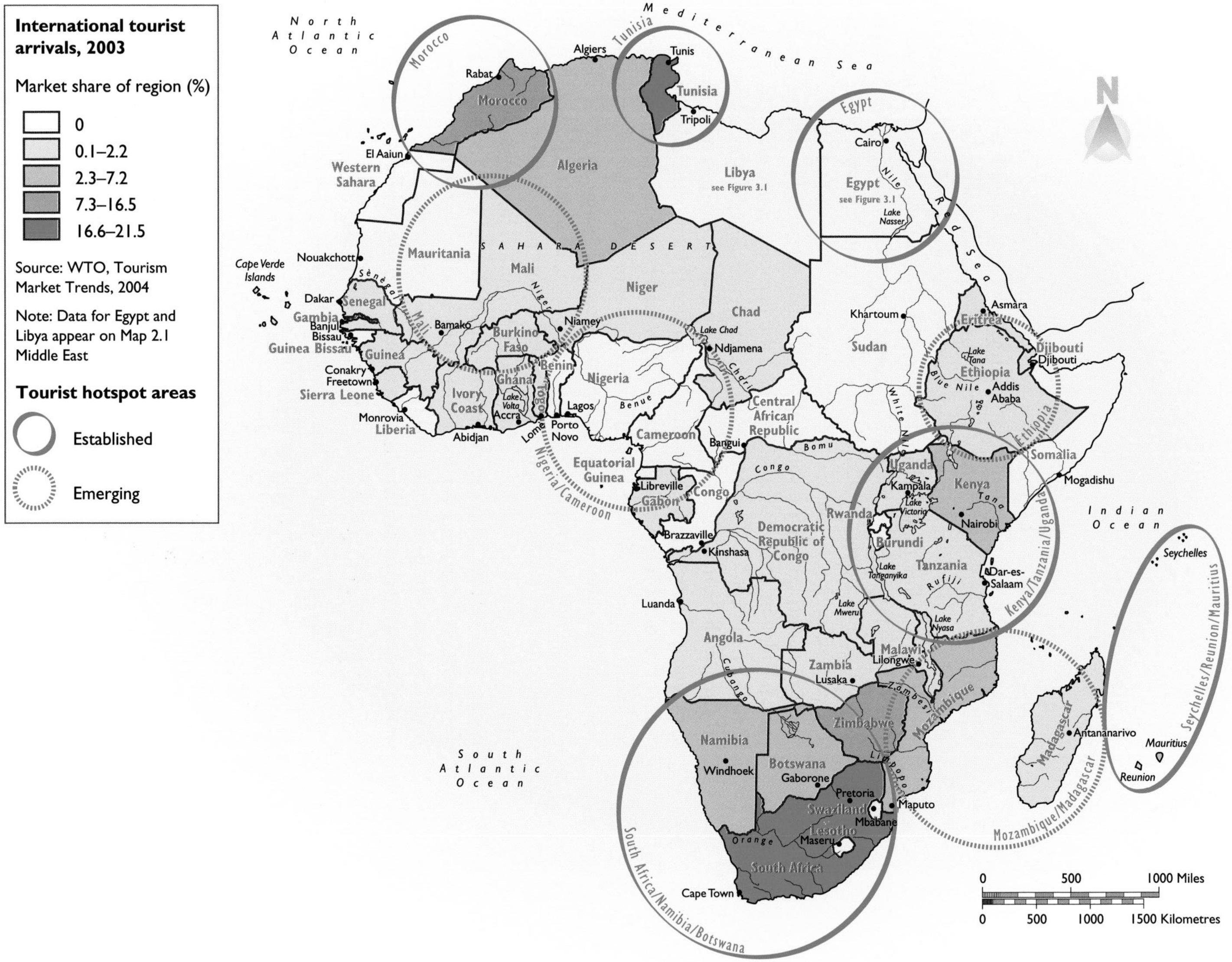

Map 3.1
Africa – international tourist arrivals 2003

International tourist arrivals, 2003

Market share of region (%)

- 0
- 0.1–2.2
- 2.3–7.2
- 7.3–16.5
- 16.6–21.5

Source: WTO, Tourism Market Trends, 2004

Note: Data for Egypt and Libya appear on Map 2.1 Middle East

Tourist hotspot areas

- Established
- Emerging

N

Mediterranean Sea

North Atlantic Ocean

South Atlantic Ocean

Indian Ocean

Red Sea

S A H A R A   D E S E R T

Morocco — Rabat
Western Sahara — El Aaiun
Algeria — Algiers
Tunisia — Tunis, Tripoli
Libya (see Figure 3.1)
Egypt (see Figure 3.1) — Cairo, Lake Nasser
Nile

Mauritania — Nouakchott
Mali — Bamako
Niger — Niamey
Chad — Ndjamena, Lake Chad
Sudan — Khartoum
Eritrea — Asmara
Djibouti — Djibouti
Somalia — Mogadishu
Ethiopia — Addis Ababa, Lake Tana
Blue Nile
White Nile

Cape Verde Islands
Senegal — Dakar
Gambia — Banjul
Guinea Bissau — Bissau
Guinea — Conakry
Sierra Leone — Freetown
Liberia — Monrovia
Ivory Coast — Abidjan
Burkina Faso
Ghana — Accra, Lake Volta
Togo — Lomé
Benin — Porto Novo
Nigeria — Lagos
Cameroon
Central African Republic — Bangui
Equatorial Guinea
Gabon — Libreville
Congo — Brazzaville
Democratic Republic of Congo — Kinshasa
Congo
Bomu

Uganda — Kampala, Lake Victoria
Rwanda
Burundi
Kenya — Nairobi
Tanzania — Dar-es-Salaam, Lake Tanganyika, Rufiji
Angola — Luanda
Cubango

Zambia — Lusaka, Lake Mweru
Malawi — Lilongwe, Lake Nyasa
Mozambique — Maputo
Zimbabwe — Zambezi, Limpopo
Botswana — Gaborone
Namibia — Windhoek, Orange
South Africa — Pretoria, Cape Town
Swaziland — Mbabane
Lesotho — Maseru

Madagascar — Antananarivo
Seychelles
Mauritius
Reunion
Seychelles/Reunion/Mauritius
Kenya/Tanzania/Uganda
South Africa/Namibia/Botswana
Mozambique/Madagascar

500   1000   1500 Kilometres
500   1000 Miles

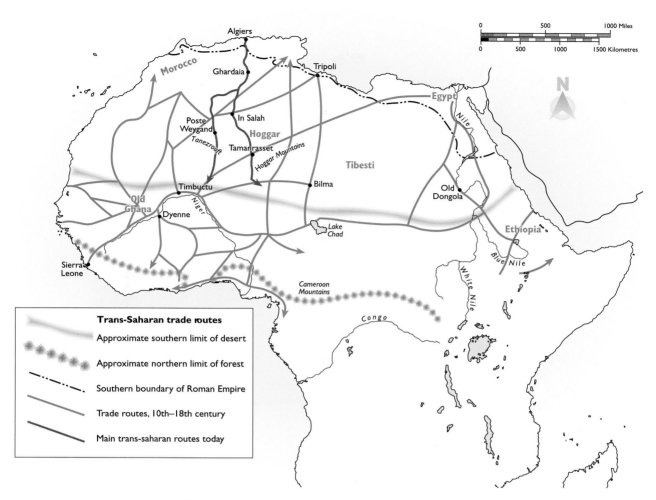

Map 3.2
Trans-Saharan trade routes

several ways. Africa was the last continent to fall under direct European rule; colonial administrations were organized at a historical moment when the state had far greater resources (communications, military technology, professional bureaucracies) than had been available in earlier centuries. The need to generate revenue from colonies led to forcible restructuring of rural African economies, often compelling local people to enter a cash economy in order to subsidize colonial rule. Culturally, Africa was held in low esteem by its colonizers, but there were important variations between the administrative systems of the colonial powers which reflected the political culture of the home country and the character of its own state institutions. For example, in France, Germany and Belgium the concept of the state stressed centralization, hierarchy and bureaucratic dominance. The British state had a distinctly different texture, with looser structure, greater diffusion of power, and more regional variation and autonomy (p. 57).

The early travel history of Africa is one of coastal exploration, followed by journeys tracing the major rivers (Niger, Zambezi, Nile etc.; Map 3.2). Before the development of air travel much of Africa was inaccessible, and even today lack of investment in air traffic control and airport infrastructure combined with political

Colonial possessions, 1930

Belgian
British
French
Italian
Portuguese
Spanish

Voyages

Dias, 1487–8 (outward)

Vasco de Gama, 1497–8 (outward)

Alternating monsoon winds

Map 3.3
Colonial possessions

instability has meant that the interior of Africa is not well served by major airlines. Contemporary airline access is still shaped by colonial rule; a brief glance at the services of Air France, partner and alliance airlines, for example, shows a close relationship with former French colonies (Map 3.3). The same is true of the routings of British-based airlines, such as British Airways and Virgin Atlantic, or by the fact that Namibia (once a German colony and then under the protection of South Africa) is served by Namib Air, South African Airways and Lufthansa. In tourism terms there is a great contrast between the volumes of international tourism received by African countries (Map 3.1), with tourism to sub-Saharan Africa being dominated by Kenya and South Africa. Many sub-Saharan African countries have high levels of poverty and illiteracy and rapidly growing populations. Domestic tourism here is insignificant compared with either Europe or Asia;[1] there are often perceived health and safety risks and difficulties in encouraging inward investment. Tourism in sub-Saharan Africa is still a developing industry, and many countries have no discernible tourism industry at all – either for political reasons (e.g. Angola) or because of lack of tourism resources (e.g. Guinea Bissau, Cape Verde Islands). Some have tourism industries in transition, which are either rapidly growing (e.g. South Africa, Namibia, Botswana) or rapidly declining (e.g. Zimbabwe), while others are at a very early growth stage and are attractive only to the business traveller or special-interest leisure travel market (e.g. Ethiopia, Mali).

Europe and Africa – early history

The writings of Herodotus (484–425 BC; see also p. 27) about North Africa and the Middle East provide a partial record of the first Saharan explorers, although some of his claims (such as the statement that a Phoenician fleet circumnavigated Africa in 600 BC) must be treated with caution. And yet Alexander the Great used his writings as a geographical reference, and even as late as the eighteenth century Sir Joseph Banks consulted the Histories of Herodotus[2] for information on the flow of the Niger. The persistent influence of the ideas of ancient geographers and historians should not be underestimated. A map of Africa produced in AD 150 by Ptolemy, the greatest of the ancient geographers,[3] was thought even by Victorian explorers to locate the source of the Nile. Ptolemy thought that the world was balanced around the Mediterranean, with the Nile to the south matching the Danube to the north. This gave rise to the idea that a great southern continent existed which would balance Europe ('*terra australis*') – an idea which persisted until James Cook reached as far as Antarctica and still found no land mass (p. 134). The western world thus knew about the existence of Africa from a very early date, but it was not until the writings of Pliny the Elder (AD 23–79) that such knowledge was widely disseminated. Pliny is often described as having written the world's first encyclopaedia, his *Natural History*,[4] an amazing compendium of fact and myth which shaped natural science for the next 1500 years. The work includes accounts of the interiors of North and West Africa, which was the extent of European knowledge until Europeans penetrated the African continent further in the nineteenth century, and his writings are credited with shaping the ambitions of many travellers and explorers, including Christopher Columbus (p. 150). Pliny himself was a Roman officer and scholar who described his *magnum opus* as containing 20 000 facts from 1000 other works, meticulously sourced and divided into 37 sections. It is an irony of fate that Pliny himself, a great academic explorer, died while investigating fumes resulting from eruption of Mt Vesuvius. Scholars drew widely on his work, only gradually realizing its errors and recognizing the differences between fact and myth.

Later sources for the geography of Africa include Al Idrisi (1100–1166), born in Cueta, who wrote an early medieval geography called *The Book of Roger*,[5] which included a map of the world in seventy sections. However, the best known of the early accounts is undoubtedly that of Ibn Battuta, born in Tangier in 1304, who set out in 1352 to travel the world – including Jordan, Arabia, Iraq, Iran, Somalia, Tanzania, the Crimea, the Balkans, Russia, Central Asia, India, the Maldives, Sri Lanka, Assam, Bengal, Malaya, Indonesia, China, Spain and the west-African states, and published an account of his travels in *The Travels of Ibn Battuta*.[6] Another major source is Leo Africanus (1485–1554); an Islamic diplomat born in Granada and educated in Fez, he travelled widely in Africa and wrote *A Geographical Historie of Africa*, which included the earliest description of the legendary city of Timbuktu.[7] Very little is known about the actual life of Leo Africanus, in spite of his well-established posthumous fame, and it has even been suggested that the man never existed and that his celebrated description of African geography was actually composed by a Venetian ghostwriter on the basis of contemporary Italian reports of Northern Africa obtained from European merchants who had been trading in North African ports since the twelfth century. In the sixteenth century Timbuktu was a major religious and cultural centre, then at the peak of its power, with a university of 25 000 students and a large library. Its description by Leo Africanus stimulated the interest of many explorers, but it was not until 1828 that the first European explorer, René-Auguste Caillié, visited 'Timbuctoo' and returned to tell the tale in three volumes published in 1830. According to Leo, the inhabitants of Timbuktu were amazingly rich and the king of Timbuktu possessed an ingot of gold that weighed over 500 kilograms. Originally this piece of gold was one of the fabulous stories about Africa circulating in medieval Arabic sources, and it became heavier with each telling but not less credible. Supported and magnified by the constant flow of new reports sent by European traders and consuls from Northern Africa, Leo's description came to represent to European readers the treasures which were available – and waiting to be discovered – in the west-African interior. His book gave a rare view of the world from the perspective of the Islamic sphere of influence, but it does not seem to have been published until over fifty years after his death. He remained a household name amidst European geographers for almost three centuries, and was unanimously respected as the most authoritative source for the political and human geography of the west-African coast and eastern Africa, until the beginning of European exploration and expansion in the African continent proved his knowledge to be outdated. The Portuguese had already successfully mapped the coasts of Africa by the early sixteenth century, but they had not been able to penetrate the interior of the continent. Their advance was checked by local resistance and lethal endemic diseases. Moreover, sub-Saharan Africa was largely forgotten after Europeans had found their way to the wonders and treasures of the New World and India.

As a result of Leo's work many European adventures tried to reach Timbuktu, and the courts of Europe were disappointed to be told by René Caillié (1799–1838) that Timbuktu was a rather poor town consisting of nothing but 'a mass of ill-looking houses, made of earth'.[8] Timbuktu seems always to have been disappointing to travellers, though inspiring memorable quotations include one from Caillié himself, who said in 1828:

> I found it neither as big nor as populated as I had expected. Commerce was much less active than it was famed to be … Everything was enveloped in a great

sadness. I was amazed by the lack of energy, by the inertia that hung over the town a jumble of badly built houses ... ruled over by a heavy silence.

Rather more recently, Sir Bob Geldof is held to have articulated the view of most modern travellers when he famously said, on first seeing Timbuktu, 'Is that it?' But despite its current lack of appeal Timbuktu was one of the major trading centres of Africa from the time of the Crusades, through which passed the west-African gold on which European finance relied. It reached the peak of its wealth and power in the sixteenth century as trading centre where salt caravans from the north met caravans bringing gold from the south. During the medieval period, and almost to the present day, Timbuktu was a significant node in the north-African network of camel caravans; indeed, Caillié himself returned from the city in the nineteenth century, posing as an Arab and joining up with an enormous caravan of 12 000 camels transporting slaves and merchandise northwards to Morocco – illustrating just how significant the volumes of caravan travel across the Sahara were, and how late they persisted.

West Africa – trans-Saharan trade and early empires

The ten million square miles of the Sahara desert (an area larger than that of the USA) is often regarded as empty space in tourism terms, and indeed by comparison with the developed countries of western Europe the numbers of visitors to its centre are very few. But there is a great deal of contemporary tourism activity on the northern fringes of the Sahara (including the southern oasis towns of Tunisia, Morocco and Libya), and a revival of interest in the great trans-Saharan trade routes for cultural tourism (Box 3.1).

Box 3.1 Trans-Saharan Travel	During the pre-colonial period between the tenth and eighteenth centuries there were at least four major north–south routes across the Sahara, each of which had numerous by-roads and feeder roads, much like the Silk Road. Routes would go in and out of favour, depending on such factors as local politics, water availability and the changing course of the great dune fields, but for the whole of this period major routes linked the African kingdoms around the River Niger (south of the desert boundary) with North Africa, from what are now Mali, Niger and Burkina Faso in the sub-Saharan Sahel belt through Mauritania, southern Algeria and Libya to the Arab countries of the north (Map 3.2). Many routes were focused on Timbuktu, which in between the fourteenth and sixteenth centuries was linked directly to Cairo and the Nile Valley by a route crossing the central Libyan desert. At much the same time a route led from the Niger to Darfur in western Sudan, joining the southern part of the Nile Valley through the western desert and Kharga Oasis near Luxor. Today's trans-Saharan tourists generally travel along two main routes, both passing through the Algerian Sahara and linking Mali/Niger with Algiers/Tunisia over the Atlas Mountains. The main Saharan artery today (much of it an asphalt road) stretches 2000 kilometres south from Ghardaia (itself 650 kilometres south of Algiers) via the Hoggar Mountains (Map 3.2), through the town of

Tamanrasset, the jumping off point for the Tassili frescos,[9] and ending in Kano in northern Niger. Near Tamanrasset there is a branch line leading directly to Mali, which is famous as the location where Mark Thatcher became lost in the 1982 Paris–Dakar Rally, but the town of Tamanrasset (Tam) effectively functions today, as for the last 3000 years, as the capital of the southern Sahara, the centre for visits to the dramatic Assekrem massif to which it is now linked by a metalled road. There is a modest amount of pilgrimage traffic to the church of Charles de Foucauld, who built a hermitage near Beni-Abbes in 1901,[10] but most visitors are bound for the Tassili National Park, whose rock frescoes were first identified and brought to the notice of Europeans in the 1930s. The tens of thousands of paintings, in at least thirty distinct styles, date from 6000 BC and are the richest source of prehistoric art in the world. However, the paintings are fading and the caves eroding as a result of visitor pressure. Some early paintings show forest and plains animals, including elephant and hippo, and a late series painted between 1500 and 500 BC depicts chariots, European-type people and horses, and suggests contact with the Mediterranean world. It seems probable that a chariot route ran from Tripoli all the way down to Gao in Nigeria. The Tassili region gradually dried up and vegetation in the Sahara could no longer support horses, making it unlikely that extensive travel on this route took place until the wholesale use of camels. The remnants of these former camel caravans (often 1000 animals at a time, though in living memory the figure was 50 000) can still be seen in Niger, crossing the dunes to the salt mines of Bilma, but few visitors go to Niger today, and those that do tend to be either aid and charity workers trying to relieve the famine of 2005 or businessmen going to its capital, Niamey. The less frequented western route goes through the Tanezrouft Mountains, passing through remote desert cities such as Poste Wegande, Reggane and Adrar, first traversed by a European in 1913 when a French Capitaine Cortier led an expedition across the Tanezrouft to Niger with three men and eight camels. Although no modern routes cross the Sahara into southern Libya, tourists are once again beginning to travel south from Libya's Mediterranean coast from the Phoenician/Roman city of Leptis Magna to the desert cities of Sabha and Ghat. These are located near the spectacular rock paintings of the Akakus Mountains, which date back to 8000 BC – an era where the landscape was grassy savannah. Although the western trans-Saharan route is less frequented, parts of it are now being visited in Mauritania, which is entering the cultural tourism scene largely as a result of the designation of its desert cities of Chinguetti and Ouadane as World Heritage sites.[11] Chinguetti is considered to be the seventh holiest city of Islam and contains spectacular thirteenth century houses, whereas Ouadane was a staging point for trans-Saharan caravans. Strangely, the nearby massif of Guelb Richat is a navigational landmark for the Space Shuttle crew.

Southern Morocco is also aiming to develop some of its Saharan sites, as has already been done in southern Tunisia. In Algeria (which has achieved rapid growth since independence from France in 1962) its fledgling tourism industry includes visits to oasis towns such as El Golea on the edge of the Grand Erg Occidental, but Algeria's reputation for harbouring Islamic terrorists and its lack of investment in a tourism structure has meant that the country only receives around one million inbound arrivals each year, mostly VFR expatriates (Map 3.1).

Although rumours of cities like Timbuktu and Djenne had circulated in Europe for some centuries and the Portuguese had been present along the west-African coast since the fifteenth century, no western power had penetrated the interior of West Africa during the subsequent 300 years. In 1796 the explorer Mungo Park reached the Niger near Segou, and described its eastern course (correcting the prevailing European view, derived from Leo Africanus, that the Niger was a branch of the Nile[12]). France, anxious to link its colonial settlements in western and central Africa, established a military presence in Niamey, and by the end of the nineteenth century there was a French/British power struggle for control of the Niger River. French West Africa, including modern Niger, was established in 1899. Tourism in West Africa is undoubtedly best developed in the former French colony of Mali, which historically was the epicentre of the great empires of ancient Ghana, Mali and Songhai, whose prosperity was based on the region's strategic location at the nexus of the camel caravan routes and the banks of the River Niger. Camel caravans still traverse the region to Timbuktu, which (together with the Dogon escarpment and the mosque of Djenné) form the tourist highlights of Mali. Travellers in this region today have the opportunity to make one of the last great river journeys of the world, along the Niger, which was known to the classical world although its source was not discovered until Heinrich Barth worked it out and found where it emptied into the Atlantic.[13] Today 1300 kilometres of the river are still navigable, and it is possible to travel by boat through most of the river which goes through Mali – although in practice few travellers do so, despite the regular steamer service (unique in West Africa) which runs only after the rains (roughly between July and December) except when the Niger is too low to be navigable. The famous mud-brick Grand Mosque at Djenne (a World Heritage site) is built in the style of the famous original constructed in the thirteenth century when Djenne was a way-station for lead, gold, ivory, wool and kola nuts from the south.

In medieval times West Africa was dominated by two great empires – Ghana (the eighth to eleventh centuries) and Mali (the thirteenth to fifteenth centuries). As the former waned, Islamic invaders from Morocco reached as far south as Senegal, bringing their religion with them. But even before the rise of the Empire of Mali an extensive trade network extended over much of western Africa south of the Sahara, pre-dating the arrival of Portuguese traders at Cape Vert (near present-day Dakar) who settled on the nearby Ile de Gorée. Almost 120 years later Sir Francis Drake stopped at what is now Sierra Leone on his voyage round the world. For the next 150 years Portuguese ships scoured the coast in search of slaves, and although the British and Dutch both became major players in West Africa, all along the coast European nations continued to trade in slaves, gold and ivory – assisted by powerful African kings, whose armies raided neighbouring tribes to procure the slaves.

The most significant figure in the pre-colonial exploration of Africa is undoubtedly Bartolomeu Díaz (1450–1500), a Portuguese navigator of noble birth sent by João (John) II to expand on discoveries already made by Portuguese on the African west coast. Díaz reached further south than anyone previously, but was then blown off course by a storm round the Cape of Good Hope before the trade route to Asia (Map 3.3) was found, which his successor Vasco da Gama succeeded in doing in 1497. Díaz claimed the land on the western coast of Africa for Portugal, and left a supply ship at Luderitz Bay in Namibia, his voyage setting the groundwork for colonial Portuguese East Africa and the foundation of the Portuguese Empire's trade links between East Africa, south-west India and Indonesia.[14]

In 1415, Portuguese soldiers crossed the Strait of Gibraltar to establish small outposts on the Moroccan coast. From this modest beginning, a momentous historical process of European subjugation of Africa was initiated. The forces of intrusion gathered momentum over the centuries, reaching their peak with the 'scramble for Africa' late in the nineteenth century. Every square inch of Africa fell at least briefly under European rule. After the Second World War, the tide of colonial domination began to recede rapidly from 1960 onwards. With the independence of Zimbabwe in 1980, only the original foreign beachheads, Ceuta and Melilla, remained under European rule. From the sixteenth to the eighteenth centuries, the main form of European intervention in Africa was the slave trade. Perhaps twelve million Africans were landed in the western hemisphere, many others having perished *en route*. This commerce was carried out from coastal establishments from Senegal to Angola; it began the remaking of African political geography, as its impetus led to mercantile African states formed around the supply of slaves. Slavery had existed in Africa long before the Europeans arrived, and still exists today, but Europeans refined it into a coastal trade which exported people to the Americas.[15] Today, one result of this is an interesting form of reverse cultural tourism that has developed in some west-African countries, especially Ghana, which are now attracting African-Americans interested in learning more about the transatlantic slave trade and rediscovering their own ethnic identities.[16] Such tourists typically visit Gorée Island, a major slave port off the coast of Senegal, as well as sites in Benin and Ghana. Three former slave forts in Ghana are now World Heritage sites (Cape Coast Castle, Elmina Castle and Fort Saint Jago).[17] In the Gambia, the village of Jufurre became a pilgrimage site for many African-Americans after the television series based on Alex Haley's 1977 book *Roots* made it famous.[18] Now, the Gambia holds an annual 'Roots' Homecoming Festival, which highlights the cultural ties between diasporic Africans and Africa. Following the Accra Declaration (Ghana, 4 April 1995), UNESCO and the World Tourism Organization (WTO) cooperated with African Tourism and Culture Ministries and the Organization for African Unity (OAU) to implement a new cultural tourism project with the principal objective of identifying, restoring and promoting sites, buildings and localities linked to the slave trade and slavery in Africa and the Caribbean.[19] Intersectoral studies were undertaken in 1999, attempting to draw up a complete list of existing sites, and there are also plans to establish tourist routes linking sites between Europe, the Americas and West Africa. The route extends from the west-African sites to locations such as Feydeau Island and the slave quarters of eighteenth century Nantes, and the plantations of Christiansted and Fredriksted in St Croix, the Virgin Islands, and is already contributing to the improvement in knowledge of the slave trade and slavery. This 'Slave Route' project was officially launched in September 1994 in Ouidah (Benin), one of the former pivots of the slave trade in the Gulf of Guinea. It aims to emphasize, in an objective way, the consequences of the slave trade, especially the interactions between the peoples concerned in Europe and Africa. Cultural tourism, based on sites associated with the Slave Route, has become a powerful educational tool. The aftermath of the slave trade has had some curious consequences for travel history, notably the return of freed slaves to settle in what is now Liberia. Liberia was chosen for the resettlement of some freed American slaves who settled there from 1822 onwards, but the USA refused to recognize any sort of formal colony, although providing symbolic support. Despite its chequered twentieth century political history Liberia maintains strong links with the USA, nominally a 'special relationship' not unrelated to use of the huge military – commercial Omega navigation station outside Monrovia as well as the 'Voice of America' transmitters which broadcast to the whole African continent. Nor are these the only African–American links. Until recently, a direct flight linked Boston USA and the town of Sal on the Cape Verde Islands (Map 3.3) for expatriate Cape Verdeans who had emigrated to New England. The biggest USA embassy in the continent is to be found in Nigeria, which also has by far the largest English-speaking expatriate community in West Africa. Thousands of Nigerians also trained and studied in the UK in the 1960s, and their children born in the UK have British passports, resulting in extensive movement of people between Nigeria and London.

The former slave forts of Senegal are not the only reason that people visit the country – currently the biggest holiday destination in West Africa, receiving more than 200 000 mainly French and German visitors each year, attracted by the beaches and wildlife tourism in the creeks of Basse Casamance. Travel within Senegal is facilitated by a good road network, the legacy of colonial rule. From about 1500 the country had frequent contact with Portuguese traders, and in 1658 the French settled on an island at the mouth of the Senegal River, named St-Louis after Louis XIV of France. By 1659 a trading fort had been established, buying in slaves and gum arabic. Just as French influence is paramount in Senegal, English links are evident in The Gambia, a tiny country consisting of the immediate environs of the Gambia River, which has a beach tourism product developed to appeal to the seasonal winter sun market from Europe.[20] The British won lasting influence over Gambia after the Napoleonic Wars, and in 1888 established a Crown Colony centred on Banjul Island, which finally became independent and a member of the Commonwealth in 1965. Tourism is based round the fifty kilometres of beach around Banjul, although there have been some limited attempts to entice tourists into the creeks and upper reaches of the Gambia River for bird-watching. Not all west-African countries have developed a tourism industry in this way. The Cape Verde Islands were uninhabited until first colonized by the Portuguese in 1462, and still maintain TAP Air Portugal flights from Lisbon to what was usually regarded as a backwater of the Portuguese trading empire. Wholesale emigration over the last 150 years has led many islanders to leave for Europe, USA and other west-African countries, and the islands had virtually no tourism until recently – no tourist offices abroad or tourist information. However, today there are direct flights between London and Sal, with an attempt to develop wildlife tourism on the islands. Portuguese influence is still very strong here, as it is in Guinea-Bissau, which was the last country on the African mainland to regain its independence (from Portugal) in 1974. Tourism has not developed in the Republic of Guinea, either, which became isolated and secretive after gaining independence from France in 1958, and only started to open its doors to tourists after the death of the dictator Sekou Toure in 1984. It remains one of the least visited countries in West Africa, with great unrealized tourism potential, since it contains the headwaters of the three great rivers of West Africa – the Gambia, the Senegal and the Niger.

In the nineteenth century, after the collapse of the slave trade, a number of western explorers and missionaries began to penetrate the hinterland of West Africa, which at that time was little known to Europeans (the slave trade having been concentrated around the coast). Mary Kingsley, a self taught naturalist, was the first European to visit several parts of West Africa by joining a cargo ship in 1893 which sailed along the coast from Freetown in Sierra Leone to the Gulf of Guinea on the coast of what is now Nigeria. The voyage in itself is remarkable, being accomplished by a woman at a time when women did not really travel anywhere, but even more remarkable is that Kingsley quietly continued to explore the Congo

River and merge into the area – in a marked contrast to some of the other early explorers such as Henry Morton Stanley (p. 59) who had been there only twenty years before, but with all guns blazing. Kingsley was deeply impressed by African culture; she was not an explorer interested in the making of maps, but was remarkable for her defence of African people against what she saw as the destructive influences of western civilization.[21] She was soon followed by others, notably Albert Lloyd who, having spent ten years working for a church missionary society in parts of the then Uganda protectorate, eventually travelled home through the great Aruwimi forest and down the Congo River, encountering groups of Batwa 'pygmies' and Abangwa people. He wrote *In Dwarf Land and Cannibal Country* in 1900.[22] It would be difficult to imagine a book title that is, in our contemporary view, more deeply politically incorrect, but Lloyd's writings generated a distinctive (and unfavourable) image of the native inhabitants of the region. Western culture has always been interested in pygmies, since they had been mentioned by classical writers from Homer to Herodotus. The study undertaken by anthropologist Colin Turnbull in the Ituri Forest (in what was then the Belgian Congo and is now the Democratic Republic of Congo) with the Mbuti pygmies generated worldwide interest in the 1960s. Turnbull was the first westerner to live with the Mbuti over a period of time (three years) and come to appreciate their culture. The publication of his book *The Forest People* in 1961 opened western eyes[23] to their culture, and today many organizations such as Survival International are concerned about their fate.

The Côte d'Ivoire (Ivory Coast) is often thought of as the least 'African' of west-African countries and has maintained strong cultural links with France, having a huge expatriate French colony and being highly developed for the French tourism market. The Côte d'Ivoire (in West Africa) and Mauritius (off the east African coast) have a tourism product aimed specifically at the French market. Apart from this, the country's main attractions are as a comfortable and relatively safe starting point for overland tours of West Africa and for its major visitor attraction constructed by former president Felix Houphouet-Boigny, who constructed the new capital at Yamoussoukro with its famous Basilica. This giant church was built between 1986 and 1990 by a huge labour force, and has 7000 individually air-conditioned seats inside plus standing room for 12 000 outside and overflow space for 300 000. The Basilica (which cost an estimated £100 million) was finally consecrated in 1990 by Pope John Paul II, only on the condition that a new hospital would be built on the site. Nearby, the Ashanti kingdom of Ghana (formerly the Gold Coast) was one of the first African countries in Africa to retrieve its independence (from the British in 1957), and at that time was one of the richest nations in the continent, with wealth derived from being the world's leading cocoa exporter and producer of a tenth of the world's gold. Economic success since independence has not been maintained, but Ghana is still regarded as an easy Anglophone country to travel in. It had, inevitably, been discovered by the Portuguese in the 1470s, who were anxious to get the gold of the trans-Saharan shipments closer to their source. The British, Dutch and French sought labour for their American colonies, and soon joined the Portuguese by establishing their own coastal forts and commercial depots in the seventeenth century, at which point it is estimated that 20 000 slaves were being shipped annually out of just one port in what is now Benin. Today's visitors are still attracted by the remains of the Portuguese trading forts protecting the maritime trade routes to the Gulf of Guinea, but major draws are Cape Coast Castle (the British capital of the Gold Coast until 1876), with its associations with the slave trade, and the Portuguese Elmina Castle, which served as the Portuguese headquarters in West Africa for over 150 years. When the Portuguese arrived in the Bight of Benin in the fifteenth century they encountered a large and flourishing kingdom whose ruler, the Oba, established trading links. However, by the nineteenth century the British Empire had become the Benin kingdom's principal partner and, after a punitive campaign against the Oba in 1897, the Benin Empire was absorbed and some of its great art treasures (such as the Benin bronzes) were sent to the British Museum in London.[24]

This complex history, including the pre-colonial trade routes, the legacy of the slave trade and the ways in which west-African countries have retained their colonial flavours, has contributed to the increasing success of the region at attracting cultural tourists. But with the exception of limited amounts of bird-watching in Senegal and Gambia, only one has serious potential for ecotourism, and that is Cameroon (Map 3.1). Cameroon has a complex colonial past and great natural diversity, and its fauna and flora were introduced to the English-speaking world in the stories of Gerald Durrell's animal-collecting trips in the 1950s and 1960s.[25] Today, Cameroon has a well-developed National Park system whose flagship is the Korup National Park in a remote corner of rainforest in the south-west on the Nigerian border, which is an up-and-coming ecotourism destination.

East Africa – the original safari destination

The same cannot be said of East Africa, where wildlife (initially as safari and now as wildlife watching) forms the basis of the tourism industry. While the travel and tourism history of West Africa is inextricably bound up with trans-Saharan trade routes and coastal trade (including slavery), West Africa has relatively few visitor attractions and low levels of visitation. But the cases of eastern and south-central Africa are entirely different. Here, travel history and colonialism are intertwined and the contemporary face of sub-Saharan tourism is to a large extent determined by the distribution of wildlife and the safari tourism industry that has grown up around it (Map 3.4). Africa's wildlife has long fascinated foreigners. Wildlife safaris remain one of the most popular forms of tourism in Africa, and an important source of revenue for countries such as Kenya, Tanzania, Uganda, Namibia, Botswana, Zimbabwe, Zambia, Malawi and South Africa. In these countries, private companies drive visitors through wildlife parks or game reserves and provide lodging in lodges or luxury tented camps nearby (Plate 3.1). Most safari tourists visit National Parks (primarily to see animals and take their photographs), although there is a supplementary market in trophy hunting.[26] The greatest draw in tourism terms is the possibility of seeing the 'Big Five' (lion, elephant, rhinoceros, leopard and buffalo). Within eastern and central Africa the most significant countries are Kenya and Tanzania, with lesser numbers of visitors drawn to Uganda, Burundi, Rwanda and The Democratic Republic of the Congo (formerly Zaire) for gorilla watching.[27]

In East Africa, the concept of *safari* (a Swahili word simply meaning 'journey') is intrinsically linked with the coming of Europeans. Yet in pre-colonial times great cross-continental journeys were being made involving caravans of porters carrying commodities such as oil, skins and rhinoceros horn out of the African interior to be traded with the seafaring people of the Swahili coast. Such trade resulted in the expansion of the great port entrepôt city of Zanzibar, and eventually became

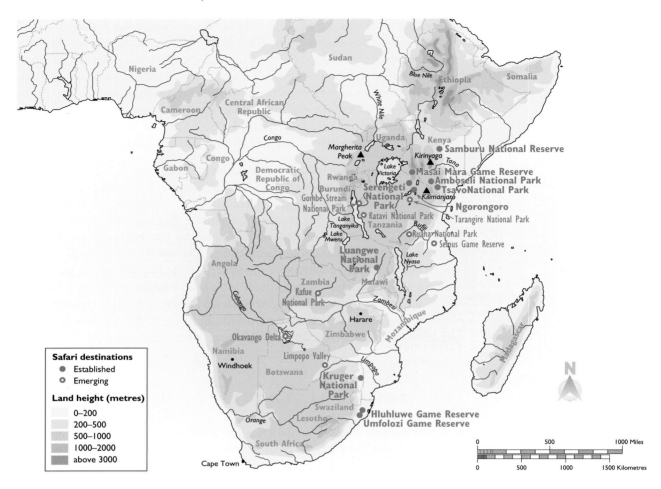

Map 3.4
Safari destinations

linked to the slave trade. In colonial times Zanzibar remained a major point of origin for safaris inland, where visitors would engage porters and secure permissions and routes. Much of the early European exploration of East Africa was motivated by interest in the course of the Nile, and in identifying its source. James Bruce (1730–1794), the first modern European explorer of Africa, travelled from Alexandria in Egypt to Ethiopia and 'discovered' the headwaters of the Blue Nile.[28] It was a journey that rekindled European interest in the interior of Africa, especially in the elusive main source of the Nile, which was identified eighty years later by John Hanning Speke (1827–1864) as being Lake Victoria. In the nineteenth century there was much dispute about this – a dispute not resolved until Stanley's expedition a dozen years later. Nineteenth century European awareness of East Africa was also closely related to interest in the events in the life of David Livingstone (1813–1873), who was a medical missionary who arrived in Cape Town in 1841, later crossing the Kalahari Desert and discovering Lake Ngami. He encountered the slave trade in the course of a second expedition to the upper reaches of the Zambezi, and resolved to dedicate his life to its abolition. Between 1853 and 1856 Livingstone made a great series of journeys throughout Africa, including a trip up the Zambezi where, in 1855, he discovered and named the Victoria Falls: 'it had never been seen before by European eyes; but scenes so lovely must have been gazed upon by angels in their flight'.[29] After his return to England he wrote up his explorations in *Missionary Travels and Researches in South Africa* (1857), which sold an extraordinary 70 000 copies – the earliest travel bestseller. Livingstone returned to Africa in 1865 intending finally to settle the debate about the source of the Nile, but nothing was heard of him for several years until his famous meeting in 1871 with H. M. Stanley, a reporter from the *New York Herald*, who greeted him with the immortal words, 'Dr Livingstone, I presume?' Together they explored the northern reaches of Lake Tanganyika and proved that Speke was right in his conclusion that Lake Victoria was the major source of the River Nile. Stanley led several subsequent expeditions and made a substantial contribution to charting of the continent.[30] Such books raised awareness of the possibilities for exploration and shooting offered by the vast unexplored terrain of East Africa.

Early in the nineteenth century, as the slave trade declined, European powers began slowly to extend their influence into the interior of Africa, creating informal zones of influence eventually supplanted by colonial annexation (Map 3.3). In the last quarter of the nineteenth century, intensifying rivalries between European powers and new military technologies (especially the machine gun) brought rapid partition. Britain, France, Portugal, Germany, Belgium, Italy and Spain divided nearly all the continent among them (Map 3.3). The shape and organization of the resulting colonies depended on the experience of the colonizer and the way in which colonial rule could be imposed over vast territories at minimal cost to imperial treasuries – a process known as 'the scramble for Africa'. The first crucial goal was to consolidate colonial control over the territory. At the Berlin Conference in 1884 and 1885, where diplomatic agreement was reached among imperial powers on major outlines of the partition, the principle of 'effective occupation' was devised. To confirm its title to a zone of African territory, a colonial power had to demonstrate to its European rivals that it exercised military control over the area; failing this, an imperial rival might snatch it away. European powers exploited Africa for labour and land, with pressure to produce commodities saleable on the international market. This was facilitated by encouraging expatriate settlement, which necessitated ignoring traditional landholding systems. By the 1920s virtually all Africa was under colonial rule, justified by European powers on the grounds that it was supplying good government and a 'civilizing' influence. However, after the Second World War a rising tide of nationalist protest in Africa challenged the legitimacy of alien occupation, with the subsequent history of the continent being, in one way or another, a story of many struggles for freedom.

In its colonies of Kenya and Uganda, the British quickly established a programme of development that followed a model tried and tested in India. They built a railway to connect the port of Mombasa with Lake Victoria in 1896, subsequently extending it to western Uganda. Before the rise of African nationalism in the 1920s, few Kenyans worked in anything except menial roles; the indigenous people of Kenya were objects of curiosity to explorers and anthropologists eager to document customs and traditions, but people such as the Maasai and Turkana became marginalized in colonial administration. By 1914, over 90 per cent of Africa was claimed by Europe.[31] This brought with it a new kind of visitor. The early travellers had been motivated by exploration and discovery (often accompanied by hardship), but the books of Livingstone, Stanley and Burton attracted a new bred of traveller who wanted comfort. Travel to East Africa was facilitated by the opening up of the Suez Canal, which made it easier to reach the area and encouraged a new breed of gentlemen tourists, usually motivated by big-game hunting. Great names of this period include Frederick Selous, the elephant hunter and naturalist, but the greatest name to arrive was undoubtedly American President Theodore Roosevelt, who engaged Selous as his 'white hunter'. After the First World War the former German East Africa became Tanganyika, held on a UN mandate by Britain. Visitors began to explore the areas that are now the Serengeti and Ngorongoro National Parks (Map 3.4), and the area around Nairobi in Kenya became home to expatriate Europeans who grew coffee.[32] These settlers were eventually supplemented by the 'Happy Valley' set.[33] The arrival of the motor car changed the face of safari in Africa for ever, and was eventually supplemented by small planes, initially delivering clients to the best shooting but now serving the growing network of very upmarket safari lodges which are the lineal descendants of pre-War predecessors. When the Prince of Wales (the future Edward VIII) came to Tanganyika on safari in 1928, he had great names such as Denys Finch Hatton and Bror Blixen as his white hunters, their ménage having been made famous in *Out of Africa* by Isaac Dinesen.[34] The safari experience was at that time at its most romantic, with rich clients able to bring with them all the comforts of home, sometimes including grand pianos and sophisticated cocktails. This remains the image of safari today, and one to which many companies are returning in order to capture the growing segment of the modern safari market with a great deal of money and a taste for nostalgia. The safari business declined during the Second World War but was to increase again in the 1950s, boosted by the latest developments in aircraft technology, such as the big four-engined aircraft Second World War bombers. The Mau Mau crisis in Kenya from 1953 again interrupted growth, but the eventual expansion of mass tourism into East Africa from the 1970s onwards allowed the safari areas to become accessible to the newly-expanding middle classes, whereas they had once been the preserve of the super-rich. This continued expansion of interest has not been without its social and environmental costs, including pressure on popular trophy species. Matters improved after photography, rather than shooting, became the favoured activity, and were assisted by the creation of game reserves under the different colonial administrations (later to become National Parks).[35]

Historically and up until the 1980s East Africa was always the preferred destination for safari-goers and wildlife enthusiasts, with both Kenya and Tanzania offering superb wildlife viewing with a well-developed safari infrastructure of operators with both permanent camps and mobile safari circuits (Map 3.4). East Africa boasts Mount Kilimanjaro, the Serengeti Plains, the Maasai Mara ecosystem and the Ngorogoro Crater. Southern Africa includes Botswana's Okavango Delta wetlands, the Skeleton Coast and Namib Desert of Namibia, the miles of coastline with diverse habitats and the Kruger National Park of South Africa, the semi-arid Kalahari Desert of Botswana and northern South Africa, and the lower Zambesi River basin – including the Victoria Falls along the borders of Zambia and Zimbabwe. Visitors to East Africa can expect to see huge numbers of animals, with the most famous spectacle being the annual migration of zebra and wildebeest between the Maasai Mara in the north and Tanzania's Serengeti in the south. But East Africa has problems with tourist densities, since most visitors stay in purpose-built safari lodges and travel in mini-vans with pop-up roofs for game viewing. There is often lack of regulation within the parks, which can result in overcrowding to the point where the vehicles may disrupt the animal's natural behaviour, and the tradition of private safaris has not really settled here although it is common further south. The revenue generated from safari tourism has made the survival of endangered species a high priority for African governments. In Kenya, for example, a single lion is worth an estimated $7000 per year in tourist income, while an elephant herd is worth $610 000 annually.[36] There is, however, a growing volume of protests from local people such as the Maasai, who have been displaced from their traditional lands to make way for wildlife parks. They often face the chronic threat of crop destruction and even attack by wild animals, and claim that their governments protect animals at the expense of people. Despite limited efforts to maximize community involvement in wildlife protection schemes, the problems remain.[37]

Tourism is critically important to Kenya, accounting for 12 per cent of GDP, generating $2.4 bn in economic activity and supporting half a million jobs,[38] overtaking coffee, tea and agriculture in a good year as the countries biggest foreign exchange earner. But problems with perceived overcrowding and security threats have led to the rise of new markets in southern Africa which offer distinctively different types of safari experience and a large number of cultural tourism attractions as well.

South Africa

The earliest history of travel to/from southern Africa (defined as modern South Africa, Botswana, Namibia, Zimbabwe, Malawi and Zambia) could be said to begin with hominid movements anytime from three million years ago, when the earliest human-like *Australopithecus africanus* communities were living in the Rift Valley of eastern Africa and highveld of South Africa. A million years ago *Homo erectus* ranged far and wide, out from Africa into Asia and Europe, but the affect of these migrations, although crucial to our species, cannot be said to have greatly influenced contemporary travel patterns, with the exception of encouraging visitation to archaeological sites in the Rift Valley and southern Africa. The first European settlers in sub-Saharan Africa encountered a variety of indigenous people, including the Khoi and San (Hottentots and Bushman) who had migrated south from Botswana perhaps before 20 000 BC. Much later (perhaps around AD 500) Bantu-speaking people migrated south, bringing with them iron-smelting and domestic livestock. The first Europeans to encounter these three groups were Portuguese sailors attempting to find a way through to the Spice Islands of Asia, who for many years had been pushing further and further south along Africa's western coast.

In 1487, a ship captained by Bartolomeu Díaz made it around the Cape of Good Hope and sailed up the east coast of southern Africa, followed a decade later by Vasco da Gama, who followed the same route but continued to head further east, landing in India (Map 3.3). Over the next 200 years increasing numbers of Portuguese, Dutch and British traders made this voyage, stopping for water and food along the African coast. The Portuguese established trading and supply posts in present-day Angola and Mozambique, where they were able to re-supply ships and also to export slaves bound for the American colonies. The legacy of this period still survives in the language and culture of these two countries. The Dutch set up the first permanent settlement in what is now South Africa in 1652 – a fort and supply station, which gradually increased in size and was later to become Cape Town. Other settlements developed and later settlers moved inland, coming into conflict with herders and San but gradually moving further to the east and north to find land suitable for settled agriculture. The Dutch colony in Cape Town was annexed by the British in 1795, and in 1820 British settlers were imported to form the nucleus of a new community. British rule was credited with ending the slave trade, but conflict between British and Dutch settlers led to the decision of a number of Dutch to set out with their families in search of new land beyond British colonial rule. Between 1835 and 1840 around 5000 people (known as *voortrekkers*) left the Cape Colony and headed east in a movement later to be known as the Great Trek – experiences crucial to the later expression of Afrikaner nationalism.[39] These pioneers encountered numerous Bantu-speaking African chiefdoms, the most significant of which were the Zulus, who had been transformed into nationhood by their powerful king Shaka Zulu. The *voortrekkers* established two separate republics of Transvaal and Orange Free State, with the British colonies of the Cape and Natal remaining very much at the backwaters of the British Empire. This changed in 1867 with the discovery of alluvial diamonds, and by 1872 it was estimated that 20 000 Europeans and many more Africans had converged on a site later to become the world diamond capital at Kimberley (Map 3.3). The subsequent discovery of gold in 1886 at Witwatersrand also attracted miners from all over the world, with the town of Johannesburg growing from nothing to 75 000 white residents by the turn of the century. The Anglo-Boer war (1889–1902) was not unrelated to this, the world's largest supply of gold, but one eventual result was the formation of the Union of South Africa in 1910. The subsequent development of an apartheid system was not seriously challenged until the formation of the African National Congress in the 1940s, with subsequent armed rebellions neutralized by the imprisonment of leaders, including Nelson Mandela, in Robben Island. The new democratic South Africa dates from 1990, when Mandela was released, subsequently to become president in 1994, yet it remains a combination of extreme prosperity for a few based on extreme poverty for the many. Robben Island has become its number-one cultural tourism destination, especially since its designation as a World Heritage site[40] and subsequent development as a visitor attraction. The tourism sector in South Africa has been highlighted as one of potential growth, especially in European markets stimulated by the favourable exchange rate of the rand, although the country's image is continually troubled by high inner-city crime rates.

South Africa has invested heavily in its National Parks system and the expansion of a tourism industry initially based around wildlife. Today, product diversification encourages visitors to visit battlefield sites of the Anglo-Boer and Zulu Wars (including the famous Rorke's Drift[41]), wine tourism in the southern Cape has become big business, and South Africa has developed major new resorts such as Sun City on the fringes of the Kalahari with five hotels, golf courses and a casino. Significantly, its flagship hotel – the 'Palace of the Lost City', completed in 1992 – is themed to resemble the classic European fantasy of a vanished Africa, sometimes described as 'Tarzan meets Rider Haggard'.[42]

Southern Africa has also developed distinctive forms of wildlife-based tourism in areas that were either politically unstable or mostly undeveloped before the 1990s, when apartheid came to an end and South Africa became a more attractive travel destination. Although South Africa has essentially the same range of wildlife species as those found in East Africa, the major difference is in their numbers and the general experience a visitor will have when viewing them. Botswana and Zimbabwe are home to 80 per cent of southern Africa's 300 000 elephants, and huge herds are a common sight along their northern borders, but southern Africa is known for its luxury tented safari camps and huge tracts of wilderness areas with very low tourist densities, making for a private safari experience unlike the mass safari tourism of Kenya or Tanzania. Southern Africa has some outstanding National Parks, but it also is dominated by huge land concessions which are owned or leased by luxury safari camp operators, and these concessions are for the sole use of the individual camp and its guests. This has led to a smaller-scale industry, with guest camps of ten to sixteen guests and one or two modified four-wheeled vehicles for the entire area, giving excellent game viewing but total privacy – an experience, indeed, far closer to the original safari spirit of East Africa than is demonstrated there today. This kind of luxury travel is the hottest safari trend of the new millennium, but it would also be possible to argue that it represents a new and sinister form of colonialism. Although sold as being ecologically friendly, some have claimed it as the new imperialism of tourism, creating an exclusion zone of reality with super-luxury tented camps (sometimes with four-poster beds, marble bathrooms and private butlers). Its opponents note the gap between the standard of living of guests at such camps and that of local people, who may have no access to medical facilities or even clean water, and may derive little benefit from expensive, privately-owned concessions. This viewpoint is opposed by many luxury travel companies, who maintain market share on the basis of conservation. For example, CC Africa (Conservation Corporation Africa), which operates in both southern and eastern Africa, claim conservation benefits including species re-introductions, and run a trust fund called Africa Foundation, raising cash from clients to empower communities through conservation.[43] This and similar operators argue that by attracting fewer travellers who spend more they can sustain both communities and wildlife. However, the concept is deeply elitist, with rooms in small lodges easily costing £500 per night. Not all operators are conservation-minded or greatly concerned with the local people, many of whom are employed only in a menial capacity.

New safari locations are also opening up in Botswana, which has followed a similar pattern to South Africa, especially around the Okavango Delta. The wildlife industry of Zimbabwe has almost totally disintegrated as a result of existing government policy, meaning not only that animal numbers have declined through uncontrolled hunting but also that infrastructure has declined. However, a change of government in the future might enable visitors once again to reach safely the outstanding wildlife parks of northern Zimbabwe, such as Mana Pools and Hwange. Namibia, too, has developed a distinctive wildlife tourism industry on the back of its interesting cultural history. Its harsh desert climate acted as a deterrent to an early European colonization, although isolated contact with European explorers, traders and hunters goes back to the arrival of Bartolomeu Díaz in the fifteenth century. Exploration of the interior was effectively blocked by the extreme conditions of the Namib Desert, which stretches along the entire length of the Namibian coast. During the early part of the nineteenth century, missionary groups from Britain and later Germany established settlements in many parts of present-day Namibia – a precursor for later German colonization. By 1878 Britain had annexed a small enclave around the port of Walvis Bay and, as a result of the Berlin Conference of European Colonial Powers of 1884, Germany was able to consolidate its dominance over the remainder of the territory. German settlers and their governor arrived and the land was parcelled out to the new settlers and large German companies, with little regard to the needs of the original inhabitants of the territory. The League of Nations mandated south-west Africa to South Africa in 1920, after which the territory was increasingly treated as an additional province of South Africa. Namibian independence and the incorporation of Walvis Bay was achieved in 1990, and modern Namibia is attracting increasing volumes of European visitors (including many German speakers) to its stunning National Parks, such as Etosha on the Angolan border. New tourism destinations are also opening up in Mozambique, now stable after thirty years of civil war. During the war Mozambique was officially recognized as the poorest country in the world, but it is now officially only the third poorest in Africa, with tourism being a major player in its economic growth. Mozambique is capitalizing on its spectacular coastline and legacy of crumbling Portuguese colonial outposts with the potential for development into resorts, and is also aiming at the low-volume, high-cost model. It includes resort islands such as Benguerra and Bazaruto, and north of Pema several new islands resorts are being created on exactly the same principle as those developed for trading purposes when the Portuguese settled on Ibo in the early sixteenth century. Other major new players in southern Africa include Madagascar (on the basis of wildlife tourism centred on its unique flora and fauna, and a fledgling dive-tourism industry), as well as the established Indian Ocean islands of Mauritius and the Seychelles.

And so the travel history of sub-Saharan Africa, which began with exploration and trade, continues into a new era. It would be possible to argue that Europe's interest in Africa has always been exploitative, and that today's tourist merely replaces yesterday's slave trader or imposed colonial administrator. To a certain extent this is true, and it is undeniable that few of Africa's tourism attractions are based on, or involve, many of its indigenous people. There are exceptions, of course, such as the *Pays Dogon* in Mali,[44] but even in the new South Africa a tourism industry has developed based on colonial and post-colonial history, and wildlife. This is gradually changing, with increased attention being paid to the heritage of Africa's Bantu-speaking groups, but there is some way to go. Product diversification in Africa has also expanded the product range offered by many African countries from wildlife to beach tourism, with the beaches of Kenya, Togo, Mauritius, the Seychelles and the Gambia all popular winter vacation spots for Europeans. Many national and local governments and private companies are now promoting eco-tourism, which is seen as environmentally and culturally sensitive, educational and locally controlled – or at least locally beneficial. Thus, host communities will see the economic value of preserving resources and biodiversity. But the recent history of tourism on the continent has shown how fragile the industry can be, and how delicate its relationships with the human and animal communities involved in any major new tourism project.

CHAPTER 4

Asia: culture and colonialism

Asia is the world's largest continent, and could be considered as containing three main geographical regions: the Middle East, South Asia (including India) and Central Asia. Despite this, in terms of travel history it makes better sense to consider the Middle East separately (as has been done in Chapter 2) because of its significance as the cradle of early civilizations and in the early development of river and sea-borne travel. Moreover, for much of recorded history the countries of the Middle East (and part of North Africa) have been under unified political control. In terms of the history of travel in Asia, several further divisions of this vast continent become apparent. Most obviously, the subcontinent of India (including Pakistan, Bangladesh and the Indian Ocean Islands), whose history is basically unrelated to that of China but closely involved with the development of sea-borne trade through the Indian Ocean and with European colonization, is a distinct area. The same is true of the countries of South-East Asia (Thailand, Indonesia, Bali, Cambodia, Laos, Vietnam, etc.), which have elements of shared political histories. It also makes historical sense to treat China separately, and to separate off the Himalayas and the pan-Himalayan region (including Tibet, Nepal, Bhutan and Afghanistan), whose travel history is conditioned by a different set of geographical determinants. However, this is very much a personal decision, and the reader may well feel that another scheme would have been preferable.

Despite its huge area and vast contrasts in culture and landscape, in world terms Asia still has only a relatively small share of global tourism (Map 4.1). As with many other areas of the world, there are also immense inter-regional differences in the kind of tourism which has developed and its relative significance to individual economies, ranging from Pakistan, Afghanistan and Bangladesh, where tourism is insignificant, to the rapidly-growing tourism industry of China. Japan has only a modest level of inbound tourism but a huge outbound industry, and countries with political difficulties, such as Indonesia, have tourism industries threatened by perceived anxieties over visitor safety. Some countries (such as Brunei) have few visitor attractions but a rapidly developing airline industry. Others (such as Indonesia) have internal variations between islands, some of which are heavily visited and others that do not even feature on the tourist map. The leisure and beach tourism product of Indian Ocean islands such as the Maldives is quite different from the cultural tourism of China or ecotourism to India's National Parks. However, there is one unifying factor – the overall appeal of southern Asia is cultural tourism (for international visitors), but levels of international visitation are insignificant compared with the huge volumes of domestic tourism, mostly related to pilgrimage. South and East Asia have a rich variety of visitor attractions related to the remains of great empires (from Angkor Wat in Cambodia to the Moghul sites of India) and also to more recent colonial history, and to its great religious traditions including Hinduism, Buddhism, Islam and Sikhism.

Map 4.1

Asia – international tourist arrivals 2003

International tourist arrivals, 2003

Market share of region (%)

- 0 or not available
- 0.1–0.6
- 0.7–2.5
- 2.6–5.7
- 5.8–9.6
- 9.7–14.1
- 14.2+

Source: WTO, Tourism Market Trends, 2004

Tourist hotspot areas

- Established
- Emerging

India

The subcontinent of India has a population of over a billion people – 20 per cent of the world's population in 3 per cent of its land area. However, despite the fact that it is now one of Asia's leading (and most rapidly growing) industrialized countries, only 15–20 per cent of the population have the means to participate in domestic tourism. Figures for domestic tourism are hard to find, but it is thought that more than 200 million domestic trips are made each year (Plate 4.1). It seems probable that this dominance of domestic travel dates back to the beginning of India's recorded history, with international arrivals growing from a mere trickle in precolonial times to their present level as a result of investment in infrastructure.

The history of travel in India is, however, very long indeed. By 3500 BC agricultural settlement had spread throughout the Indus plains, forming the foundation for the urban Indus Valley civilization of Moenjo Daro (Map 4.1). This at its height covered an area as large as Egypt or Mesopotamia and had extensive trading contacts throughout South-East Asia, utilizing simple road networks traversed on foot or with pack animals, as well as river traffic on the Indus.[1] After 2000 BC the city of Moenjo Daro itself became deserted, and within the next 250 years the Indus Valley civilization disintegrated, partly as the result of the arrival of a new wave of Aryan immigrants from the north-west who moved further and further eastwards. Small communities of Greek origin later settled in the Punjab and North-West Frontier following the invasion of Alexander the Great in 326 BC, when the wonders of India were revealed to a Greek audience for the first time – although travel at this time was still principally for military or political purposes.[2] After Alexander's retreat from the Indus the Emperor Chandragupta Maurya established the first indigenous empire to exercise control over much of the subcontinent, and eventually, under his successors, this covered all but the tip of the peninsula. Asoka, the greatest of the Mauryan emperors, took power in 272 BC and extended the empire from Afghanistan to Assam and from the Himalayas to Mysore, leaving behind a series of inscriptions recording his edicts on pillars and rocks across the continent, but this was unaccompanied by any significant developments in travel history. Within fifty years of his death the empire had disintegrated, and a period of fragmentation extended until the classical period of the Gupta Empire, which flourished until the fifth century AD. Its decline opened the way for new waves of immigrants from the north-west, among whom were the Rajputs, who probably originated outside India in central Asia. The great temples at Khajuraho in central India remain one of their most remarkable monuments.[3]

Contact between Europe, Africa and India did take place during the Middle Ages, and we owe it to the writings of the Moorish traveller Ibn Battuta (p. 50) for some idea of what medieval India was like in the fourteenth century, when Delhi had become one of the leading cities of the contemporary world. However, that came to an abrupt end with the arrival of the Mongol Timur-I-leng (Timur the Lame, or Tamburlaine), who had previously devastated much of central Asia and Russia and was to be responsible for more than five million deaths in India. His grave in Samarkhand is now a major cultural tourism destination along the remains of the Silk Road.[4] The Mughals, descendants of both Timur and Genghis Khan, came to dominate Indian politics from the founding of their dynasty by the Emperor Babur ('the Tiger') in 1526 to the death of the Emperor Aurangzeb in 1717. The Mughals left behind them a stunning architectural legacy and a profound impact on the culture, society and future politics of southern Asia. Many of India's main

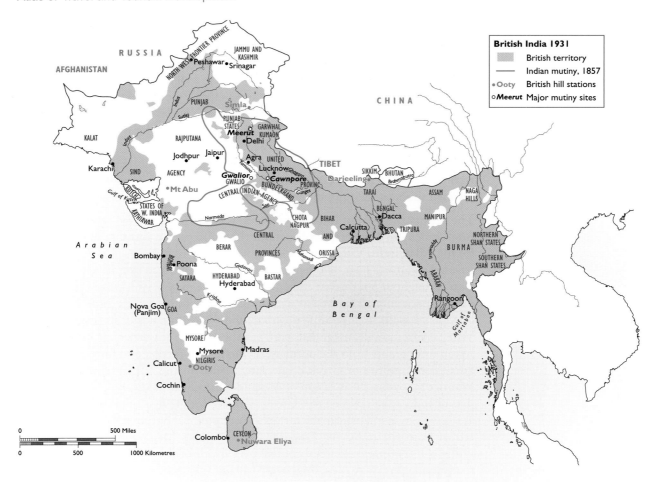

Map 4.2
British India 1931

tourist attractions are associated with Mughal rule, including the deserted city of Fatehpur Sikri, the purpose-built capital of the third Mughal emperor, Akhbar, located not far from Agra. Akhbar's empire had an extraordinarily wide network of trading links, and was probably the first Eastern civilization to impinge upon the culture of Europe since Rome. Akhbar welcomed Portuguese Jesuits to his court in 1572. His son, Jahangir, encouraged the Mughal arts of paintings, carpets and jewellery, and his favourite wife, Nur Jahan (who by 1622 effectively controlled the Mughal Empire), commissioned and supervised one of the Mughal world's most beautiful monuments, the I'timad ud-Daula – a tomb for her mother and father, located in Agra near the Taj Mahal. The Taj Mahal itself, built under Jahangir's successor, Shah Jehan, is probably the most famous monument in Asia, a culmination of the skills of Mughal craftsmen and built a tribute to his wife, Mumtaz Mahal, who died giving birth to their fourteenth child in 1631.[5]

So far the history of the Indian subcontinent had been dominated by the successive arrival of conquerors from the north-west, who achieved dominance over the indigenous population, but this was to change with the arrival of the first British traders, who established the ports of Madras, Bombay and Calcutta and eventually controlled India's sea-borne trade. The British East India Company gradually extended its power in the periphery of the weakening Mughal Empire, which eventually collapsed in 1858 after a succession of weak rulers – the same year that the British replaced indirect dominance of the subcontinent under the East India Company with formal establishment of India as part of the British Empire.[6] By 1805 the dominance of the English East India Company extended over most of the Indian subcontinent and, after its conquest of the province of Sind (1843) and the Sikh kingdom of the Punjab (1849) (Map 4.2), the boundaries of British India eventually extended to the Himalayan foothills. In the east the British annexed most of the territories of the Burmese Empire, including Assam, and by 1886 Upper Burma itself was under British rule. Several more small kingdoms in central India became incorporated, as well as the major kingdom of Oudh in 1856 after charges of misgovernment – a policy which was a major cause of the Indian mutiny of 1857. This began as a mutiny of the Company's *sepoys* (Indian soldiers), but spread rapidly before it was eventually crushed by the British after fourteen months of fighting. Several of the sites made famous in the mutiny, such as Cawnpore and Meerut, remain major cultural tourism attractions today (Map 4.2). The mutiny was a watershed in the history of British India, discrediting the Company and leading to the assumption of direct control by the British Government in 1858 through a deal which respected the (limited) autonomy of Indian princes. The implications of the British Raj for economic development were immense. A major road-building programme was instigated (which had constructed 57 000 miles of roads by 1927), as well as the development of railways to enable the export of raw materials and the introduction of profitable crops (such as tea). Between 1869 and 1929 India's foreign trade increased sevenfold, but it is doubtful whether this had much effect on India's rural majority. India now has the world's second largest railway network, utilizing 70 000 kilometres of railways and operating 7000 passenger trains per day, with an extraordinary 11 million passengers carried daily between 7000 stations. The new railway network was also used by the British for limited leisure tourism, especially for travel to the hill stations. International traveller flows were dominated by the movement of British military and civilian officials between Europe and India, mainly via Bombay, Madras and Calcutta. Indian princes also began to travel to Europe (p. 101), but such travel was very small in scale when compared with the huge volumes of domestic pilgrimage travel, which maintained patterns that were virtually unchanged from pre-colonial times and, in the case of some destinations, from very much earlier.[7]

The current distribution of tourism in India is thus related to three major historico-geographic factors: the transport legacy of India under colonial rule (Box 4.1), the religious makeup of the subcontinent, and various trends in international tourism which have brought specific destinations within India to prominence. After 1919, Congress, under the control of Mahatma Gandhi, fought actively for home rule and later for independence from Britain, which was successfully obtained in 1947. Differences between Muslims and Hindus in British India led to the partition of former British India into two separate countries (India and Pakistan) on independence, but this unfortunately left the status of Kashmir (Map 4.2) unresolved. The plans for partition in 1947[8] were hastily drawn up, with boundary designation problems in Kashmir, the Punjab and Bengal resulting in large-scale disturbances and the estimated loss of 50 000 lives, with millions becoming homeless. The situation has remained tense for the succeeding sixty years, with wars between India and Pakistan in 1965 and 1971, and continuing unrest in Kashmir. Islamic fundamentalism in Pakistan is one reason that the country has never become the international

Box 4.1: The legacy of the Raj in India

The legacy of the Raj in India included not only a language and administrative structures but also a tourism infrastructure, based around the railways, which became a foundation for modern domestic and international tourism. Even during the Raj India had developed leisure tourism destinations, particularly the hill-stations in the Lesser Himalayas and elsewhere, which became hot weather resorts for the British to escape the heat of the plains in May and June. The most famous of these is Shimla (Simla), now a substantial town with a population of *c.* 110 000, but other famous examples include Ootycamund (in the Nilgiri hills), Mt Abu (in Rajasthan), Murree (in Pakistan) and Dariling (Darjeeling) (in west Bengal) (Map 4.2). Such hill-stations developed the features of English county towns or seaside resorts, including bandstands, mock Elizabethan secular architecture, a network of churches and clubs, and a main street usually called the Mall. Although once the preserve of colonial administrators, these hill-stations have now become resorts for middle-class Indians, who migrate to them for the same reason and at the same time of year (May–June). However, they still attract incoming international tourists interested in the built heritage of the Raj or (increasingly) who use the hill-stations as the basis for walking and trekking holidays in the surrounding hills. Shimla was supposedly discovered by the British in 1819 and became the summer seat of government from 1865 to 1939, when the capital was shifted there from Calcutta and later from Delhi (1912 onwards). At the height of the Raj huge baggage trains were used to transport the business of government up into the hills, accompanied by many of the wives and families of army and government, joined for brief periods by their husbands. Travel to Shimla was facilitated by the construction of a narrow-gauge railway, the Kalka–Shimla line, completed in 1903 and running for 97 kilometres through 107 tunnels. 'Ooty' (Ootycamund, or Udhagamandalam) is located in modern Tamil Nadu in southern India in the rolling pine and eucalyptus forest of the Nilgiri hills. Here the arrival of the British was followed by that of Indian maharajahs, including the rulers of Baroda, Hyderabad, Jodhpur and Mysore, who built grand houses there and came up for shooting parties. Many of these houses have now been turned into hotels, including Fernhill, built by the Maharajah of Mysore, and Arranmore, a palace built by the Maharajah of Jodhpur. The narrow-gauge mountain railway to Ooty was famously used as the set for the railway scenes involving the *Marabar Express* in the book and film *A Passage to India*,[10] and is still visited by film buffs for that reason. Darjeeling (Dariling) in west Bengal once belonged to the Rajas of Sikkim, who granted a lease to the British to construct a hill-station which is now a favourite tourist resort for Bengalis – although since the late 1980s political disturbances have affected its popularity. Nor is it just the hill-stations that have metamorphosed from exclusive destinations for the ruling classes to mass tourism destinations. After independence in 1947, over 500 princely states, varying in size from the equivalent in area to France down to that of a small English county, left a legacy of palaces, many of which have been opened to visitors though still being run by the princely family and retaining much of their original character. In Rajasthan the palaces of some maharajas have now been converted into luxury hotels, notably the Lake Palace at Udaipur and the Rambagh Palace at Jaipur, which form part of a new class of heritage hotels.

tourism destination that India is. Indeed, in Pakistan tourism represents only 1 per cent of GDP and its development is hampered by poor infrastructure, problems with cross-border travel, and difficult terrain. Yet in the time of the Raj, what is now Pakistan was the North-West frontier of British India, immortalized by Rudyard Kipling and connected to India via major historic routes such as the Khyber Pass.[9] Pakistan also has a Mughal legacy, as its second city, Lahore, was Akhbar's capital for the fourteen years between 1584 and 1598. He built the massive Lahore Fort on the foundations of a previous fort, and enclosed the city within a red brick wall boasting twelve gates. The last of the great Mughals, Aurangzeb (1658–1707), gave Lahore its most famous monument, the great Badshahi Masjid and the Alamgiri gateway to the fort. Lahore also has a legacy of colonial buildings (many built in the style known as 'Moghul Gothic'). Hindu and Muslim fundamentalism in India has had some limited impact on the development of the country as a tourism destination, although this has been helped by western cultural influences mainly resulting from the legacy of British rule. However, the Portuguese had actually arrived in the region much earlier and had spheres of influence, especially in Goa. But Goa, together with enclaves of French influence such as Yanao, Ghandernagore, Pondicherry, Mahé and Karkal, were mere spots on an essentially British-dominated continent.

Tourism in contemporary India is still dominated by domestic travel, particularly for pilgrimage to temples, shrines and other sacred sites associated with any of India's major religious traditions. Modern pilgrimage is multifunctional and multi-purpose, and involves huge numbers of people – for example, the 15 million people who go to Tirupati in Andhra Pradesh in southern India every year, 75 000 on auspicious days; and the millions who visit locations such as Varanasi (Benares) on the Ganges steps, where the stepped *ghats* are the focus for ritual bathing and cremations. Many pilgrimage locations, including Varanasi, have also become tourist attractions, such as the city of Amritsar, home to the 400-year-old Golden Temple, which is the heart of the Sikh religion. Amritsar is living community, the spiritual and temporal centre of Sikh faith, but is hardly visited by non-Indians or non-Sikh tourists. Fifty thousand people per day are fed free of charge at the temple of Guru Nanak. Major festivals and events also influence domestic tourism patterns; it is thought that over sixty million people celebrated the Hindu Maha Kumbh Mela festival in Allahabad in 2001.[11] There are also substantial volumes of tourism to Buddhist sites, including the birthplace of the Buddha at Bodhgaya, which also attract Buddhist pilgrims from all over the world on a route which follows that taken by the Emperor Ashoka in the third century BC. Today, some Buddhist sites have become especially attractive to overseas visitors, especially the town of Dharamshala, seat of the exiled Dalai Lama and home to India's expatriate Tibetan community. Modern Indian pilgrimages often include elements of tourist travel, reflecting the changing cultural and economic aspirations of emerging middle and elite classes in India. Traditional pilgrimages drew crowds of visitors for particular annual events, but present forms of pilgrimage, which create huge floating populations of visitors at pilgrimage centres, have immense social and environmental impacts.

Outbound tourism flow during the Raj was confined to members of the British army and colonial superstructure, plus a few wealthy Indian princes. Even today India has a very small volume of outbound tourism, mainly connected with VFR trips to Britain and with outbound tourism to neighbouring countries, especially Nepal. However, incoming tourism is flourishing and is now the third largest earner of foreign exchange, attracting eight million international visitors per year. The vast majority of foreign visitors (except those from Bangladesh and Pakistan) arrive by air through Delhi, Bombay, Calcutta and Madras (Chennai) – perpetuating the inbound arrival pattern of the Raj. Current international trends in tourism have made India a fashionable destination and conditioned the development of its tourism portfolio. The traditional 'Golden Triangle' of cultural tourism, centred on Delhi and including Agra and the Taj Mahal, has been supplemented by new destinations such as Kerala in south India, whose popularity is related to its fame as a centre of *ayurvedic* medicine and also for its distinctive cuisine (Map 4.1). However, not all areas of India are equally accessible; peripheral states, including Arunachal Pradesh, Manipur, Mizoram, Nagaland and Sikkim, still require 'Inner Line' permits, much as they did under colonial rule. Wildlife tourism is also flourishing, based on India's 54 National Parks and 370 sanctuaries, including the National Parks associated with Project Tiger, such as Ranthambhore.[12] Major tourism areas today include the Himalayan foothills (including the high plateaux of Leh and Ladakh[13]), the Corbett National Park and Shimla, popular for trekking, climbing and rafting. The 'Golden Triangle' (Delhi-Agra-Jaipur-Bikaner-Jaisalmer-Jodhpu-Udaipur) (Plate 4.2) is still the main attraction, focused around the most spectacular sites of Mughal and Rajput India, but also including sacred Hindu sites such as Varanasi. Central India is less well visited but southern India is growing rapidly, with visitors going to new destinations in Tamil Nadu and Kerala, as well as the traditional beach resorts of Goa. Goa, a Portuguese colony, demonstrates the sea routes which have linked India to Europe, the islands of the Indian Ocean and the rest of South-East Asia. Map 4.3 reflects the direction of the monsoon winds that moved the sailing ships across the Indian Ocean. In the winter the winds blew to the south-west, bringing the ships down the coast of East Africa. In the summer the winds reversed direction and went north-east, bringing the ships up to Arabia and India. From the African coast the traders picked up wood for buildings, ivory, ostrich feathers, and even slaves. The trading network was vast, and goods from as far as China were brought to the eastern coast of Africa by the Arab traders, and later by the treasure ships of Zheng He from Ming dynasty China.

Such trade routes started early. Goa's history stretches back to the third century BC, when it formed part of the Mauryan Empire and its harbours and wide rivers made it a significant trading base for successive Indian empires. For this reason it became a Portuguese base from 1510, since the Portuguese were hoping to control the spice route from the east and had a strong desire to spread Christianity. Jesuit missionaries, led by St Francis Xavier, arrived in 1542. By the middle of the sixteenth century Portuguese control had expanded throughout Goa, and eventually the colony became the viceregal seat of the Portuguese Empire of the East, which included various East African port cities, East Timor and Macau. However, competition from the British, French and Dutch in the seventeenth century, combined with Portugal's inability to adequately service its far-flung empire, led to a decline. Goa achieved independence in 1961 and eventually became India's twenty-fifth state, a centre for beach tourism and a famous hippy hang-out during the 1970s.[14]

The maritime legacy seen in Goa can also be seen in Sri Lanka, at the heart of Indian Ocean trading routes. After the opening of the route round the Cape of Good Hope by Vasco da Gama in 1498, the island was brought into direct contact with western Europe; the opening of the Suez Canal in 1869 further strengthened trading links with the west. Sri Lanka has a written political history dating from the sixth century, and a history and culture much influenced by its proximity to India.

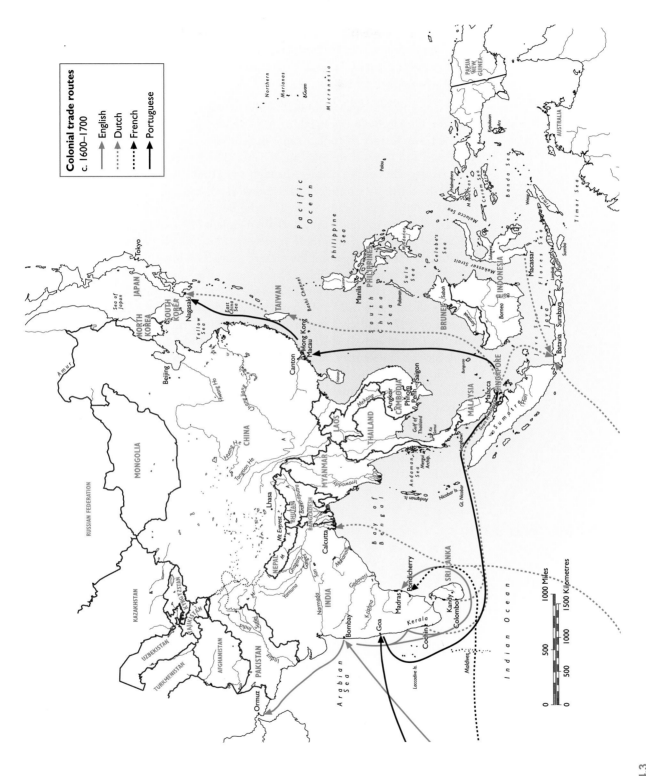

Map 4.3
Colonial trade routes 1600–1700

RUSSIAN FEDERATION

MONGOLIA

KAZAKHSTAN

UZBEKISTAN

TURKMENISTAN

TAJIKISTAN

KYRGYZSTAN

AFGHANISTAN

PAKISTAN

INDIA

NEPAL

BHUTAN

BANGLADESH

MYANMAR

CHINA

LAOS

THAILAND

CAMBODIA

MALAYSIA

SINGAPORE

INDONESIA

BRUNEI

PHILIPPINES

TAIWAN

SRI LANKA

NORTH KOREA

SOUTH KOREA

JAPAN

AUSTRALIA

PAPUA NEW GUINEA

Beijing

Lhasa

Mt Everest

Calcutta

Bombay

Goa

Cochin

Kerala

Madras

Pondicherry

Kandy

Colombo

Ormuz

Canton

Macau

Hong Kong

Nagasaki

Tokyo

Saigon

Phnom Penh

Angkor

Manila

Malacca

Batavia

Surabaya

Macassar

Amur

Hwang Ho

Yangtze

Hong He

Mekong

Salween

Irrawaddy

Brahmaputra

Ganges

Indus

Sutlej

Yamuna

Son

Narmada

Godavari

Krishna

Mahanadi

Chindwin

Sea of Japan

Yellow Sea

East China Sea

Pacific Ocean

Philippine Sea

South China Sea

Sulu Sea

Celebes Sea

Banda Sea

Molucca Sea

Flores Sea

Timor Sea

Java Sea

Gulf of Thailand

Andaman Sea

Bay of Bengal

Arabian Sea

Indian Ocean

Bahi Channel

Makassar Strait

Strait of Malacca

Sumatra

Java

Borneo

Sabah

Mindanao

Luzon

Palawan

Ko Samui

Mergui Archip.

Andaman Is.

Nicobar Is.

Gt. Nicobar

Laccadive Is.

Maldives

Northern Marianas

Guam

Micronesia

Halmahera

Ceram

Buru

Sumba

Lombok

Bali

Timor

Palau

0   500   1000 Miles

0   500   1000   1500 Kilometres

Its fabled wealth attracted Arab traders very early on and it was frequently invaded – as early as the thirteenth century by a Buddhist king from Malaya who tried to capture the island's significant relics of the Buddha, and then 200 years later by a fleet of Chinese junks sent by the Ming emperors. The Portuguese, Dutch and British had arrived in the early seventeenth century, and the British controlled the whole island after 1815. Sri Lanka eventually obtained independence in 1948, six months after India and Pakistan. The port of Galle was significant even when Ibn Battuta visited it in 1344.

Just as Goa and Sri Lanka demonstrate the sea routes linking India with peripheral areas, the kingdoms to the north of India (especially Nepal, Bhutan and Sikkim) link the travel history of India to that of central Asia, across the high passes of the Himalayas and towards the plateau of Tibet. The Khyber Pass is a fifty-three kilometre (thirty-three mile) passage through the Hindu Kush mountain range, connecting the northern frontier of Pakistan with Afghanistan. At its narrowest point, the pass is only three metres wide. It is the best-known land route between India and Pakistan, and has had a long and often violent history, traversed by conquering armies and used as a major trade route for centuries. Until the 1970s, Kabul in Afghanistan was a staging point for western tourists on overland routes to India. The history of that arid and mountainous country was summarized in Eric Newby's much-loved travel book *A Short Walk in the Hindu Kush*,[15] but current travel to the region is all but impossible. Afghanistan was devastated as a result of the Soviet invasion of 1979 and civil war from long-standing tribal feuds, with the fundamentalist Taliban actively discouraging visitation between 1996 and 2001. The cultural legacy of the country (and thus its unrealized tourism potential) was brought to public attention by much-publicized destruction of Buddhist monuments at Bamayan by the fundamentalist Islamic Taliban in 2001. The Buddha statues of Bamayan, built between the third and fifth centuries, represented a classic fusion of Buddhist and Grecian art and were located along the Silk Road, along which camel caravans plodded between China and Rome. The Buddhas survived attacks by Genghis Khan and others for more than 1600 years, but were destroyed by the Taliban in 2001, to global outrage.[16]

The Silk Road

Marco Polo was the son of a Venetian tradesman, and was probably aged seventeen in AD 1271 when he set out on a journey to China with his father and uncle, who had already travelled there before him. Their route took them through the Persian Gulf, Afghanistan and the Gobi Desert, taking four years to reach the Mongol emperor Kublai Khan's courts at Xanadu. Kublai Khan took a liking to Marco Polo and sent him on missions to distant corners of his empire; Polo remained in his dominions for at least sixteen years before eventually returning home to Venice and dictating the story of his twenty-five years of adventures while in a Genoese prison. The book, *Il Milione*,[17] was circulated all over Italy, although European ignorance of the civilizations of the Far East often made it seem to be a work of fiction. Even today the fantasy element in the book convinces some scholars that he did not make the journey, because he gave elaborate accounts not only of what he saw but also of what he had been told, and muddies the waters with stories of unicorns and men with tails. As European influence spread westward, many of Marco Polo's accounts were seen to be true and the book was used as valuable source of geographical and cultural information. Almost 200 years later Christopher Columbus used Marco Polo's description of Cipangu (Japan) as a goal for his voyage towards the setting sun.

Marco Polo travelled along The Silk Road, which first became a real intercontinental route (as opposed to a complex of local trade routes) around 100 BC and lasted (arguably) until the fifteenth century, when newly-discovered sea routes to Asia opened up. Today, the World Tourism Organization's (WTO) Silk Road Project is reviving interest in this ancient route through tourism.[18] In the ancient and early medieval worlds, silk, porcelain, furs, spices, gems, gunpowder and paper travelled west from China through cities such as Antioch, Babylon, Erzerum, Hamadan, Bukhara and Samarkand, and were exchanged for cosmetics, silver, gold, amber, ivory, carpets, perfume and glass. Culture, art, philosophy and belief systems travelled the Silk Road alongside the merchants, bringing Buddhism to China and assisting the spread of Islam and Christianity.

The Silk Road was in fact many routes, not just one, and is often considered to originate in Italy and Greece, with 'feeder' routes from Egypt, Arabia, Africa and Central Asia. It crossed Turkey and passed through what is today the Islamic Republic of Iran, which is just beginning to emerge into the cultural tourism market with limited tours to Silk Road cities such as Esfahan (Isfahan). For centuries part of the Silk Road wound its way south from central Asia, across some of the highest mountains in the world, down through modern Pakistan. Subsidiary routes passed through countries yet to develop their full tourism potential, such as Kazakhstan, Kyrgyzstan, Tajikistan and Turkmenistan, which sit at the heart of central Asia, with China to the east and the Indian subcontinent to the south. There are indications that goods from India passed through the Republic of Georgia and Azerbaijan centuries before there was trade from China heading west on the main Silk Road. The extreme eastern end of the Road could be considered as the Democratic People's Republic of Korea, with the Korean peninsula providing a cultural bridge between the Asian continent and sea trade routes to Japan.

Since 1991, coinciding with the independence of the five central Asian republics, there has been a revival of interest in the Silk Road for cultural exchange, trade and tourism. Encouraged by this development, the WTO decided to create the long-term Silk Road Tourism Project to unite the tourism development and marketing agendas of Silk Road countries under one banner. In 1996 an overall marketing plan was suggested, and further steps have included the compilation of an exhaustive inventory of all tourism resources along the Silk Road, including attractions, facilities, accommodations, transport and information; now used by the Silk Road countries as an effective tourism marketing tool. The WTO project has stimulated the development of infrastructure and superstructure in its participating countries, particularly with regard to new hotel accommodation, improved accessibility, internal transportation, human resource development, and other management actions taken to improve the overall quality of the Silk Road tourist destinations. Special-interest tourism (mainly focused on the cultural, historical and environmental resources of participating countries) is developing fast, along the Silk Road, to countries and regions previously inaccessible to western tourists. Moreover, travel along today's Silk Road is greatly facilitated by easier land and air transportation. Today's typical Silk Road travellers might take a month's tour, with an itinerary taking in China, Kazakhstan, Kyrgyzstan and Uzbekistan, visiting Xian, the Great Wall, the Turfan depression, Urumqi, Kashgar and the cities of

Uzbekistan (Map 4.4). Alternative Silk Road itineraries enable visitor access to the Tien Shan Mountains, and to the southern Silk Road around Hotan, the Pamir Mountains and Kashgar, including (relatively) comfortable drives though the heart of the Taklamakan Desert, once the most feared geographical obstacles in the ancient route. Although accommodation may be basic, business is brisk for such tours. Supplementary itineraries include Armenia (easily reached by direct flight connections from London to Yerevan, with tours of the historic sites of Armenia and Georgia – including the Aghpat Monastery World Heritage site and a drive to Tbilisi in Georgia), and an exploration of the Caucasus Mountains. Of all the Silk Road countries it is probably, with vastly increased western visitation to the Silk Road cities of Samarkhand, Bokhara (Plate 4.3) and the WHS city of Khiva,[19] Uzbekistan that has benefited most.

However, Marco Polo was not the only early source for information about central Asia. In 1412, Ruy Gonzalez de Clavijo, a Spanish diplomat, travelled to Turkistan as an ambassador from the Court of King Henry III of Castile and Leon to attend the Court of Timurlaine at Samarkand. This journey required five months of sailing across the Mediterranean to Constantinople, over the Black Sea, followed by an overland journey on horseback to Turkistan. Timur welcomed them but died before they left the country, leaving Ruy Gonzalez to write an account of their trip that gave the Spanish an insight into Persia and central Asia.[20] Much later in history, Nikolai Przhevalsky, a Russian lieutenant-colonel, was sent in 1870 by the Imperial Geographical Society of St Petersburg to explore southern Mongolia. With only two companions he covered 7000 miles in three years over largely unmapped territory. He is particularly well known for his travels in and around the Gobi Desert, which included being the first European to visit Lop Nor since Marco Polo, 600 years before. His most famous legacy is the discovery of the last truly wild horse, named after him, and his writings, which give the west a picture of Mongol life and survival strategies in the tough climate of the Mongolian plateaux.[21] This area had been the heartland of the Mongol Empire in the thirteenth century, and has remained remote, landlocked and sparsely populated ever since. Mongolia moved from communism to a free market economy in the 1990s, after the collapse of the Soviet Union, and has since developed limited amounts of incoming international tourism aimed at visitors interested in the traditional lifestyles of Mongolian pastoral nomads and also, increasingly, at wildlife-watching in newly designated Protected Areas. Przhevalsky's writings fired the imagination of the Swedish geographer Sven Hedin, who made many journeys in central Asia, starting (at the age of twenty) in 1885. His was the first scientific expedition aimed at crossing Asia from west to east via the Pamirs and Taklamakan Desert.[22] Hedin made two unsuccessful attempts to reach Lhasa, but was still the first European to explore Tibet's trans-Himalayan mountain range and to prepare a detailed map of the country. Today's traveller along the Silk Road can no longer expect such great discoveries, and the journey is facilitated by train charters on the stretch of the Silk Road from Xian to Urumqi, which connects with the caravan route to Kashgar.[23] Hedin also explored the Lop Nor Desert and Silk Road oasis of Lou-Lan, and became the first westerner to see the ruins (later studied in depth by Aurel Stein) at Dandan-oilik and Karadong. In 1900 Mark Aurel Stein began the first of four expeditions which traced the Silk Road in central Asia, collecting data on little known regions. He found the 'Cave of a Thousand Buddhas' series of temples in the Taklamakan, which were filled with early Buddhist manuscripts that had lain there untouched since the seventh century. Stein justified his removal of the manuscripts

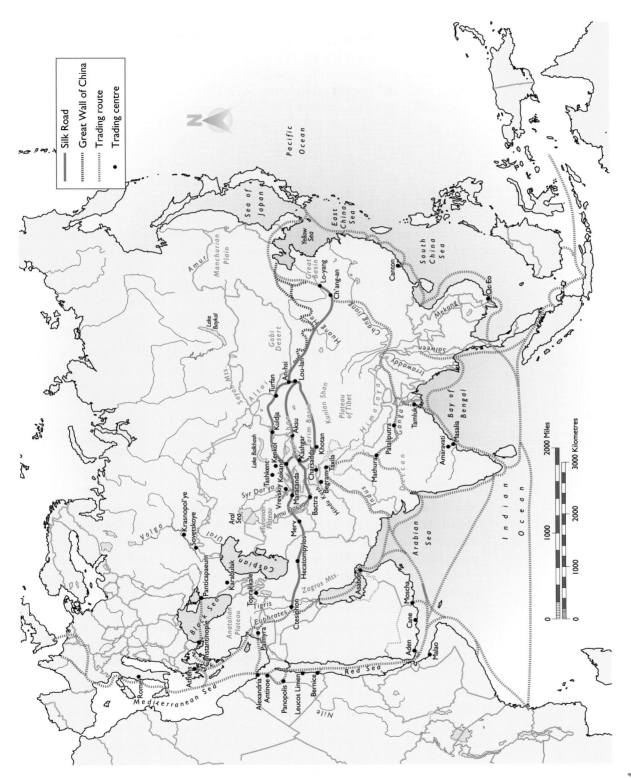

Map 4.4
Silk Road

by arguing that if left they would be stolen or destroyed; most ended up in the British Museum. Although he did not realize it at the time, many were documents recording far earlier travels, and indeed had been brought back by Hsuan Tsang, the Chinese Buddhist monk and pilgrim, from his travels in India in AD 602–604. Tsang went on a sixteen-year voyage to gather Buddhist teachings in India and translated them into Chinese. He defied an imperial order restraining citizens from leaving China, and made a 40 000-mile journey on horseback, returning to China in AD 645 (to a hero's welcome) with information on the cultures, climate and products of the places visited.

The Himalayas

The Hindu kingdom of Nepal was closed to the outside world until the 1950s, when it was discovered by hippies, overland travellers and climbers and made a fashionable exotic destination. Indeed, the capital, Kathmandu, is one of the world's exotic names and often figures on 'must-see' lists (Plate 4.4). Nowadays tourism to Nepal is affected by political uncertainties, including an ongoing Maoist rebellion (mainly in the west of the country), but Nepal is still popular as the world's major trekking destination. Awareness of its possibilities was created by writers such as Peter Matthiessen, the American naturalist and author, whose book *The Snow Leopard* describes the region of Dolpo.[24] The previously sealed kingdom of Lo (Mustang) was opened to travellers for the first time in 1994.[25] Mustang's appeal was that it preserved the traditional Tibetan Buddhism in a country that had been inaccessible, after the traditional culture of Tibet itself was destroyed following the Chinese invasion of 1952. Tibet is another fantasy destination for western travellers, whose views of it have been conditioned by the mythical Shangri-La of James Hilton's *Lost Horizons*.[26] The flight of the Dalai Lama and the visual images of the Potala Palace and the empty wastelands of Tibet have made it a desirable destination to visit, helped by its perceived inaccessibility (both geographically and politically) and cultural remoteness.

This western interest in the traditional culture of Tibet is not a twenty-first century phenomenon. In the nineteenth century two missionaries made illegal journeys into Tibet disguised as Buddhist lamas, travelling for two years and finally arriving, as part of a caravan of 2000 people and 4000 animals, in Lhasa in January 1846. The Chinese Imperial Commissioners had them expelled after two months and did not permit them to set up a mission, but their accounts of contemporary Tibetan life stimulated much interest. The first western woman to reach Tibet was also a missionary, Anne Taylor, who arrived in 1887 dressed as a Tibetan nun after a 12 000-mile journey. However, European influence in Tibet really started with the 1903 Younghusband expedition, which took place at the height of Kipling's so-called 'Great Game'[27] – the strategic manoeuvring of Britain and Russia for control of the area. The Russian tsarist regime was intent on expanding into Afghanistan, western China and independent kingdoms on India's northern frontiers, which threatened the British hold on the subcontinent. Sir Francis Younghusband was chosen to lead a military expedition into Tibet and establish relations with the Dalai Lama in order to edge out the Russian presence. The expedition was a disaster, as Younghusband's troops were massacred and it became clear that there was no Russian presence, but Younghusband developed a deep affection for Tibet which influenced the rest of his life. The carving on his tombstone is a relief depicting Lhasa.

China

It has been estimated that there are more than 14 000 different visitor attractions in China, including ninety-nine historical and cultural cities and thirty World Heritage sites, and the country now has eight billion domestic/international tourists. China has a landmass of nearly 9.6 million square kilometres – almost one-fifteenth of the world's land – and extends across five climate zones.

In ancient China, travel was more a cultural phenomenon than an economic activity; landscapes, mountains, natural and cultural scenery have a sentimental meaning to the Chinese. Pilgrimage, educational travel and health-related travel have all taken place in China since the earliest times, but until the travels of Marco Polo in the thirteenth century there was no international tourism and the western world knew nothing of the country. Under the Han dynasty in China (206 BC–AD 220) the empire was unified under a single sovereign, and the expansion of the Han brought China into contact with the 'barbarians' that encircled their world, bringing military commercial gains. Military expeditions were sent against the Xiongnu (name given to the various nomadic tribes of central Asia) to the north, who posed the greatest threat to China, and these were successful in providing China with access to the Silk Road routes to Europe. Chinese diplomats also opened links with central Asian tribes, and the great Chinese explorer Zhang Quian provided the authorities with information on the possibilities of trade and alliances in northern India. During the same period, Chinese influence penetrated into what would later be Vietnam and Korea. Under the Tang dynasty (AD 618–907) the empire reached its greatest extent, far north of the Great Wall and far west into inner Asia. The rich repository of texts and paintings at Dunhuang in Gansu shows the importance of the Silk Route.

During the seventh and eighth centuries, great cities such as the capital Chang'an, the Yangzi port of Yangzhou and the coastal port of Canton became crowded with foreign merchants. Buddhism, introduced into China during the first century, flourished, and Buddhist monasteries became great centres of learning and cultural activity with a pivotal place in the network of communications between China and other parts of Asia. The Tang dynasty (c. 1200 years ago) set up maritime trading routes that were to establish China (temporarily) as a great sea power, 200 years before Spanish Portuguese and British started their voyages of exploration. China started sea trade as alternative to using the Silk Road, partly to export its fragile ceramics, which were not yet durable enough to survive prolonged overland trips. Export by sea was the logical alternative, but the Chinese were at first forced to rely on Arab seamen, who had perfected the *dhow* as an ocean-going vessel. The wealth that China created through its maritime exports enabled the country to build its own navy, and by 1237 China was the predominant global sea power, with 52 000 seamen and a vast fleet. This is supported by archaeological evidence, such as the wrecks of Batu Hitam off Indonesia, which have yielded 60 000 pieces that formed part of the cargo of eighth century porcelain traders being exported from China aboard an Arab *dhow* to Malaysia, India and what is now Saudi Arabia.

China has also had its share of early travel writers. In AD 639, the great Buddhist master Zhang Quian (Xuan Zang or Hsuan Tsang) set off for the home place of the Buddha and toured the whole of India.[28] Genghis Khan was recognized as supreme ruler of the Mongols in central Asia in 1206, penetrating the Great Wall of China in 1213 and capturing Beijing in 1215. The Mongol Empire which was bequeathed to his descendants stretched from Ukraine to Korea and the northern limits of what is now Vietnam. Under his grandson, Kublai Khan, a new dynasty emerged in China, the Yuan. The Mongol conquests resulted in the so-called *Pax Mongolica* in inner Asia; land routes were reopened and European missionaries and traders made their way to from Europe to Asia. Foreigners were easily incorporated into the ethically complex and religiously diverse empire. The Mongols controlled China for less than a century, and in the early part of the succeeding Ming Empire relations with central Asia deteriorated and Emperor Yongle launched the first of seven great maritime expeditions in 1405. This consisted of a fleet of more than 60 large vessels and 255 smaller ones, carrying nearly 28 000 men. His fourth and fifth expeditions, in 1413 and 1417 respectively, travelled as far as Aden on the Suez Canal, and brought back embassies from Egypt. At the end of Yongle's reign China retreated into itself, and by the middle of the sixteenth century coastal provinces were being harassed by pirates. Ships from Europe arrived in China, and in 1557 the Portuguese gained the right to establish a permanent trade base in Macau. Traders were followed by missionaries, and the Jesuits, led by Matteo Ricci, made their way inland and established a presence at the Chinese Court, making an impression with their skills in astronomy. They remained active in both the court and the provinces until their activities were curtailed in 1720. We tend to think of China's trading relationships as being with Europe and the rest of Asia, but the Portuguese presence also linked China directly to trade in the New World. New crops (such as potatoes and maize) were introduced, and silver from the Americas was used to pay for Chinese exports such as tea, porcelain and ceramics. The second half of the sixteenth century saw something of a commercial revolution. The early Qing (Manchu) emperors had welcomed foreigners, but from the reign of Yongzheng (1722–1735) missionary activity was banned in the provinces, and under Quianlong (1736–1795) strict controls were placed on maritime activity, which from 1757 was limited to Canton. Gradual development of the trade in opium in the nineteenth century was stopped in 1839, which resulted in the Opium Wars – one result of which was the signing of the Treaty of Nanking, which ceded Hong Kong to the British in 1842. Britain agreed to hand back the entire colony to China when the lease of the New Territories expired in 1997, and this was done. Macau, the oldest European settlement in Asia, returned to the People's Republic of China in 1999.

The growth of the European influence in China ended after the Boxer rebellion of 1900, with the Qing Empire quickly collapsing and a provisional Republican government being established in 1911. During the period of the nationalist revolution and subsequent civil war, international travel was greatly curtailed. The People's Republic of China was established in 1949 under Mao Zedong, but the 'cultural revolution' of 1966–1970 destroyed not only millions of people but also much of China's ancient culture and buildings, and millions of works of art. China's trade and diplomatic contacts with the outside world were not restored until the 1970s, and in 1976 were further battered by the violent suppression of demonstrations in Tienanmen Square. However, in the contemporary world China's tourism became a significant economic activity alongside the country's modernization – although inbound travel to China does actually have rather a long history. The establishment of the first foreign travel agency by Thomas Cook took place in 1841, and the founding of the first national travel service, the China

Travel Service (CTS), in 1923 marked the real beginnings of an international tourism industry. The CTS had the primary function of facilitating the travel of overseas Chinese to China, but its successor, the China International Travel Service (CITS), in 1954 catered for non-Chinese visitors, and this was followed in 1964 by the Travel and Tourism Bureau, now the China National Tourism Administration, as a policy-making body for overseas. There are now more than 7500 domestic and international travel agencies in the country, allowing both inbound and outbound international travel to flourish. In 1978, the first year after implementing economic reform, China received *c.* 1.809 million inbound arrivals. Domestic travel expanded from VFR to conferences, student holiday travel, shopping and recreation, and the distances people travelled also began to increase. This period in China has been compared in significance to that of Thomas Cook in the nineteenth century in Europe. Between 1991 and 1996, corresponding to the eighth National Five-Year Plan, international tourism expanded rapidly, and today tourism is considered to be a major growth industry with investment in marketing, facilities, infrastructure, management and organizational change (Map 4.5). For the first time in its history outbound tourism is significant, but still only 1 per cent of the population has the ability to travel abroad.

China is attractive to overseas tourists, partly because of its ancient civilization and partly because of its long period of modern-day isolation giving it a sense of mystery and adventure. Because of its huge size and virtually unlimited capacity to develop new destinations and products, China will eventually become a major player in the world tourism market by 2020; however, its products are currently cultural with little in the way of beach, shopping, cruise, sport and adventure travel.[29] Ecotourism in particular is very poorly developed, as China's environmental problems are severe, but business travel remains significant. There is a marked east–west divide in China's contemporary tourist regions, with many of the natural and cultural attractions being along the coast and eastern China – including Beijing, Shanghai, Jiangsu, Zhejiang, Fujian and Guangdong. The western region, which includes Xinjiang, Ningxia, Guangxi, Yunnan etc., is far less developed for tourism.

Japan

Chinese influence once extended far beyond its existing borders, into Korea, much of South-East Asia and Japan. Japan, made up of the four main islands Honshu, Hokkaido, Kyushu and Shikoku, is a destination of immense variety. It is still dominated by domestic tourism, such as the vast number of people who travel to observe the *sakura* (cherry-blossom viewing), around the time of the Japanese New Year and the 'Golden Week' holidays in early May. The *obon* season occurs mid-August, when Japanese travel to visit the graves of their ancestors, and there are many other seasonal festivals and events, as well as domestic travel to spa and ski resorts. During the Heian period (AD 794–1192) Japan received cultural delegates from China, and under the Genji rulers the emperor himself became merely a figurehead, with actual government being carried out by powerful *shoguns* and their factions. During the Kamakura period, the Mongols under Genghis

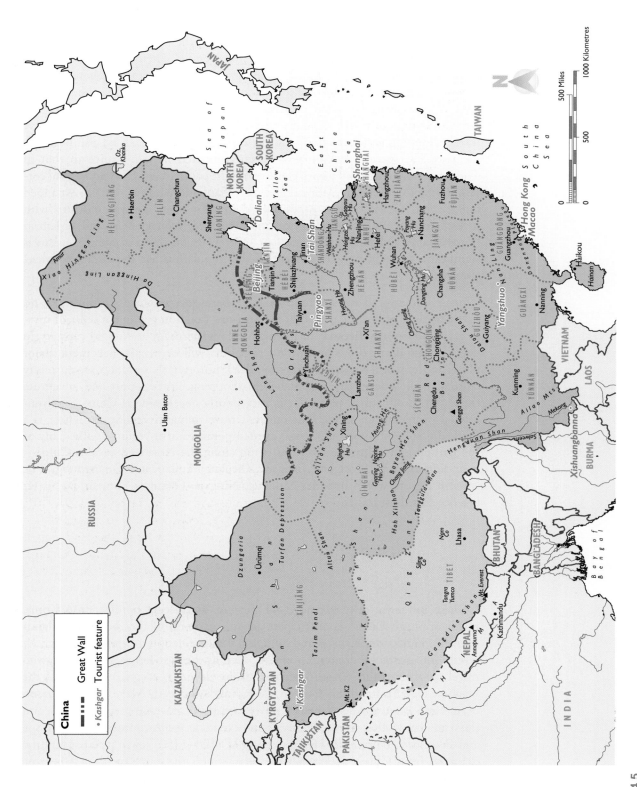

Map 4.5
China

Khan tried, in 1174 and 1181, to land at Hakata in northern Honshu, but a destructive typhoon wrecked both the fleet and 100 000 warriors. This idea of a *kamikaze* (divine wind) was resurrected in the Second World War as the name for Japanese suicide pilots making a second attempt to save Japan from invasion. During the Edo or Tokugawa era (1603–1867) Japan had extensive contacts with European traders and missionaries, to the point where its government felt threatened – especially by Christianity, which was suppressed with the martyrdom of thousands. Only the Dutch were permitted to trade in Japan, and only through the port of Nagasaki on the southern island of Kyushu. The Portuguese were banned in 1639, after the exclusion of the English and Spanish. The succeeding two centuries saw Japan sealed off from the outside world, with little internal mobility either except for military action. Outbound travel was strictly forbidden under the rule of the Tokugawa *shoguns*, and even after the Meiji restoration of 1868 it was permitted only for business or study. Commodore Perry of the US Navy arrived in 1853 with a demand that Japan open its doors to trade; with Yokohama and other ports opening, Japan gradually modernized under the Meiji emperors, acquiring a modern army and navy. In the twentieth century these forces were employed against Taiwan, Korea, China and eventually the USA and Allied forces in the War of the Pacific, with Japan entering that conflict after its raid on the American naval base of Pearl Harbour in Hawaii. The Pacific War ended in Japan's defeat and the dropping of two atomic bombs on Hiroshima and Nagasaki. Occupation by alien (mainly American) forces followed. The Peace Memorial museum of Hiroshima has become a major visitor attraction and World Heritage site, and the economic power-house that is modern Japan is now the largest generator of tourists in the Asia-Pacific region. It has been politically stable since 1945, with restrictions on outbound leisure lifted in 1964 and actively encouraged in the late 1980s as a way of restructuring Japan's trade balance with the outside world and promoting mutual understanding.[30]

South-East Asia, Indonesia and Malaya

South-East Asia comprises the mainland countries of Myanmar, Laos, Cambodia, Thailand and Vietnam, plus the Malay peninsula and the islands of Indonesia and the Philippines. The development of tourism in South-East Asia can be divided into three distinct periods; pre-colonial, colonial and post-colonial (the latter including the twentieth century wars). During the pre-colonial period there was limited European awareness of the richness of the cultures of South-East Asia, but this changed rapidly with the arrival of the first colonial explorers in the sixteenth century (Map 4.3). This was followed by 400 years of tussles between indigenous and colonial powers, which has left a rich architectural and cultural legacy. During this period incoming travellers included merchants, army or government officials, with limited volumes of leisure travel. Mass leisure tourism to South-East Asia is thus a relatively recent phenomenon, having remained relatively small in scale until after the 1970s (with the end of the Vietnam War and the development of the jumbo jet). Today's tourism is still beach-dominated and seasonal (mainly December–February), but trends include increased diversification into cultural tourism and ecotourism. The region has large volumes of domestic tourism dominated by pilgrimage either to Buddhist sites (in Vietnam) or to Catholic shrines (in the Philippines), and substantial business travel. Present patterns of incoming international leisure tourism into the area are responding to the development of city and transit centres, especially the main air hubs of Bangkok, Kuala Lumpur and Singapore, together with cultural tourism based around historic and religious sites and shopping, especially in Thailand and Singapore (Map 4.1). The destination image of South-East Asia for Europeans is highly age-dependent. For people in their seventies it results from the events of the Second World War, including the Japanese invasion of Singapore and the US-dominated war in the Pacific. For post-war 'baby boomers', the area is inextricably linked with the Vietnam and Korean wars of the 1960s and 1970s. Today, new destination images are related to the frequency with which the area features in travel programmes and feature films, as well as the entry of new destinations such as Cambodia, Vietnam and Laos – which appealed initially to backpackers, but are now attracting a more mature market as their infrastructure develops. Recent problems with tourism development in the area include the effect of terrorist attacks (such as the Bali bombings of 2003 and 2005) and natural catastrophes such as the 2004 tsunami, which devastated many coastal areas, discouraged travel to the region and led to job losses and business closures.[31] Bird flu is likely to be a factor in 2006–2007, as is the potential escalation of terrorist activities by Islamic fundamentalists.

The existence of South-East Asia was known to Europe from Roman times; Malaya was known in Europe as early as the second century, and appears on the early second century map of Ptolemy as 'Golden Chersonese'.[32] Moreover, South-East Asia was in medieval times the seat of powerful ancient kingdoms, the remains of whose secular and religious monuments remain significant for contemporary tourism in the area. Vietnam had contact with the west as far back as AD 166, when the Roman Empire was under the control of Marcus Aurelius. China and India traded with scattered South-East Asian communities from around that time, with succeeding centuries seeing the emergence of powerful states, including the empire of Angkor in the interior of present-day Cambodia. The Angkor Empire in the ninth to fourteenth centuries AD eventually included most of what are now Thailand, Laos and Cambodia, with an economy based on agriculture and a sophisticated irrigation system. Its greatest monuments are to be seen at Angkor itself, with interest stimulated by their rediscovery. The 'lost city' of Angkor, built when the Kymer civilization was at its height, became a centre of intense European popular and scholarly interest after the publication in the 1860s of *La Tour du Monde*, an account by the French naturalist Henri Houhot of his voyages.[33] Archaeologists and philologists started work at the site in 1908, but the excavations were interrupted from the early 1970s by the Vietnam War, although they were later resumed, revealing an immense complex of temples and structures forming a huge administrative and religious centre. Angkor Wat is the world's largest religious building, and the nearby fortified city of Angkor has walls twenty kilometres (twelve miles) round and six metres high. Recent visitor interest has been stimulated by easier air access via the nearby town of Siem Riep, increased visitor safety, and the publicity generated by the use of the site as a backdrop for the film *Tomb Raider* in 2000.[34]

A similar rediscovery of a lost archaeological site and its extraction from covering jungle was made on the island of Java, where the colossal temple of the Borobodur was built during the early part of the ninth century at the time of Java's Buddhist heyday. With the decline of Buddhism, it, like Angkor, was abandoned, and it was only rediscovered in 1814 when Sir Stamford Raffles governed Java.[35] A US$25 million restoration project returned the temple to its former state and it forms the basis for tourism in central Java, together with the nearby city of Yogyakarta, which is Java's cultural capital, and the huge port of Surabaya, famous for its Dutch colonial architecture. In Myanmar (ancient Burma) the city of Bagan remains the principle tourist attraction, with thousands of temples and ruins dating from the eleventh to the thirteen centuries spread over a forty-kilometre plain, built by the Bamar Empire. The decline of the Bamar Empire was accelerated by the sack of Bagan in 1287 by the Mongol emperor, Kublai Khan. Myanmar receives low levels of international visitation and has been virtually sealed off from the outside world since 1962, when a repressive military regime took control of the government. Many human rights groups urge tourists not to visit Myanmar.[36]

Although there was at least limited awareness of South-East Asia from an early date, Europe's first serious interest in the area relates to trade – particularly with the Spice Islands of Indonesia,[37] whose nutmeg, cinnamon and pepper were once valued more highly than gold. Marco Polo mentions the Spice Islands in his 1292 account of his Asian journey, which generated European interest in the search for a fast sea passage to the islands. At first the European interests in the region were confined to controlling shipping via alliances and agreements with local authorities, but in 1519 Ferdinand Magellan set off from Europe with instructions to sail round the world and extend Spain's trading empire into the Pacific. Magellan reached the Philippines in 1521 (and died there on Mactan Island), and by 1571 the Spanish had established a headquarters at Manila, from where they gradually took control of the whole region. For 250 years, Spanish governors, priests and traders travelled across the Pacific to Manila in galleons which set out from the Mexican port of Acapulco, Manila's lifeline to Spanish power. Mestizo Mexican troops also made the journey in the huge (up to 2000-tonne) wooden-hulled vessels which sailed almost a third of the way around the world, sometimes stopping at the Spanish base on the island of Guam. The Spanish traded Mexican gold and silver for the spices, Chinese porcelain, brocade silks, jade, ivory, gems and lacquer goods of Asia, which were shipped to the markets of Europe and North America. The ships were preyed on by pirates in the Sulu Sea (a problem that still exists today), which has resulted in tales of lost galleons laden with treasure which haunt the islands of the Philippines even today. This profitable trade route continued in existence even while Spanish power in Europe gradually declined after the English defeat of the Spanish Armada in 1588, eventually waning until the Philippines became a backwater.

European footholds in Asia started in the sixteenth century when, on the Malay peninsula, the port of Melaka (Malacca/Molucca) also attracted early European interest, falling first to the Portuguese in 1511, then to the Dutch and subsequently to the English. The Spanish established themselves at Cebu in 1565, later invading Manila, but it was the Dutch (whose area of influence centred on Java and Sumatra) who monopolized European trading links with Asia for 200 years at a time when the Spanish, French and, later, the English were beginning to think of the colonial possibilities of the region. The British took advantage of Napoleon's occupation of Holland to establish a brief presence in Indonesia under Sir Stamford Raffles in 1811–1816, but the Dutch retained control of much of Indonesia until its independence 130 years later.

European merchants and missionaries started to trickle into Vietnam in the early sixteenth century, including Alexandre de Rhodes, a French Jesuit missionary who developed the *quoc ngu* script still used for written Vietnamese. France had a foothold in Vietnam and imposed a Treaty of Protectorate in 1883, extending French influence over Cambodia and Laos, which had formerly been part of the great Thai kingdom. Siam (Thailand) was the only South-East Asian nation to remain independent, with its kings gradually modernizing the country to produce a state which acted as a buffer between British and French zones of colonial influence. In 1824 Burma (Myanmar) was invaded by the British, who captured Rangoon; France occupied Vietnam in 1862; and in 1898 the USA annexed the Philippines in the aftermath of the Spanish–American War. The remnants of these various colonial activities have left a legacy of colonial tourist attractions which persists to the present day. In southern Cambodia, for example, the town of Kep-sur-Mer was founded as a colonial retreat for the French elite in 1908, and today acts as a destination for wealthy Cambodians interested in gambling and watersports – a pattern not dissimilar to the changing tourist usage of India's colonial hill-stations such as Shimla (p. 71).

British interest in Malaya was related to a search for tin, with British inroads into Sarawak and Saba and Singapore memorably chronicled by Somerset Maugham's tales of colonial life in Malaysia.[38] Malaysia's colonial history, complete with golf courses and rose gardens, is still an important tourist attraction today, particularly with the tea plantations of the Cameron Highlands. However, the region's tourism product also includes cultural tourism based round the indigenous Dayak (a word used for the aboriginal non-Muslim people of Borneo) groups such as the Iban and Bidayuh in Sarawak. The oldest British settlement in Malaysia, pre-dating both Singapore and Melacca, is actually the island of Pulau Penang (Betelnut Island), founded in 1786 by Captain Francis Light on behalf of the East India Company, who acquired possession of the nearly uninhabited island by allegedly firing silver dollars from his ships' canons into the jungle to encourage settlement. This soon grew into the small town of Georgetown, later known as Penang.

The two World Wars of the twentieth century collapsed these European empires and provided leverage for independence movements. Today's South-East Asian countries struggle to unite a land mass that shares only a diverse colonial legacy. With the thawing of the Cold War, South-East Asia gained renewed stability and vitality. Singapore emerged as the star of the region, with Vietnam, Laos and Cambodia gradually opening to foreign trade, regional collaboration and tourism. Only Myanmar remains closed today. During the Second World War the Japanese linked with the Burmese Independence Army (BIA) to drive the British out of Myanmar, and declared it an independent country. Mandalay was the seat of the Burmese kings until the arrival of the British, and the Golden Buddha of Mahamuni Paya and the Golden Boulder of Kyaiktiyo are still major domestic pilgrimage sites. However, the unsavoury image of Myanmar has been compounded by adverse publicity regarding opium poppy growing in the lawless regions of the Shan state on the Thai border, still controlled by powerful drug lords. The area forms part of the so-called 'golden triangle' of Thailand, Myanmar and Laos, where opium became a cash crop as early as the 1600s for the region's ethnic minority groups, and from where it was exported as part of the Asian spice trade.

Singapore was founded by Stamford Raffles in 1819 and prospered as a trading hub for South-East Asia, attracting large-scale Chinese immigration. British control over Singapore was ended abruptly on 15 February 1942, when the Japanese invaded Singapore and ran it for the rest of the war with great brutality. The Japanese incarcerated many British in Changi prison, a site still visited by families of those who were killed there. Singapore has become the shopping and stopover capital of Asia (rivalled only by Bangkok), and is now trying to encourage tourists to visit the remains of its colonial past, including the old Parliament House, cathedral and Concert Hall. Its Chinese legacy is also being revived, with the restoration of many buildings and the Thian Hock Keng Temple, as well as the development of a Chinatown Heritage Centre. Thailand also contains many tourist attractions related to the Japanese invasion. A new museum near Kanchanaburi tells visitors the story of the Thailand–Burma railway, which resulted from a Japanese plan to connect Yangon in Burma with Bangkok in order to transport military supplies. It was constructed by captured Allied soldiers plus Burmese and Malay captives, who were used as slave labour to build the 415-kilometre 'death railway' where more than 1000 died. Its most famous individual location is the Kwai River bridge, made famous by the film *Bridge On the River Kwai*.[39] Today's bridge comes complete with a sound and light show. However, such cultural tourism attractions form a minor element of Thailand's modern tourism portfolio, which is based on beach tourism on the southern island, such as at Phuket, an ancient crossroads of Malay Chinese and Indian traders, and on shopping in Bangkok. Both Bangkok and Singapore represent the legacies of 2000 years of worldwide trading links. In the north of Thailand the city of Chiang Mai has a famous night bazaar which is legacy of the original Yunnanese trading caravans that stopped here along the ancient trade route between Simao in China and Mawlamyaing on Myanmar's Gulf of Martaban coast. Today's market is the main attraction for visitors to the arts and cultural centre of Chiang Mai, seen as the Asian equivalent of Marrakech with its cooking and language classes and potential expeditions to visit the hill tribes. Thailand's hill tribes are famous in tourism history terms for the role they have played in the development of the early literature regarding the social and cultural impact of tourism.[40] Early studies were made of visitors to these ethnic minorities, such as the Akha Hmong, Karen Lisi and Lahu Mien people, whose distinctive clothing and belief systems attracted early tourist interest. Subsequent analysis of the impact of tourism on these hill tribes, who probably number more than half a million people living in the mountainous regions of north-western and western Thailand, suggest that tourism has been a mixed blessing, protecting some indigenous cultures from government-induced change but creating ethnic fossilization and almost theme parks as a side effect.

Independence was won by the Philippines in 1946, Burma in 1948 and Indonesia in 1949, and in 1957 an independent Malaysia was founded. The British retreat from Singapore occurred in 1965. However, progress towards democracy and independence was halted in 1973 when Saigon fell to the north Vietnamese, and after a brutal civil war the Khmer Rouge took over Cambodia from 1975–1979, killing two million Cambodians and destroying the cultural legacy of the country. For this reason very little tourist visitation took place to Cambodia until the late 1990s, after an UN-facilitated peace accord, and even today the tourism infrastructure is limited. Cambodia and Laos both retain a strong French influence, evidenced in the collection of Buddhist and French colonial architecture that comprises Luang Prabang in Laos, now on the World Heritage List. The legacy of the Khmer Rouge has contributed the dark tourism[41] attractions of the 'killing fields' of Choeung Ek, just outside the capital Phnom Penh, where 17 000 people died. Laos, which has a reputation as South-East Asia's most relaxed country, is a remote and mountainous region which maintained village life through the arrival of the French 100 years ago, and through the period of 1965–1973 when Laos was bombed by the US because of the north Vietnamese presence in the country.

Two million tons of US bombs dropped in Laos, 30 per cent of which failed to explode, producing extensive no-go areas for tourism. After the end of the Second World War, the independence movement in Vietnam under Ho Chi Minh and his communist-dominated Viet Minh led efforts to be free of French rule with a famous battle fought in May 1954, when Viet Minh forces overran the French garrison at Dien Bien Phu. Subsequently, the Geneva Accords of mid-1954 provided for a temporary division of Vietnam between a communist-dominated National Liberation Front (NLF) or Viet Cong North and the South, giving a temporary division along the Ben Hai River. These zones were divided by a demilitarized zone (DMZ) (of which contemporary tours can be taken today), but this did not last. The USA committed its first combat troops to the Vietnam War in 1965 in support of the south (based at Hanoi), and from then until the Paris Agreements of 1973 (which led to Vietnam's eventual reunification) the Vietnam War accounted for the deaths of some 58 000 American servicemen. Today's dark tourism into the region includes many military sites, including the Vinh Moc tunnels utilized by the Viet Cong, plus the similar (though more commercialized) tunnel network at Cu Chi. In the Cu Chi district alone there were over 200 kilometres of tunnels, part of which have been reconstructed at two sites near the villages of Ben Dinh and Ben Duoc. The Cu Chi tunnel network, in the outskirts of Ho Chi Minh City, stretched, at the height of the war, from Saigon to the Cambodian border. Other sites, such as the Khe Sanh Combat base, the Truong Son National Cemetery and the Museum of Ho Chi Minh City (in modern Saigon), with its model of the infamous 'tiger cages' used to house Viet Cong prisoners,[42] have become not only tourist attractions but also pilgrimage sites for US soldiers and their families, for whom the memory of the Vietnam War is still very fresh.

The tourism development of the region has also been influenced by more recent acts of war and terrorism. Bali, which gained independence from the Dutch only in 1949, had become the most significant tourism destination in Indonesia following rapid development of its tourism infrastructure, but the bombings of 2002 and 2005 demonstrated its fragility and the extent to which the island has come to rely upon its tourism industry. The two factors are interconnected, as the increased prosperity of the island and the massive over-development which accompanied it raised Bali's international profile, making it a target for investors and terrorists alike. Bali diversified from its hippy beach image, promoting spa tourism, upmarket boutique hotels and the galleries and craft complexes of centres such as Ubud. The 2002 bombings killed more than 200 people, with the industry gradually recovering only to be affected by further incidents in 2005.

Europe: change and continuity

As we have already seen, many of the first developments in travel technology, including the wheel and the domesticated horse, originated in Asia, as did the earliest farming cultures and, later, the first urban civilizations of the Nile Valley and Mesopotamia. For the earliest farming cultures of Asia, travel was a domestic business involving access to local market centres or (more rarely) international travel by a few merchants or explorers in search of rare natural commodities. The rise of great empires in the Near East necessitated volumes of military and political travel (on foot or by water, only much later using horse-drawn vehicles), but the focus of the ancient world remained firmly in Asia until the rise of the classical civilizations of Greece (and later Rome) from the sixth century BC turned it towards the Mediterranean, where it remained for a thousand years.[1] After the disintegration of the Roman Empire, the early medieval period was marked by disruption in trade and travel both on land and by sea, with the network of Roman roads disintegrating and easy road-based travel on a Roman scale not achieved until the eighteenth century. We have already seen that this was to change with the emergence of new ports and intra-European trade routes in the fifteenth century, with the dominance of Italian cities such as Venice and Genoa not only over trade in the Mediterranean but also, via routes across the Arabian Sea and Indian Ocean, over sea routes linking Europe with Asia. The resumption of the Silk Road following the Mongol Empire restored the greatest highway in the world, but there has not been a unified transport system since the fifth century. The sixteenth century voyages of discovery opened up entire new continents to travellers, just as the transport improvements of the nineteenth century Industrial Revolution drove a movement towards the establishment of colonial empires by European powers. Continuous improvements and innovations in travel technology and infrastructure have permitted the development of the cheap, rapid international travel that we have today. A glance at Map 5.1 shows that the heartlands of travel in western Europe are, as they have always been, France and Spain, but internal travel within Europe has become considerably easier since the formation of the European Union (EU). The origins of European integration date back to the end of the Second World War, which left Europe in ruins and prompted the search for a lasting peace and, in particular, the need to bring about lasting reconciliation between France and Germany. One of the first initiatives was the European Coal and Steel Community (ECSC), established by the Treaty of Paris in 1951. On 9 May 1950, Robert Schuman, the French Foreign Minister, proposed that French and German coal and steel production should be 'pooled'. Belgium, Italy, Luxembourg and the Netherlands joined France and Germany in setting up the ECSC and merging national interests in these industries. In 1957, the six members of the ECSC formed the European Economic Community (EEC) and began the process of developing a common market for goods and services. The Treaties of Rome,

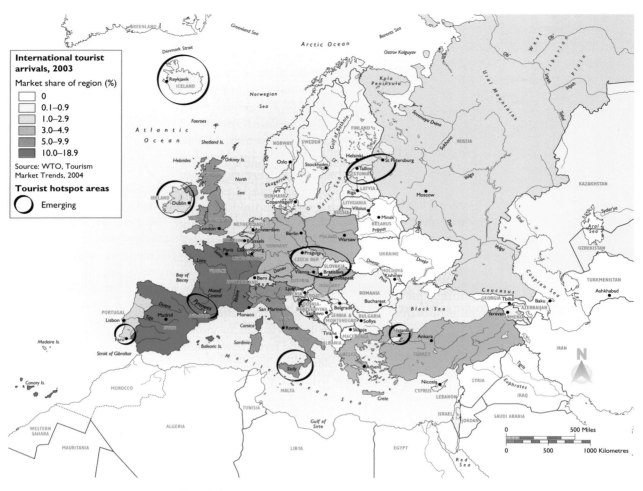

Map 5.1
Europe – international tourist arrivals 2003

signed in March 1957, created the EEC and the European Atomic Energy Community. The Common Agricultural Policy to support farmers was also established. Since 1957 the EEC has seen five stages of enlargement, and now brings together twenty-five countries in what is known as the European Union (EU).[2] Denmark, Ireland and the United Kingdom joined in 1973; Greece in 1981; Portugal and Spain in 1986; Austria, Finland and Sweden in 1995; and Cyprus, the Czech Republic, Estonia, Hungary, Latvia, Lithuania, Malta, Poland, Slovakia and Slovenia on 1 May 2004. The first direct elections to the European Parliament were held in 1979; before that, its members were drawn from national parliaments.

Another notable development took place in 1987 with the coming into force of the Single European Act, which set out the timetable for the creation of the Single Market by 1993. This brought about the world's largest trading area, and the free movement of goods, capital, people and services. The term 'European Union' was introduced by the Maastricht Treaty in November 1993. The Treaty established new areas of European cooperation in foreign and security policy, and in justice and home affairs. The new Treaty also set out a timetable for economic and monetary union and for the introduction of a single currency. Further enlargement of

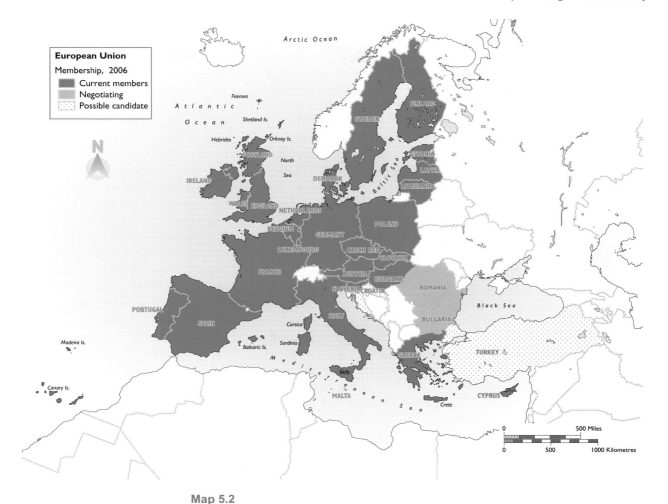

Map 5.2
EU membership 2006

the European Union is on the cards, as more countries from Eastern Europe and the Mediterranean have applied to join (Map 5.2). In order to allow the EU to function effectively with a much larger membership, member states agreed to a new EU Treaty in Nice in December 2000. A special Convention proposed a constitutional Treaty setting out new arrangements to enable an enlarged EU to work. In February 2002 the euro became the sole currency of twelve EU countries. Denmark, Sweden and the UK remained outside the eurozone. The ten new countries will adopt the euro only when they are able to fulfil certain economic criteria – namely, a high degree of price stability, a sound fiscal situation, stable exchange rates and converged long-term interest rates. The European Central Bank contributes to the decision-making on future euro members. The numerous travel implications of the EU are seen, for example, in easy Eurail passes. These offer a wide range of options, including unlimited rail travel in eighteen European countries for periods of up to three months, and can include free transportation on the boats of many shipping lines, such as some international connections between Italy and Greece, Sweden and Finland, and Germany and Finland. Free transportation is also offered on national tracks such as the Rhine cruises and the boats on many of the Swiss lakes. However, although such cross-border initiatives are helpful, it is the loosening of passport and customs controls, combined with the widespread adoption of a single currency, that have really facilitated movement within Europe today.

The Europe of today is a miscellany of more than thirty national cultures on a modest land mass. Its great cities, such as Amsterdam and Prague, are living museums, illustrating the way its past and present coexist. Modern metropoli such as London, Berlin and Milan drive the world's cultural trends (if not its technology). A traveller in Europe can visit the remains of 3000 years of civilization in its archaeological and historical sites (Plates 5.1, 5.2), see its architectural legacies, eat its different foods. Europeans still think of themselves as occupying the cultural and artistic heart of the world, with its science and innovation being driven from Asia and the Americas. And Europe is constantly changing, not just in the number of countries that comprise it (as a result of EU expansion) but also in its ethnic and religious composition. In AD 313 Emperor Constantine converted to Christianity and made it Rome's official religion, and after the Roman Empire had fallen in the West the churches' existing independent hierarchy of Popes often assumed state power. The Roman Catholic Church dominated the political, artistic and cultural life of Europe for nearly 500 years until the Protestant Reformation of the 1520s, inspired by the teachings of Martin Luther, resulted in parts of Germany, Switzerland, Scotland, Hungary and England breaking away from Rome. Today, traditionally Catholic countries like France have a large Muslim minority, thanks to immigration from former African colonies, although Islam (which emerged in Saudi Arabia in the seventh century) has had a permanent presence in Europe and North Africa since the twelfth century – largely due to military conquests, particularly of Spain and the Balkans. Croatia, Bulgaria and Romania are negotiating to join the EU, possibly as early as 2007, and Turkey is also hoping for membership, which would substantially alter the religious balance of Europe.

The shape of Europe today is constantly evolving. In geographical terms, it is possible to divide Europe into four sections; western Europe (dominated in land mass terms by France and Germany), Mediterranean Europe (dominated by Italy, Spain and Greece, together with the Mediterranean islands), central and eastern Europe (Poland, Hungary, and eastern European countries formerly part of the USSR) and northern Europe (the Scandinavian countries together with Russia) (Map 5.1). But this is for convenience only; using this system England might be placed with Sweden, whereas culturally it has more in common with France. Turkey, hoping for EU membership, has been considered in this book as part of Asia for sound historical reasons. On the whole, the contemporary traveller within Europe has the advantage of good communications networks, except on the continent's outer fringes, together with a rail network that was fully developed by 1914. Terrorism is only just becoming significant in Europe, with the 2004 bombing of Madrid trains and terrorist bombings in London in 2005 giving cause for concern, and the future development of the EU will be significantly affected by whether its voters accept the newly developed European constitution in 2006. Sorting out the complexities of travel history in Europe is an immense task, so the reader will find that the approach taken in this chapter involves one specimen issue being examined in depth, to illustrate appropriate developments in the period.

The great literary tradition of the classical world includes the writers of Greece and Rome – the Greek philosophers, including Aristotle, Plato and Socrates, followed by the politicians and writers of Rome (Cicero, Ovid and Virgil). However, it also includes historians such as Herodotus, geographers such as Strabo,[3] and

Julius Caesar himself (100–44 BC), who qualifies as a geographical writer. Caesar, who expanded the Roman Empire throughout Gaul and pioneered a new route through the Alps, wrote the first accurate historical description of Britain, France and much of western Europe. His eight volume work *Conquest of Gaul*[4] gives us an account of the shape and feel of the Graeco-Roman world two millennia ago, together with its travel patterns and natural resources. At its peak the Roman Empire stretched from England to the Sahara and from Spain to Persia. By the fourth century it was in terminal decline, although Roman emperors in Constantinople hung on for another thousand years. The Empire's western half was toppled by Germanic tribes in 476, which marked the start of the Middle Ages in western Europe. In 768 King Charlemagne named his lands the Holy Roman Empire, and its territory passed into the hands of the Austrian Hapsburg's in the thirteenth century; they then became the continent's dominant political power. Elsewhere an alliance of Christian nations repeatedly sent troops to reclaim the Holy Land from Islamic control, with the Crusades between 1096 and 1291[5] setting the stage for centuries of skirmishes with the neighbouring Ottoman Empire as it took control of Asia Minor and parts of the Balkans from 1453 onwards. Europe's Renaissance began in the mid-fifteenth century, and saw a rebirth of Europe's artistic and cultural traditions. Religious changes after the Reformation broke the dominance of the Roman Catholic Church (except in the Mediterranean region), and the French Revolution in 1789 was about political power, with Napoleon Bonaparte (1769–1821) crowning himself Emperor. His efforts to colonize all Europe ended in defeat at Waterloo in 1815, but the civil laws he introduced in France in 1804 would spread the revolutionary ideas of liberty and equality across the globe. After vanquishing Napoleon Britain became a major world player, with the invention of the steam engine, railways and factories. The Industrial Revolution and the need for new markets accelerated the colonization of countries around the world, extending a process that had begun in the voyages of exploration and discovery of the sixteenth century. The end of the Hapsburg Empire was hastened when Serbia was accused of backing the assassination of the heir to the Austro-Hungarian throne in 1914 – an event that precipitated the First World War. Adolf Hitler rose to power in Germany, with the annexation of Austria and parts of Czechoslovakia and the invasion of Poland in 1939 sparking the Second World War. During the final liberation of Europe in 1945, allied troops from Britain, France, the USA and the USSR uncovered the full extent of the genocide that had occurred in Hitler's concentration camps. The allies carved out spheres of influence in Europe and Germany was to avoid any military resurgence. Differences in ideology between the western powers and the Communist USSR resulted in the division of Europe by a notional 'Iron Curtain', behind which was the vast territory of the USSR, which also controlled East Berlin and most of Eastern Europe. The 'Cold War' lasted until 1989, when the Berlin Wall fell, and Germany was unified in 1990. A year later the USSR was dissolved, with Czechoslovakia, Hungary, Poland and Bulgaria becoming multiparty democracies. However, the downfall of the Eastern bloc created issues in Yugoslavia when nationalist leaders seized the chance to stimulate political unrest. All these events, and the subsequent development of the EU, have shaped the political boundaries, influenced communications, impacted on national culture and resulted in the dynamic and complex Europe of the twenty-first century. They have also determined destination attractiveness; controlled patterns of trade, travel and (later) tourism; and contributed a tangible artistic, cultural and archaeological legacy that forms the core of Europe's cultural tourism product.

Although routine leisure travel was interrupted following the end of the western Roman Empire, trading activities did continue (albeit in a more disconnected fashion) throughout individual provinces and around the Mediterranean. However, after the conversion of the Roman Empire to Christianity in AD 312 pilgrimage also became a significant travel motivator in Europe and the circum-Mediterranean world, not only as a result of the fact that bishops and other church officials (and their staff) were allowed to use the Roman military road network (*cursus publicus*) but also as Europeans developed an interest in visiting the Holy Land in the Near East. Such pilgrims had the choice of overland routes or travel by sea, with many choosing a combination of methods, often embarking for the final sea voyage at any of the ports (such as Marseilles) in the south of France.[6] The numbers of travellers making the long journey from Europe to Jerusalem increased after Emperor Constantine cleared the site of Christ's crucifixion in Jerusalem and built a church over it (the modern Church of the Holy Sepulchre), but wealthy European travellers (often female) from the fourth century onwards also wanted to see a wider range of biblical sites. The best known is Egeria from Gaul,[7] who took an overland route to the east and also travelled up the Nile in Egypt as far as Thebes. She seems to have come either from north-western Spain or the Rhone area of Gaul, and travelled to Jerusalem as part of a trip that lasted three years in the early 380s AD. The *Itinerarium Egeriae* (or *Peregrinatio Aetheriae*) is part of her letter to some women back home, covering about four months of the trip, although Valerius, a Spanish monk of the late 600s, has added some portions, in which he described for his fellow monks the contents of those parts of her manuscript that had been lost. Egeria seems to have been an educated woman who wanted to make her readers at home share vicariously in her experiences; the surviving description speaks of her journey from Constantinople to Jerusalem.

An early guidebook for Christian pilgrimages had been drawn up by an anonymous writer in Bordeaux by AD 333, with a subsequent rise in popularity of many biblical attractions, including not only the sites in Jerusalem, Galilee and Judea associated with the life of Jesus, but also attractions as diverse as the desert monasteries of Wadi Natrun in Egypt's Eastern Desert and the 'stylite' Christian hermits who lived on pillars. The most famous of these became very popular tourist attractions, including St Simeon Stylites, who lived near Antioch in AD 423 and gradually increased the height of his six-foot wide living platform over the thirty years of his occupation so that it eventually became a sixty-five foot pillar, with visitors admitted to the base of the pillar only after 3 pm. From the late fourth century such pilgrimage journeys became harder as the strong military control of the western Roman Empire disintegrated under pressure from Germanic tribes, including the Vandals and the Visigoths, and the waters of the Mediterranean became infested with pirates. However, the needs of pilgrims were catered for by a network of hospices for Christian travellers, providing food and shelter in return for a donation, and these hospices were supplemented by the network of abbeys and monasteries which grew up throughout Europe and offered hospitality and accommodation to pilgrims and other travellers. The decline of this network in England after the Dissolution of the Monasteries removed the accommodation infrastructure that had been associated with it, and was not to be replaced until the introduction of inns (and, later, hotels) 300 years later. Such hospices have survived into the present day, when pilgrimage has once again become a popular activity (see Box 5.1).

| Box 5.1: | In the Middle Ages, three major long-distance Christian pilgrimage jour- |
| Compostela | neys dominated for Europeans – to Jerusalem, to Rome and to Santiago |

Box 5.1:
Compostela

In the Middle Ages, three major long-distance Christian pilgrimage journeys dominated for Europeans – to Jerusalem, to Rome and to Santiago de Compostela in north-west Spain, where the remains of St James the Great, the patron saint of Spain, are supposedly buried.[8] The pilgrimage to Santiago started after the discovery of the bones of St James early in the ninth century, heavily promoted by local church authorities keen to make the city a place of pilgrimage, partly for financial reasons and partly because the Spanish church at that time was struggling against the Muslim Moors (p. 96). Moreover, the Holy Sepulchre at Jerusalem had come under Islamic control from 1078, virtually stopping Christian pilgrimage traffic to the Holy Land. Pilgrim numbers were at their height during the twelfth century, then dwindled due to the Reformation and other political factors, but made a significant comeback during the twentieth century and are now steadily increasing. The traditional method of undertaking the pilgrimage is on foot by walking the 'Way of St James' (Camino de Santiago), although today the city of Santiago de Compostela itself can be accessed rather more easily by Ryanair from Stansted airport (p. 106). Pilgrims have been walking the Way since the ninth century, but in 1987 the last 800 kilometres of the ancient route from the Spanish monastery of Roncesvalles in the foothills of the Pyrenees to Santiago itself became the first European Cultural Itinerary. This allowed the Spanish Government access to European funding sources to develop the route, with the result that it is now better maintained than at any time in its history and is way-marked for ease of access. The medieval pilgrim could join the many routes which comprised the Way (just as the Silk Road was, in practice, a composite of many different roads) at different locations through France and Spain. The routes coalesce near Roncesvalles, and the whole Way today still offers pilgrim accommodation in traditional hospices, although these are supplemented by hotels and guest houses. Today nearly 100 000 people walk or ride the Way but, unlike the medieval pilgrims who had to return along the same route, today's travellers generally utilize more modern forms of return transport. However, this volume of traffic is nothing compared to that at the height of the Camino's popularity in the eleventh and twelfth centuries, when half a million pilgrims made the journey each year, from all parts of Europe. Then, as now, pilgrims were awarded a *compostela* (certificate of pilgrimage), which in medieval times entitled them to stay in pilgrim shelters on the return journey. The scallop shell that was the symbol of the journey was carried back from Santiago by returning pilgrims, but today has become the logo of the Way. Modern visitors often buy a shell without completing the pilgrimage, thus unconsciously aligning themselves with the medieval *coquillards* (pseudo-pilgrims), who did the same thing to obtain free accommodation.

Just as the land-based pilgrimage routes to Compostela were becoming established by the ninth century, the sea routes of Europe were receiving increased volumes of traffic as a result of the Viking activity which dominated early medieval Europe from AD 800 to 1200, as the Vikings travelled from their homelands in Scandinavia across the oceans and waterways of four continents. Viking ships penetrated most of western Europe's navigable rivers and inland waterways, travelled to the Black Sea via the rivers of Russia, and voyaged around the Mediterranean as far as North Africa, the Near East and the Caspian Sea. Vikings crossed the Atlantic to found colonies in Iceland, Greenland and Canada, and maybe also made it as far south as along the present-day coast of the United States (p. 113). The Norse sagas tell us that the explorer Leif Ericsson went further, becoming the first European to set foot in North America. Viking warriors raided and looted their way across Europe and parts of Asia, and many more of them lived in communities scattered along the coastlines of Norway, Denmark, Sweden and, later, Iceland and Greenland.[9] Such epic journeys were made possible by unrivalled skill in ship-building. Viking ships came in a number of different shapes and sizes, depending on their function, including broad-beamed cargo ships (*knar*) and fast warships (*drakkar*) with a shallow draught capable of sailing in only one metre of water and holding a payload of thirty tonnes plus a full complement of warrior oarsmen. A Viking ship could be as much as thirty metres long, made of overlapping oak (or pine) boards and capable of travelling at a speed of twelve to fourteen knots with full sails and a good breeze. Vikings used coastal landmarks for navigation during the day, with deep water navigation based on the sun, the stars, knowledge of prevailing winds and currents, and the flight of birds. With neither variety of ship needing a harbour, the Vikings were able to land on beaches or riverbanks anywhere. Modern knowledge of Viking ship-building has been improved by the finds at Roskilde Fjord, twenty miles west of Copenhagen, where, at the end of the tenth century, a number of naval barricades were built in order to protect the important Viking trading centre of Roskilde from attacks. Five Viking ships had been sunk as a barricade, all of which have been excavated and are on display in Roskilde. Roskilde Cathedral was started in 1170 on the site of Denmark's first Christian church, built by the Viking king Harald Bluetooth in AD 980, and made a World Heritage site in 1995.

Just as northern Europe descended into a cultural vacuum during the second half of the first millennium, great changes in southern Europe were happening as a result of the Muslim conquerors, known as the Moors, who brought with them a substantial Islamic intellectual legacy greatly influenced by Greek philosophers such as Ptolemy of Alexandria. The Spanish occupation by the Moors began in AD 711 when a Berber Muslim army, under their leader Tariq ibn-Ziyad, crossed the Strait of Gibraltar from northern Africa and invaded the Iberian Peninsula. Roderick, the last of the Visigoth kings of Spain, was defeated at the Battle of Río Barbate, and by AD 719 the Moors had conquered the entire area from the coast to the Pyrenees. Moorish dominance continued until AD 1085, when the Spanish city of Toledo was re-conquered by Christian crusaders, with the result that much of the accumulated Arab knowledge was translated and made available to the rest of western Europe.[10] The episode is immortalized in film by the heroic portrayal by Charlton Heston of the Spanish knight Rodrigo Díaz ('El Cid'), although actually the battle in which he died in the film probably never happened. Like Spain, Portugal was to be culturally influenced by the Moors, who ruled and occupied Lisbon and the rest of the country until well into the twelfth century. They were finally defeated and driven out by the forces of King Alfonso Henriqués, who was aided by English and Flemish crusaders. African (Moorish) presence can be seen everywhere in Portugal; in the architecture of many of the buildings, which are still of Moorish design, as well as the *fado* songs, which owe much to the influence of the Moorish musicians of centuries ago. Even the design of the traditional Portuguese fishing boats (*rabelos*), with their large red or white sails, which ply the Douro River to fetch wine from the upper valleys, are derived from the transport boats of Lagos in Nigeria. The best known legacy of Spain's Moorish rule, though, is undoubtedly to be seen in the city of Grenada, famous for the Alhambra Palace.

Created originally for military purposes, the Alhambra was an *alcazaba* (fortress), an *alcázar* (palace) and a small *medina* (city), all in one. The fortress had existed since the ninth century, but the Alhambra was built by the Nasrite emirs, starting in 1238 and continuing under successive Moorish kings until the early fifteenth century. The Alhambra became a Christian court in 1492, when the Catholic monarchs (Ferdinand and Isabel) conquered the city of Granada and returned Spain to Christian rule. The Palace later fell into disrepair, but was declared a national monument in 1870 and has since been protected and restored. It was first added to the World Heritage List in 1984, and is now visited by more than two million tourists each year. Pressure on the site has become so great that it has become necessary to limit access by offering timed tickets so that 'only' 7700 tourists a day are allowed.[11]

In fifteenth century Europe, after the fragmentation of the medieval period, the pattern of local domestic travel – motivated by fairs, festivals and events and punctuated by longer trips (only undertaken by a very few) for political, religious or military purposes – was to be significantly changed as a result of the Renaissance. In the fifteenth century, European art and culture again became significant travel motivators, with the Renaissance (which began slowly in the Italian city-states of Florence and Venice following the rediscovery of Graeco-Roman culture, and spread gradually through Europe over the next several centuries) epitomized by the work of great masters such as Leonardo da Vinci and Michelangelo. The invention of the printing press in 1450 contributed to the spread of ideas during the Renaissance and the following period, often known as the 'Enlightenment', from the mid-seventeenth to the mid-eighteenth century – a time also referred to as the 'Age of Reason', since at this time science and human logic predominated over religion in cultural development, particularly as a result of ideas from writers and philosophers such as Voltaire and Rousseau.[12] This stimulated an interest in the beauty of the natural world and ultimately led, via the discoveries of the Age of Exploration, to the nature-based tourism and ecotourism of today.

At quite a different level, this appreciation of the beauties of mountain scenery led not only to the popularity of mountain walking among Edwardians and Victorians but also the emergence of the Alps for the first time in history as a tourism destination in its own right. Switzerland gradually emerged as a popular destination for the appreciation of landscape, and evolved after the late nineteenth century into the centre of an entirely new type of tourism based around skiing, after Lunn developed the first ski tours in the 1880s. The emergence of skiing as a leisure activity can be traced back to the mid-nineteenth century in western Europe (although skis as a means of transport were used much earlier in northern Europe and North America, for practical reasons), starting with a group of social skiers in Norway in 1868, followed by more focused skiing clubs.[13] At that time Europe's Alpine regions were popular venues for summer walking holidays; winter holidays seem to date from 1866 as the result of an initiative by an enterprising hotelier at St Moritz. In 1905 the Olympic Games included skiing in its programme for the first time, which stimulated a steady growth of interest, and by the beginning of the First World War in 1914 a fledgling Swiss ski industry had emerged, catering primarily for British and German skiers at resorts such as Davos, Zermatt and Wengen (Box 5.2). However, these resorts had no lifts specifically for skiers until the 1930s, so much time was spent in walking and climbing back up the slopes. English visitors had traditionally travelled to Switzerland during the summer months while in winter society went to the Mediterranean, with population destinations including the Côte d'Azur and Egypt.

Box 5.2:
Ski resorts

The vogue for winter sports started with the development of fashionable resorts such as St Moritz, with its famous bobsleigh run. This initial diversification of European summer Alpine vacations into the winter sports market was followed by the first purpose-built resorts, starting with Megeve in 1933. Growth was rapid after the end of the Second World War, related to speedy improvements in equipment and clothing (which made the sport safer and more comfortable), easier access to ski destinations as a result of increased numbers of family cars, and generally rising living standards. In the late 1940s and the 1950s a second phase of ski resort development took place in France, including such centres as Courcheval, Meribel and Tignes, which not only offered plenty of skiing but also excellent off-piste and après-ski facilities. The skiing boom continued in the 1960s with the creation in Europe of new fully-integrated ski stations, and in the 1970s with technological changes to metal skis. However, the European ski industry matured in the 1980s, with supply outstripping demand and forcing the closure of some less well-managed destinations. New eastern European destinations (particularly Romania and Bulgaria) came on line after the break-up of the USSR, offering cheaper ski vacations than the traditional Alpine destinations, but in a less attractive atmosphere. Just as new resorts have developed so have new types of skiing, although traditional (downhill) skiing still dominates over cross-country skiing (especially popular in Scandinavia), mono-ski, ski touring and (much later) snowboarding. Contemporary mountain resorts also need to cater for non-skiers, who might require facilities for winter walking, bobsleigh, skating or skidoo (snowmobile). It is estimated that the current ski market includes at least seventy million skiers worldwide, fifty-five million of whom are downhill skiers, with Europe having more than 50 per cent of the global ski market, followed by the USA, Canada and Japan. The European ski market is evolving faster in eastern Europe, with highly affordable resorts in Bulgaria and Romania attracting both groups and first-time skiers. In the future, it seems probable that the mountains of the Polish Tatra, Czech Republic, Slovakia and Slovenia will expand their ski industries if sufficient investment capital is available. However, Europeans are increasingly turning to the American and Canadian resorts, partly because of their more reliable snowfall. A recent UNEP report[14] predicts that a warmer climate could in the future present between 37 and 56 per cent of ski destinations with such low levels of snow that lower-altitude destinations (such as the Swiss resorts of Wildhaus and Unterwasser) will have acute difficulty in attracting tourists. At present, 15 per cent of Swiss ski resorts are deemed to have unreliable levels of snow, and this number could increase to nearly 40 per cent in thirty to fifty years. Unpredictable and unreliable patterns of snowfall are expected to increase in the coming decades, with lower-altitude destinations like those in Germany and Austria likely to be the worst affected. It seems probable that the ski industry will vanish from lower mountain resorts as the snow line rises between 200 and 300 feet in the next 50 years. Under a worst-case scenario, none of Austria's ski resorts will be economically viable by 2070, working on the presumption that temperatures will rise by 3.4°C by this date. Climate change has already caused problems in Scotland, where the ski industry began in the early 1960s at five centres, most notably Aviemore. Rising temperatures have meant less snow at Scottish resorts, and the number of skiers has fallen by more than 70 per cent over the past fifteen years. It seems theoretically possible that Europe's ski industry may have lasted not much more than a century, its beginning rooted in the appreciation of landscape and its end in the changing environmental conditions precipitated by a long chain of events initiated by the Industrial Revolution.

Just as interest in the natural world was stimulated by the writers of the Age of Enlightenment, a wave of interest in the classical world was stimulated again by the writings of Goethe and Byron, so that a young gentleman of the eighteenth century taking a Grand Tour would be expected to appreciate the wonders of the classical world, its environmental context and the artistic legacy of the Renaissance. This whole notion of 'student travel', so significant in the modern world, has a history dating back more than 300 years. The writer Adam Smith noted in 1776 that in England, more and more young people were being sent to travel in foreign countries immediately up on leaving school and without going to university.[15] It was his view that, on the whole, they returned home much improved by their travels. Whether or not this is always true of their descendants today, travelling within a 'gap' year before attending university, still remains to be seen, but student gap-year travel has created a major contemporary travel phenomenon, now diversified by people taking a recreationally-motivated break from careers later in their working lives and utilizing much the same travel structure. Despite the cultural motives of the first Grand Tours, Adam Smith also noted that students often returned home more unprincipled, more dissipated and more incapable of any serious application than when they left, and attributed this to the fact that the students were so young and had not formed useful habits of study. European travel undertaken as an eighteenth century Grand Tour would have been considerably less comfortable (or safe) than its equivalent today, and vastly more expensive. Local tolls and taxes and the unreliable rate of exchange of foreign currency meant that travellers had to take with them enough money to cope with all eventualities, the gold which they carried making them a target for thieves and the unscrupulous. Today's gap-year travellers are generally taking a break between school and university life. Within the UK, although precise numbers are unavailable, it seems probable that at least 100 000 students defer university entry in this way each year. The provision of travel facilities for gap-year students has become an established branch of the travel industry, driven by websites and specific guidebooks.[16] Like their eighteenth century predecessors, today's European gap-year travellers seldom travel for the whole period, with a common pattern involving several months of backpacking followed by a period of volunteering at a developing world project, or learning new skills. However, unlike their predecessors, today's gap travellers are more likely to be female than male, and are also more likely to be paying part of the cost themselves. There is an increasing trend for people to do something constructive with their gap year rather than just travelling, and this can include cultural tours and language lessons abroad (continuing the cultural motivation); however, others might gain diving qualifications or become ski instructors. The travel company STA Travel carried out a survey of 5000 UK students and young people, and found that 65 per cent of them planned to take a gap year, with 41 per cent intending to travel to Australia, 29 per cent to Asia and 28 per cent to the USA. Backpacking round the world remains as popular as ever, with today's young European travellers having Australia as their number-one destination, facilitated by low-cost round-the-world flights which start at less than £700. Many organizations (such as Raleigh International[17]) exist to provide gap-year students with exotic volunteer projects abroad, which can cost between £2000 and £5000.

The development of spas and health resorts throughout Europe in the eighteenth century has already been discussed, together with the slow transition from visiting spas (and later coastal resorts) for health reasons to their success as pleasure resorts when augmented by entertainment and a full range of visitor services. This was facilitated by the development of the stagecoach in the seventeenth century, which travelled on fixed itineraries along fixed routes initially within the UK and then within established networks throughout Europe. It was a method of travel that remained popular for 200 years. The accommodation that developed along stage-coach routes between major cities brought custom and prosperity to the villages, exactly paralleled in the American motel strips following major lines of communication which developed in the USA following the large-scale adoption of the motor car as a preferred means of travel (p. 121). Life in seventeenth and eighteenth century 'watering places' resembled in many ways life on a cruise or in a small winter sports hotel, where the company is of limited numbers and self-contained, rather than life in a modern seaside resort, where the individual is submerged in the crowd.[18] Social life could be exclusive, and it was not until the eighteenth century, when travel and tourism filtered down the social scale, that watering places gradually changed into holiday resorts, by which time the position of traditional watering places was already being challenged by small seaside fishing villages, which attracted the followers of sea bathing. In the UK, Brighton was being visited by holidaymakers in 1730; by 1786 Blackpool had emerged as a popular resort, its emergence related to the increasing volumes of tourism and changing patterns which meant that the resources appropriate to small numbers could no longer cope. British seaside resorts, which had grown as a result of the Industrial Revolution, declined as a result of the development of the package holiday in the 1970s, when economical travel to warmer beaches became a reality. Attempts to reinvent many of the resorts have met with some success; Bournemouth now has a cosmopolitan population related to its numerous language schools and growing reputation as a party town. Blackpool has become a major conference centre, and Brighton is a short-break destination with a reputation for culture and the arts. The traditional long-stay resorts, like St Ives and Newquay in Cornwall, are benefiting from the tendency to take domestic short breaks, and also from the rise of the surfing market, the development of new food-based visitor attractions, and the possibility of flying to Cornwall from London – thus avoiding a long rail or road journey. However, not all seaside resorts have been able to adapt, and their failure has created high unemployment and economic distress in places such as Skegness on the east coast, and problems in Hastings which, having lost its holiday trade in the 1970s, is now using its Victorian seaside hotels as hostels for the homeless and new immigrants.[19]

The age of rail

Travel as exemplified by the Grand Tour of the eighteenth century was largely confined to wealthy males, but from the middle of the nineteenth century things began to change as Thomas Cook founded a company that aimed to make travel universally affordable by organizing a wide range of cheap day trips to seaside towns, special events and places of historical interest. Longer tours appealed to the middle classes, including teachers and doctors, who had both the time and the money to travel further afield, and Cook's Tours also provided a safe and socially acceptable environment for unaccompanied women. The development of modern travel patterns owes much to Thomas Cook, the founder of the package tour, whose early activities were intrinsically linked to transport developments such as the train and steamship, since his firm acted as the link that enabled the passenger to book ocean liners, trains and hotels all in one go.[20] Cook's Tours and Travel Agency started in 1841, and developed rapidly. Ten years later Cook made travel arrangements for visitors to the Great Exhibition in Hyde Park, which was held for six months in Joseph Paxton's Crystal Palace, made of 293 655 panes of glass. The Great Exhibition, which attracted more than six million visitors, was the largest single visitor attraction ever opened in Europe, and had a tremendous effect on the development of subsequent visitor attractions. Cook's overseas tours to Paris started in 1855, and by 1864 he was running tours across the Alps into Italy. The coming of the railways made large-scale organized travel possible for the first time, although Thomas Cook initially had difficulty in persuading steamship and railway companies to accept his business, as they worried about the new excursion culture and wanted to avoid paying commission to travel agents. This situation is still evident today in many travel companies, which encourage direct on-line booking by customers rather than utilizing the services of travel intermediaries. Other milestones included the launch of a hotel coupon scheme in 1868, Cook's Continental Time Tables in 1873 and, even more splendidly, the setting up of an Indian Princes Department in the 1890s to cater for incoming aristocratic Indian families. Cook also made travel arrangements for Indian princes to attend Queen Victoria's Golden Jubilee celebrations in London – a major undertaking, since one prince brought with him 200 servants, 50 family attendants, 20 chefs, 10 elephants, 33 tigers, 1000 packing case and a small howitzer.[21] The firm of Thomas Cook grew and adapted as the demands and sophistication of tourists increased, and evolved from the provision of simple excursions through guided tours to fully independent travel before the firm eventually dissolved in its original form during the Second World War, after 100 years of operation.

The expansion of new seaside resorts was greatly facilitated by the development of the European railway network after the 1840s, which not only created a utilitarian network permitting the circulation of raw materials, manufactured goods and business travellers but also created new opportunities for easier long-distance travel and luxury travel. And it is here that two names predominate: the *Orient Express* and the Trans-Siberian Railway.

The *Orient Express*, whose inaugural journey from Paris to Istanbul took place in 1883, is probably the most famous luxury train of all time. As a concept it appealed to the rich and famous before the introduction of regular air services, in much the same way that Concorde was to do a century later. The history of 'luxury' train travel can be traced back to 1864, when the innovative railway builder, George Mortimer Pullman, created a train in Britain that featured the ultimate in nineteenth century technology and opulence, and was far more advanced than anything that existed in Europe. In the 1870s the first sleeping carriages and parlour cars in Britain came into service, and for the first time meals were served on board a train. Georges Nagelmackers, a young Belgian railway enthusiast, also began building luxury railway carriages and gradually proceeded to do for continental train travel what Pullman had for Britain. In 1883 the first Orient Express train service was inaugurated. The initial route ran from Paris to Giurgi (on the River Danube in Romania), via Strasbourg, Vienna, Budapest and Bucharest. By the turn of the century, the great age of rail travel was in full swing. The Simplon Tunnel – at twelve-and-a-half miles, the world's longest – was built in 1906, cutting the trip from Paris to Venice significantly, and by 1921 the Orient Express service was running an extended Simplon–Orient Express route to Istanbul. The 1920s and 1930s were the heyday of the legendary train, whose opulent service included elaborate meals and fine wines for the wealthy and aristocratic classes of Europe, perfectly evoked in Agatha Christie's most famous work, *Murder on the Orient Express*.[22] However, the heyday of the *Orient Express* stopped with the Second World War, after air travel became faster, cheaper and more convenient. So pervasive has this luxury image been that the train was re-invented in 1982 as the *Venice Simplon–Orient Express*, using restored art deco 1930s-style sleeper carriages, Pullman and restaurant cars. The legend has also been exported, as tourists can enjoy a similar experience on board the *Eastern & Oriental Express* in South-East Asia, the *Great South Pacific Express* in Australia, and the *Road To Mandalay* in Myanmar.

Although the Trans-Siberian Railway has never had the luxury image of the *Orient Express*, it too became legendary, and in many ways has replaced the Silk Road in the popular imagination as a means by which Europe and the Far East are linked. Today, tourism along the route is so significant that it has a *Lonely Planet* guide all of its own.[23] It is the world's longest and most famous train route, crossing the whole continent; it starts in Moscow, passes through European Russia, crosses the Urals (which separate Europe and Asia) and continues into Siberia's taiga and steppes to finish in Vladivostok – the Russian Far East coast on the Pacific Ocean (Map 5.3). The 9000-kilometre route goes through seven time zones, and through cities such as Yekaterinburg (where the last Tsar of Russia was executed), Novosibirsk in Siberia, Irkutsk on Lake Baikal, and Ulan Ude. A loop north of Vladivostok goes through Russia's Far East, including a rarely visited spur round the north of Lake Baikal. The Trans-Siberian Railway was constructed between 1891 and 1916 to protect Russian Pacific Ocean territories, and the main route between St Petersburg and Vladivostok was already complete by 1903; however, it took a further thirteen years for the many temporary constructions to be replaced by permanent bridges, tunnels and stations. Until the completion of the Trans-Siberian Railway there had been no permanent link between the European and Asian parts of Russia. Pressure from Japan, China and England to remove Russia's Asian territories also increased Russia's desire to strengthen its possessions by a rail link, to facilitate development of its Siberian and Pacific shores. Nowadays the Trans-Siberian Railway is still very important for Russia; the route is the shortest way between Europe and Asia, and Russia is making money by transporting goods from China and Japan to Europe. Today's tourists can travel the entire length in six days, but most make stopovers along the way, utilizing one of the three modern routes into which the Railway diversifies after crossing Siberia – one following the route of the original Trans-Siberian Railway, a second crossing Mongolia between Moscow, Ulan Bator and Beijing, and a third linking Russia with China along the eastern border of Mongolia (Map 5.3).

Map 5.3
Trans-Siberian Railway routes

The age of air

By the beginning of the nineteenth century many of the characteristics of modern tourism could be seen, and subsequent developments were destined to add considerably to the volume of traffic within Europe. As we have already seen, the invention of steam was rapidly followed by the first passenger air travel. By 1939 there were regular flights between London and all major European cities, which increased exponentially after 1970 with the development of the jumbo jet. With the advent of the cheap package holiday in the 1970s, the focus of European leisure tourism turned very much towards the Mediterranean coasts and islands, initially to the Costa Brava, driven by UK-based companies.

The earliest package holidays from Britain to Spain were in the Costa Brava out of technical and geographical necessity, due to the limited range of propeller aircraft, although many package holidaymakers travelled by coach. However, the limitations of the Spanish road network and the length of the drive between Spain and the UK soon caused coach travel to be replaced by air travel. During the 1970s, jet aircraft became the standard form of transport to Spanish coastal resorts, with new airports being developed at Alicante and Malaga (in addition to the earlier one near Girona), which opened up sunnier areas with more room for high-density hotel (and later apartment) development. The Costa Blanca and Costa del Sol quickly eclipsed the Costa Brava as the leading package holiday destinations. Hotels and apartments were hurriedly constructed at places such as Benidorm and Torremolinos to cater for the new industry. Today, new building on the Spanish coastal resorts is dominated by villas and apartments, rather than hotels, and these are often bought by northern Europeans (especially the British) as second homes. Despite the diversification of the package holiday market fifteen million Mediterranean packages are still sold from the UK each year, but numbers are declining relative to the rest of the travel market (especially in relation to urban short breaks and independent long-haul adventure travel). Spanish resorts established in the 1970s have since lost market share to Tunisia and Turkey, despite attempts to regenerate tired resorts like Lloret del Mar or Torremolinos, often said to be suffering from 'destination fatigue', by enhancements in hotel quality. The rapid and unplanned speed of development that took place on the Mediterranean coast of Spain after the Second World War led to some well-documented negative impacts. In the closing decade of the twentieth century, however, the Spanish Government took steps to rationalize development by adopting a more sustainable and planned approach.[24] This includes the twin-track formulation of new tourism development plans to improve the quality of the well-established Spanish tourist resorts (*Plan de Excelencia Turística*), and the development of new tourist resorts in municipalities where tourism activity did not previously exist (*Plan de Dinamización Turística*). Today's Spanish 'costas' have expanded into eight distinct areas. The Costa del Sol in central Andalusia is centred on Marbella, which was developed initially as an exclusive resort by wealthy Europeans in the 1950s, and in the 1960s by aristocrats such as Prince Alphonso von Hohenlohe, founder of the Marbella Club. It is still the most popular region for affluent middle-aged northern Europeans buying holiday and resort property, with incoming mega-rich Arabs and Russians concentrating on the expensive harbour and surrounding resort of Puerto Banus. The Costa Brava (north Catalonia) was the original resort area to be developed in the 1970s, followed by the Costa Blanca (in Valencia), which now has the highest concentration of expatriate Britains in the whole of Spain. Its elderly resorts, including Torremolinos and Benidorm, are at the centre of an expanding region of new housing developments. However, the Costa Dorada (south Catalonia) is much more prestigious, with a holiday product focused on some attractive seaside towns and the Ebro River Delta Nature Reserve. The Costa Calida in Murcia has developed fairly recently and is famous for both its golf and its market gardens, and has a more authentically Spanish feel, with the Costa de la Luz (western Andalusia) famous for windsurfing and the Costa Verde (north-west Spain) for its coastal scenery and culture (including Santiago de Compostela, p. 95).

Some 'classic' Mediterranean resorts such as Ibiza have developed a reputation for being party towns, so that the family market is going elsewhere. Indeed, at least one major package tour company has completely abandoned the Costa Brava in Spain, where the package holiday was pioneered, and another is reputedly thinking of doing so. Newer family holiday destinations, such as Croatia, Tunisia and Turkey, are seen to be better value for money, although Spain still remains the major destination for European short-haul 'fly and flop' holidays, with travellers nowadays making increasing use of budget airlines.

Budget airlines

The budget airline idea dates back to 1971, when Southwest Airlines carried its first passengers on no-frills, low-cost services from Dallas, Houston and San Antonio; a mere three years later it carried its millionth passenger.[25] By 2000 Southwest Airlines had become the fifth largest major airline in America, now operating over 2600 flights every day. This phenomenal success was to be copied in Europe by Ryanair (see Box 5.3), which in 1986 introduced a Dublin to London route with an introductory fare of £95, compared with scheduled fares of more than £200. European airline deregulation in 1997 permitted considerable expansion in budget airlines and there are currently twenty-six major carriers, including regional airlines (e.g. Air Scotland) and spin-offs from scheduled airlines (e.g. bmibaby). The concept has revolutionized short-haul European travel patterns, especially the urban short-break market. It is increasingly affecting business travel, stimulating demand for new leisure travel destinations and making more established destinations easier and cheaper to reach. Budget airlines offer low prices and e-tickets with the minimum of frills (such as free food and drink), and utilize smaller airports with lower landing fees. Their simple aim is to carry as many passengers as possible for the cheapest fare. European budget airlines carry twenty-three million passengers per year to more than a hundred destinations within Europe, with fares as low as £10 return (as of spring 2006).

Box 5.3: Ryanair	Map 5.4 shows the routes of Ryanair, which evolved into a no-frills airline copying the Southwest model, pruning non-profitable routes and reorganizing both fleet maintenance costs and the pricing structure so that today Ryanair is Europe's largest scheduled carrier, serving twenty-one European countries. The budget airline market is highly dynamic. Map 5.4 shows that Ryanair routes could be utilized to facilitate a pilgrimage to Knock, a city break to Dublin, a short-haul holiday to Brittany (Dinard), the Loire Valley (Tours) or the Dordogne (Bergerac) in France, or access to southern France via Carcassonne, Perpignan and Montpellier. All these routes have become popular with the owners of second homes in France, and, indeed, the availability of a budget airline destination is increasingly influencing second-home purchase patterns. In 2006 Ryanair will carry over 35 million passengers on 288 low-fare routes across 21 European countries. It utilizes 12 European bases and a fleet of over 100 brand new Boeing 737–800 aircraft. New planes have been ordered to allow Ryanair to double in size to over 70 million passengers by 2012. Its continued expansion has broken Lufthansa's virtual monopoly in Germany and opened up new regions of Scandinavia, facilitated by the establishment of continental European bases in Milan, Stockholm, Rome and Barcelona. A passenger travelling from Stansted in early 2006 has the option of more than 85 routes, with new destinations constantly coming on line. Even domestic travel has been revolutionized, since services are available between London and Blackpool, Newquay and Glasgow. Recent additions to Ryanair include Kaunas in Lithuania, and Lamenzia in Italy.

Budget airlines serve the classic European city-break destinations (Rome, Milan, Vienna and Venice), as well as less familiar airports (such as Bari in eastern Italy, from which a trans-Adriatic ferry is available to Dubrovnik in Croatia). Increasingly, budget airlines are also serving ski destinations and are offering places no-one has heard of, such as Bydgoszcz in Poland. Budget airlines also service cities that are staging major festivals and events (e.g. the Mozart festival in Salzburg), but perhaps the hottest and certainly most fashionable short-break destination to develop as a result of cheaper air access is the Czech city of Prague, a town of importance

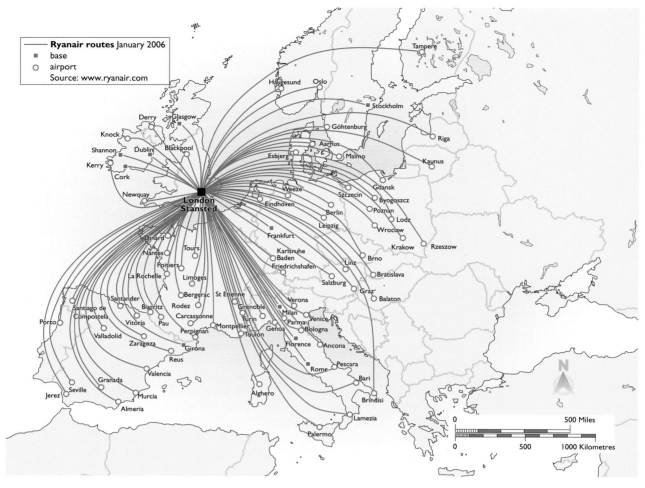

Map 5.4
Ryanair flight routes (late 2005)

since the tenth century and now reached via budget airlines such as bmibaby, Easyjet, Flybe and Jet2. It is marketed as the perfect short-break destination, and has become extremely crowded between Easter and September. Tourists sightsee on foot, visiting Hradcany Castle, Charles Bridge, and Josefov, the old Jewish quarter. Some specialized budget airlines are placing entire countries on the short-break market. Helsinki, for example, and the lakeside town of Tampere are now served by the Flying Finn airline from Stansted, and Iceland Express is flying to Reykjavik, also from Stansted. It seems likely that this remarkable growth will continue, marked by increasing competition between major players (currently bmibaby, Ryanair and Easyjet). Just as European airlines copied Southwestern, so budget airlines are springing up all over the world, and can now exist in New Zealand, South Africa, Brazil and Australia, as well as in Asia.

Contemporary Europe

Today's pattern of travel within Europe bears little resemblance to that which existed in the 1970s, but Map 5.1 confirms that in the Europe of 2006 France and Spain still remain dominant in terms of international tourist arrivals, followed by the UK and Italy. France is one of Europe's most visited countries and, like America, has a huge domestic tourism industry. Once the western boundary of Europe, today France stands firmly at its crossroads. Its Gallo-Roman legacy is found in the south and typified by the amphitheatre at Nîmes and the Pont-du-Gard.[26] The medieval cathedral of Notre Dame in Paris is Europe's most visited sacred site, attracting an estimated twelve million visitors a year; the influence of recent history is also seen in Lille, which was once a grimy industrial centre and, after having been designated European capital of culture in 2004, is now famous for its art museums and attractive old town, although such popularity is also connected to easy access via the services of Eurostar trains. Although the development of the Channel Tunnel has revolutionized access between England and France, twenty-two million people still travel through Calais each year, with between forty-five and fifty-four car ferries from Dover arriving each day. The trading legacy of southern France is shown in the city of Bordeaux, where 'Entrepôts Laine' was built in 1824 as a warehouse to store the rare and exotic products of France's colonies, including coffee, cocoa, peanuts and vanilla; it also holds the Museum of Contemporary Art. A different kind of legacy is seen in Lourdes in the foothills of the Pyrenees, where a vision of the Virgin Mary appeared to Bernadette Soubirous in 1858 in a series of eighteen visions. Bernadette was declared a saint in 1933 by the Vatican, and five million visitors now come to the side annually, of whom over half are pilgrims – including many invalids seeking cures.[27] The port of Marseilles has an African–Middle Eastern feeling, with easy links to Morocco; ferries leave from here for Corsica, Sardinia and Tunisia, just as they have always done.

Significant volumes of international tourists are now received by central and eastern Europe (and Turkey, although the effect of the 2006 outbreak of bird flu will undoubtedly have a significant impact). Map 5.1 indicates some areas that are rapidly expanding as leisure tourism destinations, including the Baltic states, the Czech Republic and Poland, Sicily, Portugal (driven by demand for golf), Ireland and Iceland. In eastern Europe, Bulgaria is now building a tourism business utilizing new Spanish-run hotels. Croatia has now recovered from the Balkans War, with the World Heritage site of Dubrovnic becoming a popular destination, as are its beach resorts. The countries of Bosnia and Herzegovina have always been at a European crossroads, but have little international appeal; however, Bulgaria and Romania are becoming popular for their Black Sea beaches and are hoping for EU membership by 2007. The relaxation of border checks within the boundaries of the EU has significantly assisted intraregional travel, as has the adoption of the euro, which from 1999 has been used in the euro zone (comprising Austria, Belgium, Finland, France, Germany, Ireland, Italy, Luxembourg, the Netherlands, Portugal and Spain). Greece was not included at the time but joined in 2001, with the euro also circulating in the French Overseas Departments of Mayotte and St Pierre et Miquelon, and in Monaco, Andorra, San Marino and the Vatican.

In central Europe Vienna remains a major destination for cultural tourism, and is a major flight hub between western and eastern Europe. The ancient river routes down the Danube are still operated during the summer season. The Czech Republic encapsulates the history of Europe as a whole. The so-called 'velvet revolution', the bloodless overflow of the Communist regime in 1989, has helped Prague to become one of Europe's top tourism capitals, with visitors moving around on the efficient Czech railway network. There are new countries, such as Belarus, that have still to develop as tourism destinations. Belarus was under Nazi occupation during the Second World War, and is known chiefly to the outside world today for being just over the border from the 1986 nuclear disaster at Chernobyl in Ukraine, which left a quarter of the country seriously contaminated. In 1991 Belarus achieved independence from the USSR, but it has yet to make its mark on the tourism map.

In northern Europe, the city of Bruges has become a major short-break destination, and is now mainly pedestrianized. Bruges, Ghent and Ypres boomed in the thirteenth and fourteenth centuries, on the manufacturing and trading of cloth. The medieval town of Bruges reached its peak in the fourteenth century, after which the waterway linking the city to the sea silted up, leaving the city suspended in time.[28] Visitors see it as a perfectly-preserved medieval city, although actually it was actually partly rebuilt in the nineteenth and twentieth centuries in a medieval style. Visitors often travel south to the battlefields of Ypres, where more than 300 000 Allied soldiers were killed during four years of fighting in the First World War, which left the medieval town flattened. The area is dotted with cemeteries and memorials. Battlefield tourism is becoming increasingly popular, with some British companies having been pioneers in the field.[29] Britain itself, receiving under 10 per cent of Europe's tourism arrivals, once ruled 20 per cent of the planet and sparked the Industrial Revolution. It has produced the world's most ensuring cultural icons, and its small size combined with its immense diversity of landscape and culture makes it a major player in tourism terms despite (or because of?) being one of the world's most densely populated nations. Visitors to the UK can see a microcosm of the history of Europe, from Neolithic and Bronze Age structures at Stonehenge and Avebury to the remains of Roman towns and fortifications such as Hadrian's Wall, and a network of spectacular medieval towns and castles, including the castles of Edward I in Wales.[30] Houses and places of the Age of Exploration, the Tudor period in England, can be seen at Hampton Court, and the great northern industrial cities were built upon the Industrial Revolution and still exhibit its heritage. Scandinavian countries have always had low visitor numbers, with few developed attractions, huge land areas, transport difficulties and a low population base, with the exception of major capitals such as Oslo and Stockholm. Few international visitors travel around Denmark, with the exception of its capital Copenhagen, but other attractions include the Viking Ship Museum at Roskilde, which was a thriving trading port throughout the Middle Ages. Estonia is now famous for its beautiful fifteenth century capital, Tallinn, and its old town, with growing volumes of tourism since it joined the EU and became accessible by low-cost flights. Finland, sandwiched between Sweden and Russia, is a beautiful country of lakes and forest riding on a wave of high-tech revolution, but travellers here are usually drawn by its unspoiled natural environment and particularly by Lapland – one of Europe's last great wilderness areas. It is particularly bicycle-friendly, as is Amsterdam, with the UK also developing a network of bike routes facilitated by the transport initiative SUSTRANS.[31]

If it were possible to choose a place that sums up the travel history of Europe, the Bay of Naples might be a good candidate. In Roman times wealthy citizens built villas in the hills around Rome and on the shoreline to Naples and beyond, especially in the area of the Bay of Naples near the Sorrento peninsula. Luxurious homes with terraces and piers thrust far out into the water were clustered together so thickly in the second century BC that the poet Horace, writing at the end of the first century BC, remarked that even the fish were feeling cramped.[32] With the transition from Republic to Empire the popularity of this resort area was maintained; indeed, Emperor Tiberius spent the last ten years of his life at a huge villa in Capri. The most desirable Roman villas around the Bay were located actually on the shoreline, so that aristocrats could fish out of the windows, and the largest might comprise up to five storeys, all with porticos giving extensive sea views. Social life included dinner parties, rides along the shore in litters, and excursions around the Bay in oar-propelled yachts. The similarities between these early seaside resorts and today's Mediterranean coastal developments are therefore immense. In the first two centuries AD less wealthy Romans also began to take breaks from summer heat of Rome in the Bay area, taking rooms in boarding houses at Baiae, Puteoli or Naples, just as happened in the Spanish 'costas' or, indeed, in British coastal resorts such as Brighton. The shoreline around the Bay was rich in natural hot springs, leading inevitably to development into seaside resorts. Indeed, the town of Baiae, ten miles west of Naples, was Rome's first summer resort, and remained a favourite leisure tourism destination for several hundred years. The line of seaside villas eventually joined up the original fishing ports into an almost continuous classical costa, although each town retained its own personality; Baiae was favoured for spa recreation while Naples was thought to appeal more to intellectuals. Even in the dying days of the western Empire, Romulus Augustulus, the last Roman emperor in the west, when exiled from the capital in AD 476, was sent to live at the Bay of Naples. The eruption of Vesuvius that destroyed Pompeii in AD 79 wiped out some estates, but most remained (steadily disintegrating) into the beginning of the early medieval period. Today's visitors come to see the remains of Pompeii and Herculaneum buried during the eruption, which killed 2000 people. Capri is still a popular holiday resort, easily reached as a day trip from Naples and now very commercialized, with boat trips through the famous 'Blue Grotto' and tours of Tiberius' villa. Sorrento epitomizes the southern Italian mass tourist resorts, though the nearby fifty-kilometre long Amalfi coast appeals more to the higher end of the market. Nearby Positano has clear Moorish influences on its architecture, and the three Greek temples at Paestum demonstrate the sea links of the classical world. Ferries from Naples still connect the Aeolian Islands and Capri. Newer influences include the world of film, since the region of Matera was the location for the filming of Mel Gibson's controversial *The Passion of the Christ*[33] and is visited for this reason and also for its *sassi* stone houses, now a World Heritage site, with tourism to the region helped by budget airlines flying into Bari. Although the travel and tourism history of Europe is complex, the threads that developed even in prehistoric times remain clear today, despite millennia of political upheaval and technological innovation.

North America: expansion and revolution

A glance at Map 6.1 emphasizes the huge size of the North American continent; the USA and Canada occupy 14.3 per cent of the world's land area and are home to 5.1 per cent of the world's population. With this immense size comes immense diversity, in both people and landscape. The populations of the USA and Canada are concentrated on the coastlines, with large coastal cities such as Vancouver, Seattle, San Francisco, Los Angeles and San Diego dominating in the west, and Toronto, Boston, New York, Washington DC and Miami dominating in the east. North America has often been described in tourism terms as resembling a ring doughnut, with the great population centres of the coasts driving outgoing international tourism and receiving most inbound visitors, but the centre dominating domestic tourism and, increasingly, attracting international visitors. The USA spends more on, and receives more from, international travel than any other country in the world with a sophisticated travel infrastructure. Each day more than 15 000 planes take off from USA airports, and travel and tourism is responsible for 12 per cent of USA jobs. The situation in Canada is rather different although both countries share an emphasis on domestic tourism; however, in Canada this is directed more to the great outdoors than to managed visitor attractions. There is a huge amount of intraregional travel; nearly 80 per cent of visitors to Canada come from the USA, and more than 50 per cent of visitors to the USA come from Canada.

Travel within the continent is dominated by domestic airlines, although there is a substantial volume of cross-border traffic by road.[1] In addition to the established vacation areas of California, Florida and Hawaii, new tourism hotspots include Alaska, the Pacific north-west, New Mexico and the Rocky Mountains, from Arizona through to the ski resorts of Alberta and the Atlantic provinces of Canada (especially popular with the USA short-break market). Domestic tourism is facilitated by a high rate of recreational vehicle (RV) ownership, the willingness to travel long distances for a vacation (facilitated by the continent's excellent road network), seasonal migration (especially by retired people) to the southern USA from the north and Canada (so-called 'snowbirds'), and a high rate of second home ownership. The cruise market both from and around North America continues to grow, especially in Alaska and Hawaii. However, inbound tourism to North America was severely affected by the terrorist activities of 11 September 2001 and continuing anxieties about domestic security. Recent environmental disasters such as the 2005 hurricane Katrina, which wiped out New Orleans, and increasing numbers of tornados in the Midwest have affected tourism patterns. Domestic tourism continues to grow, helped by a high standard of living and (especially in Canada) an extremely high quality of life. Both inbound and outbound VFR tourism are closely related to the political and social history of the

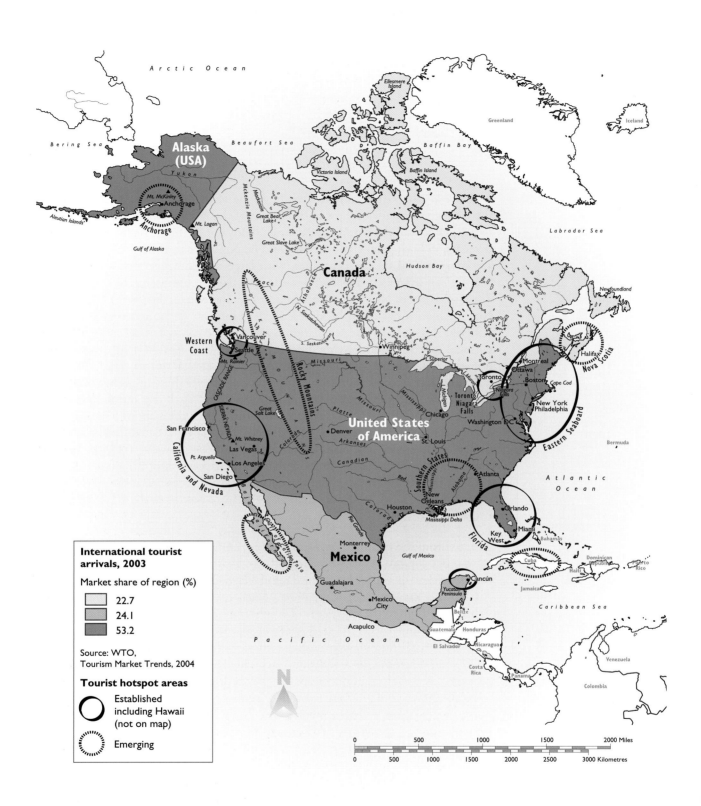

International tourist arrivals, 2003

Market share of region (%)

	22.7
	24.1
	53.2

Source: WTO,
Tourism Market Trends, 2004

Tourist hotspot areas

Established
including Hawaii
(not on map)

Emerging

Map 6.1
North America – international tourist arrivals 2003

continent, including links related to previous waves of immigration from Ireland, Mexico, Puerto Rico and (for African-Americans) west Africa. The historical links between America and Great Britain are demonstrated by the fact that 40 per cent of America's visitors come from the UK, which is also the most popular outgoing destination for residents of the USA and Canada. Travel motivators for incoming visitors include historical images (often fictional) of the 'Wild West', which stimulate visitation to US states such as Texas. Much more recently, the USA invention of the theme park[2] has stimulated both international and domestic tourism to new destinations such as Orlando. The travel history of the continent is bound up in a saga of east–west migration (at least in the post-colonial period), with successive travel innovations ranging from wagon trains to railroad and long-distance routes such as Route 66 aimed at bridging the east–west coast gap. The North American tourism landscape is driven by both its transport connections and its visitor attractions, the latter including remains of the history of the continent, starting with its indigenous people.

Discovery and colonization

It now seems probable that humans first arrived in North America somewhat before the previously accepted date of 20 000–30 000 BC,[3] most probably over a land-bridge that linked Alaska with Siberia, covering what is now the Bering Strait. These first people proliferated and eventually diversified into numerous hunter-gatherer groups roaming widely on foot across the continent, but leaving little evidence of their presence. After the development of settled agricultural communities the archaeological record becomes richer, and some of the early paleo-Indian sites have left the remains of complex settlements – such as those that may be seen today at Chaco Canyon in New Mexico (Plate 6.1) and at Head-Smashed-in-Buffalo Jump near Calgary in Alberta.[4] The European 'discovery' of America came very much later, and European awareness of the vastness of North America in any meaningful sense postdates Columbus's arrival in the Bahamas in 1492. However, it seems likely that travellers from further north in Europe had arrived considerably before him. Legend says that St Brendan (AD 489–570) travelled to a 'Promised Land', possibly America, in the early sixth century. Brendan lived at a time when Irish monks were leaving their land to spread the gospel and travelled to the Hebrides, Shetland and Faroe Islands. A tenth century manuscript, *Navigation Sancti Brendani* (the voyage of St Brendan), talks of a leather boat with supplies for forty days. The explorer Tim Severn recreated this journey across the Atlantic in 1976–1977, sailing in a small ox-hide covered boat, proving that St Brendan could indeed have accomplished this remarkable feat of navigation.[5] Even though Brendan's arrival in North America cannot be absolutely certain, it is generally agreed that the Vikings, travelling in sophisticated sailing/rowing ships, did reach the continent. Leif Ericsson, son of Erik the Red (Eirik Thorvaldsson), is a character in several of the Icelandic sagas which first appeared in manuscript form in the thirteenth and fourteenth centuries. In the *Saga of Erik the Red*, Ericsson, returning home to Greenland from Norway, gets lost and encounters a land rich in salmon, vines and wheat. The writer of the *Saga of the Greenlanders* says that he heard about this country from another lost Viking and went to investigate, finding a glacial 'flatstone land' (perhaps Baffin Bay), a 'land of forests' (perhaps Labrador) and Vinland 'Meadowland'.[6] The precise location of these landings has never been determined, but the reference to the growing of grapes suggests that it may be in the south. Ericsson spent a year there before he and the other Vikings returned. A Viking-Age settlement with evidence of Norse artifacts has been uncovered on the northernmost peninsula of Newfoundland at L'Anse aux Meadaux in Newfoundland (Plate 6.2), with the remains of a small group of stone and turf buildings (the largest sixty feet long) similar in style to those used in Iceland and Greenland and dating to around AD 1080.

Christopher Columbus's 1492 expedition had the backing of Spain, which meant that the news of his discoveries were widely disseminated in Europe, and quickly followed up by a number of other explorers as soon as they were able to obtain financial backing. In 1513 Ponce de Leon sailed round the string of islands now known as the Florida Keys in search of the mythical 'fountain of youth', making landfall on the Atlantic coast of modern-day Florida near the resort of Daytona Beach, where the small Ponce Inlet marks the place. Much of this early exploration was motivated not by science or scholarship but by a search for myths or treasure or (in the case of Cortés and the other *conquistadores*) for both. Nor were the Spanish the only Europeans to explore this New World. In 1524, Giovanni de Verrazano led a French group who explored the coast from Carolinas to Canada (Map 6.2). Later expeditions pushed further into the fur-rich interior of the Midwest and Canada, to be followed eventually by traders and missionaries. Jacques Marquette, a French Jesuit missionary, travelled up the Mississippi and was one of the first Europeans to document the interior of North America.

The mid-Atlantic area was sparsely settled when the first Europeans arrived, with probably fewer than 100 000 indigenous people, mainly Algonquians and Iroquois Native Americans (First Nations). French fur trappers and traders on the St Lawrence River reached the New York region in the mid-sixteenth century, and in 1609 Henry Hudson found and named the Hudson River. The French soon had rivals in the Ohio Company, which was a group of British entrepreneurs formed to develop and control the Ohio valley. Their explorations helped precipitate the French and Indian Wars of 1754–1761, after which Britain gained all the lands west of the Mississippi. In 1497 John Cabot charted the eastern coast of Canada, a voyage that was directly responsible for the claim that England 'owned' North America. There was a strong English presence in the waters around North America all through the sixteenth century – indeed, the activities of Sir Francis Drake against pirates and the Spanish in the Caribbean reached as far as San Francisco. English efforts to colonize the eastern seaboard were marked by failure and starvation for much of the sixteenth century, but victory over the Spanish Armada in 1588 focused their minds on the economic possibilities offered by a New World. A group of businessmen started a colony in Jamestown, Virginia, in 1607, followed by the arrival of the Pilgrim Fathers at Plymouth, Massachusetts, in 1620. Neither met with initial success and both were saved from starvation by local First Nations, who gave them food and showed them how and when to grow local crops. So successful was this relationship that the thankful Pilgrims threw a harvest festival which has come to be known as Thanksgiving, and remains one of the busiest times of the year for domestic travel in contemporary America.

The history of European settlement on the eastern seaboard can be illustrated by looking at specific localities. For example, the first European settlements on the islands now known as the Hamptons were whaling and fishing ports established as early as the 1640s, but by the late nineteenth and early twentieth centuries the ultra-rich had built secluded big estates there[7] and today the resorts have become

Plate 2.1
Contemporary tourist pressure at the pyramids of Giza, outside Cairo

Plate 2.2
Harvesting frankincense gum
in Oman

Plate 2.3
A remnant of the ancient cedars of Lebanon in the Quadisha Valley

Plate 3.1
Cheetahs on parade for tourists
at Okonjima Guest Farm,
Namibia

Plate 4.1
Domestic tourism at the Qutub Minar complex, New Delhi

Plate 4.2
The ancient trading city of Jaisalmer, Thar desert (India)

Plate 4.3
Islamic architecture in central
Bokhara on the Silk Road,
Uzbekistan

Plate 4.4
Hindu temples in central Kathmandu, Nepal

Plate 5.1
The remains of the Forum and start of the Appian Way, Rome

Plate 5.2
Old and new at Westminster
Abbey, London

Plate 6.1
Pueblo remains at Chaco
Canyon, New Mexico

Plate 6.2
Reconstructed Viking longship at L'Anse aux Meadaux, Canada

Plate 6.3
The World Heritage walled city of Quebec, Canada

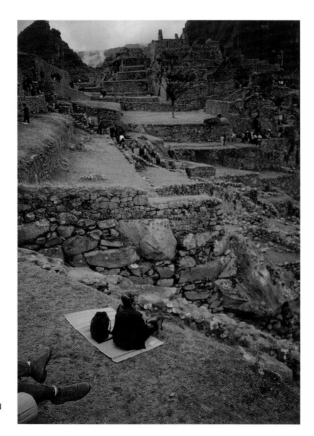

Plate 7.1
Visiting the Inca site of Machu
Picchu, Peru

Plate 8.1
Visitors climbing Uluru (Ayers
Rock), Australia

Plate 8.2
Carved *moai* statues on Rapa
Nui (Easter Island)

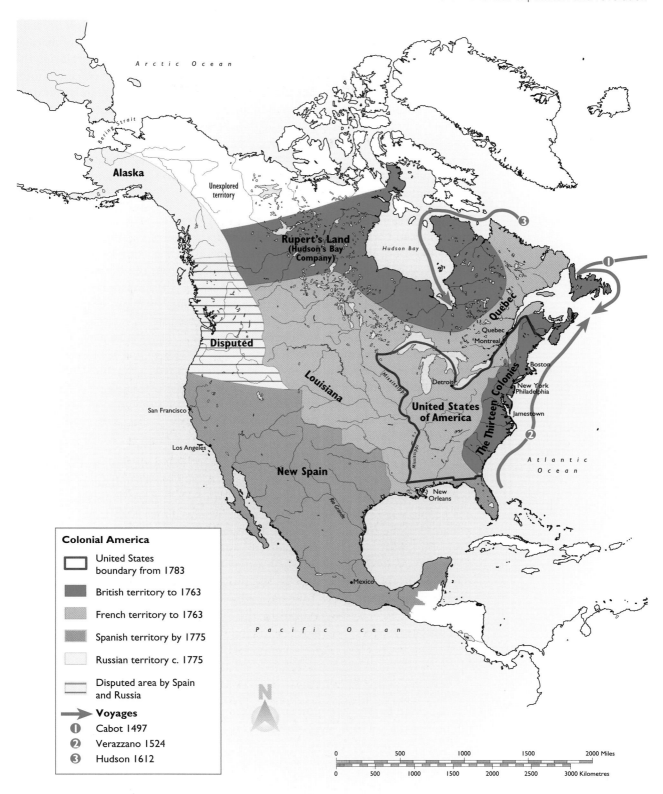

Colonial America

- [ ] United States boundary from 1783
- British territory to 1763
- French territory to 1763
- Spanish territory by 1775
- Russian territory c. 1775
- Disputed area by Spain and Russia
- → **Voyages**
- ① Cabot 1497
- ② Verazzano 1524
- ③ Hudson 1612

Map 6.2
Colonial America

a fashionable get-away for the rich and famous. A similar cycle of prosperity happened in Martha's Vineyard in Massachusetts (named after the daughter of mariner Bartholomew Gosnold, who found wild grapes on the island when exploring the coast in the sixteenth century). Martha's Vineyard was a whaling settlement until the early twentieth century, but after the age of steam it became a popular vacation resort. Gosnold himself was a representative of the second wave of mariners (following Columbus and Cabot) who explored the coast of New England in the early 1600s and opened the coast up for colonization. European settlement began in earnest with the landing of the Pilgrims at Plymouth in 1620, and ship-building thrived along the coasts – especially in Maine, with prosperous settlements based on fishing, whaling and commerce.

In 1642 the British founded the royal colony of Virginia, and a decade later a royal grant enabled Lord Baltimore to establish an independent Catholic colony that he called Maryland. To resolve early territorial disputes between Maryland, Pennsylvania and Delaware a pair of English astronomers mapped out the Mason–Dixon line, which was later to represent the boundary between the industrial north and the slaveholding south. The lifestyle of these early colonists remains of perennial fascination to Americans and visitors alike, as witnessed by the success of sites such as Colonial Williamsburg, an historically accurate restoration of part of the town of Williamsburg which, between 1699 and 1780, was the capital of England's largest richest and most populous colony. Its restoration started in the mid-1920s with a US$70 million contribution from John D. Rockefeller, and today the visitor can see dozens of authentic seventeenth and eighteenth century houses in the 173-acre restored district, although purists object to a certain theme park quality in the costumed interpretation.[8]

The Dutch established a foothold at what is now New York, and in 1624 a group of Dutch settlers bought Manhattan Island from local First Nation people for some beads and trinkets. Eventually the relationship between colonists and indigenous people was to deteriorate into conflict as newcomers stole tribal lands, culminating in the Indian Wars of the 1870s and the events following the battle of Little Big Horn, which were finally to consign the surviving Native American tribes to the reservations which they occupy today.[9] One of the great ironies of the travel history of America must be the successful twentieth century attempts by First Nation communities to attract white North American and international tourists to those very reservations by the development of casinos and their surrounding resorts.[10]

From the sixteenth century onward, European sailors had also been trying to find a passage to the north of the American continent. Martin Frobisher, born in Wakefield, Yorkshire, made the first attempt in 1576 to find the North-West Passage route to Asia from the north Atlantic over the top of the American continent, but this was not successfully accomplished until more than 330 years later by Roald Amundsen. Frobisher did reach Labrador and Baffin Island, where he and members of his expedition were first to encounter the people they called Eskimos ('eaters of raw meat') but who called themselves simply Inuit. Eyewitness accounts from Frobisher's expedition were collected by Richard Hakluyt.[11] During the seventeenth and eighteenth centuries the English set up colonies on the eastern seaboard, removing the Dutch from New Netherlands in 1664 and changing its name to New York. In 1733 Georgia became the last of the thirteen original colonies which then stretched south from New Hampshire (Map 6.2).

Economically the colonies began to grow, based on the wealth of lumber and the development of boat-building, manufacturing and fishing, and eventually on the growth of export crops such as tobacco in the Carolinas and Georgia.

Within the hinterland of North America the greatest revolution in transport during the century was undoubtedly the introduction of the horse, which revolutionized the lives of the Plains Indians. The population of North America grew steadily; by 1700 it is estimated that there were 250 000 colonists living in the area that is today's United States of America. Word of the opportunities spread around Europe, with immigrants arriving from Germany, Scotland and Ireland as well as England swelling the total to 1.6 million by 1760. However, travel between Europe and North America was still mainly for political, military or commercial reasons, although by the mid-1700s it was not unusual for a limited amount of visiting friends and relations to take place, especially with the increased speed and reliability of the transatlantic voyage and with a more developed infrastructure in North America. It was inevitable, with such a rapid growth of population, that more land would be required. By the mid-1700s much of the usable land east of the Appalachian Mountains had been colonized, with settlers pushing further into the Midwest. Here they ran into French colonists, who had been trading with the First Nations, but successfully continued their westward expansion. Subsequent tensions between colonists and the British Government led to the American Revolution in the mid-1770s (with George Washington leading the American forces), the publication of the Declaration of Independence in 1776 and the gaining of full independence in 1781, with Washington as the first President of the United States.[12]

This continued westward expansion resulted in Kentucky becoming, in 1792, the first state west of the Appalachians. In 1803 President Thomas Jefferson offered (successfully) to buy the vital port of New Orleans plus the area that today is Louisiana and Mississippi from the French for $15m, and eventually huge tracts of French-owned land in the north-west were added, doubling the size of the United States. With the Louisiana Purchase of 1803 the US had acquired vast new territory west of the Mississippi, and President Thomas Jefferson decided that it was time for it to be mapped. He appointed Meriwether Lewis and William Clark to lead an expedition through the region via the Missouri and Rocky Mountains to the Pacific. The expedition gathered in St Louis and set out from St Charles, travelling via what are now Kansas City, Omaha, Sioux City, Bismark in North Dakota, and across Montana. Lewis and Clark crossed the continental divide south of Dillon but then turned north to the Idaho–Washington border, finishing at Astoria on the Pacific coast. They left in May 1804 with forty men and finally reached the Pacific in November 1805, setting off for the return trip six months later, having covered 8000 miles, made detailed maps, navigated uncharted rivers and came into close contact with many First Nation people, as well as a nomadic population of French and Scottish trappers. The two-hundredth anniversary of this great journey, marked by numerous events and special exhibitions in 2006, will doubtless encourage many modern travellers to try and retrace their route.[13] Among Lewis and Clark's great discoveries were the Missouri River and the Rocky Mountains; their expedition was undoubtedly the single most significant exploration event in the United States since its initial 'discovery' by Europeans. The findings of Lewis and Clark opened up the eyes of North America, and eventually of the world, to the beauty, richness and variety of the North American continent in a way that had never been possible before. The great prairie lands west of the Mississippi which Lewis and Clark crossed were later to be settled by sequential waves of incoming colonists, pushing the indigenous First Nations westwards and making the cowboy a figure of global mythology. The success of Lewis and Clark and the information which they obtained encouraged other adventurers, with wagon trains going west until the completion of the transcontinental railroad in 1869.

In the 1800s, following America's independence, relationships between Britain and America remained tense and prevented leisure travel, with the USA declaring war in 1812. The conflict was inconclusive, but one of its major outcomes seems to have been a diminution in the volume of transatlantic travel (even for commercial purposes). 'Fortress America' began, to all intent and purposes, in 1814, and in 1823 President James Monroe issued the Monroe Doctrine that said that North and South America were hereafter closed to European colonization. This, of course, became a keystone of US foreign policy. It also (partly) accounts for American reluctance to be drawn into European affairs (America did not enter the First World War until 1917 and the Second World War until extremely late, despite repeated pleas from the Allies, and after the destruction of the USA naval base at Pearl Harbour in Hawaii by the Japanese in 1941).

Pleasure and leisure contact between Europe and America was minimal during the nineteenth century, and even today Americans are famously insular. The later history of travel within North America is dominated by domestic (internal) travel, conditioned by technological developments from the expansion of the railway through to the evolution of today's airline network which connects all America. Following in the direction of the Lewis and Clark expedition was the first step in opening up the wonders of the North American continent and, as such, laid the foundation stone for all later internal exploration and, indeed, for American domestic travel. Even today, the primary direction of American domestic travel is east–west rather than west–east, with the long-settled and urbanized states of the east sending travellers to the hedonic destinations of California and Hawaii. This is clearly a great simplification, yet Americans remain more fascinated by their romantic Midwestern past (frequently distorted in Hollywood movies) than by their British colonial roots. It is the Texan, rather than the Bostonian, who is regarded as the father of the nation, and there is still a lingering tendency to regard Europe as effete and Asia as potentially dangerous. Correspondingly, incoming European visitors are often drawn to the America that they hope to recognize from the movies rather than the edgy, sophisticated and cosmopolitan cities that dominate America today. North American cities grew substantially during the early twentieth century, with some – such as New York, San Francisco, Washington DC, Quebec, Charleston and Los Angeles – becoming more distinctive than others. The bombing of New York's Twin Towers on 11 September 2001 did, however, have an enormous global affect on tourist confidence in the USA as a safe destination. Before the attack the USA received more than fifty-one million international visitors per year, whereas in 2003 these numbers had reduced to forty-one million and it seems probable that the former level will not be regained until 2007.

The making of modern America

Travel within the vastness of the North American hinterland was assisted by various transport developments in the nineteenth century. In 1825, the Erie Canal linked New York City (then the commercial centre of the country) with the raw materials of the Great Lakes. From the 1830s, hundreds of miles of railway lines were built (the railway was, of course, a British invention) linking the remote Midwest to the markets of the east coast.[14] Continental USA took its current shape in the 1830s and 1840s, after the resolution of a conflict with Mexico (which had won independence from Spain and controlled today's Texas and California) resulted in the addition of Texas in 1845 and California in 1850. Pressure from settlers travelling westwards along the Oregon Trail eventually caused the British to relinquish claims to Washington and Oregon in 1846.

The wealthy cotton plantations of the south had become successful using imported slave labour, which was eventually banned in all states north of Maryland in 1804. In 1860 Abraham Lincoln, a member of the antislavery Republican Party, was elected President in a campaign where slavery was the main issue, and in 1861 the southern states formed the Confederate States of America and declared war on the United States by attacking Fort Sumpter in Charleston, South Carolina. The next four years of the Civil War are thought to have cost well over a million lives, and when the Confederation, under General Robert E. Lee, surrendered at Appomattox in April 1865, the social and economic shape of the USA had changed forever.[15] However, African-Americans continued to fight for equal rights up until the 1960s – a fight that is far from won, even today. One legacy of the slave trade is that many of today's African-Americans have become interested in discovering more about their ethnic backgrounds, generating an interesting international tourism link with West Africa and the Caribbean, which has become commemorated in the UNESCO 'Slave Route' project (p. 54). Conversely, the vanished world of the luxurious southern plantations immortalized in films such as *Gone with the Wind* is extremely attractive to incoming international tourists who visit the antebellum houses of Charleston and Savannah and the plantation homes of the Deep South in a rapidly-growing sector of the cultural tourism industry.

The 'Southern' heritage of the Virginias, Carolinas, Georgia, Tennessee and Louisiana is capitalized on by today's tourism industry. More major battles of the Civil War were fought in Virginia than any other state. North and South Carolina are increasingly popular as golf and vacation destinations. The legacy of the French and Spanish colonists of the Americas is seen most clearly in Louisiana, with the Creoles of New Orleans and the Cajuns of southern Louisiana. New Orleans has conventionally been regarded as the cultural capital of the South, although the devastating effect of the 2005 hurricane means that it will be some time before its tourism industry recovers. New Orleans was a famously cosmopolitan site, birthplace of jazz, with its historic French quarter and the clubs and cabarets of Bourbon Street. However, the arrival of Hurricane Katrina also pointed out to the world that the city was still home to an immense black underclass, African-American descendants of the slaves imported to work on the cotton and tobacco plantations of the South. They have left no architectural legacy – unlike the European plantation owners, whose splendid houses dating back to the 1700s are scattered throughout the south, with some famous examples in Savanna (Georgia) and Charleston (South Carolina). Steamboats still ply the Mississippi, as they did over 150 years ago, including the *Delta Queen*. This is the oldest steam-driven paddle-wheeler and, its gleaming Victorian brass now refurbished, it is now designated as a National Historic Landmark.

After the end of the Civil War the two ends of the transcontinental railway network were finally joined up in 1869, so that the West was opened for even more rapid colonization as the more reliable railroad replaced the old incident-prone wagon trains. An open immigration policy meant that in the 1870s tens of millions of immigrants arrived from Europe and Asia (a process which has resulted in considerable volumes of VFR travel today between America, Ireland, Scandinavia and central/eastern Europe), many hoping to claim the promised forty acres of land for their own homestead. Alas, this expansion was achieved at the expense of the remaining First Nation groups in a pattern characterized by the gradual removal of their ancestral lands by allocation to incoming settlers, accompanied by numerous broken agreements and land settlement treaties. By 1870 few Great Plains First Nations had not succumbed to this genocide, their downfall hastened not only by inward migration from settlers but also by the wholesale slaughter of the buffalo on which their economy depended – a slaughter greatly facilitated by the railroads, which imported the hunters and exported the meat and hides.

Railways linked the major cities of the east coast by the 1840s and the population grew rapidly, starting with Irish immigration in the 1840s and 1850s. Work available in the newly-industrialized cities of the Great Lakes brought successive waves of immigration from Ireland (early and mid-nineteenth century), Germany (mid–late nineteenth century), Scandinavia (late nineteenth century), Italy and Russia (turn of the century), southern and eastern Europe (early twentieth century), and many African-American migrants moved north after the Civil War. The 151-foot high Statue of Liberty, constructed by French sculptor Bartholdi, was unveiled in 1886 on a small island in New York harbour as a monument to these immigrants, and is usually combined by today's tourists with a visit to nearby Ellis Island, the country's main immigration station from 1892 to 1954, through which passed more than twelve million immigrants.[16]

In 1925 the Erie Canal between Albany and Buffalo connected New York and the Hudson River with the Great Lakes and the Midwest. The canal system helped to open up the continent's interior and promote the industrial developments of cities. As a result of the opening of the canal New York became the port for the whole country as well as a major centre for trade and finance, and by 1830 its population had grown to 250 000. Further developments such as the Planning Commission of 1811, which gave Manhattan its distinctive street grid, and the Croton Aqueduct of 1842, which brought 72 million gallons of fresh water daily, contributed to the design and function of the city which we know today. Severely limited space in the downtown business district led to the multi-storey office buildings, known as 'skyscrapers' from the late nineteenth century. The tourism historian of the future will also undoubtedly remark that the destruction of perhaps the most famous skyscrapers, the 110-storey Twin Towers of the World Trade Centre in Manhattan's financial district, on 11 September 2001, killing 3000 people, marked yet another watershed in the development of New York and, indeed, of American tourism. From that day onwards America was reminded that it had not been excluded from the world's war against fundamentalist terrorism. The events of 9/11 have left their mark on American tourism, as on every other aspect of American life – effects far more profound than the drop in inbound and outbound travel that took place straight afterwards. In the New York tourism landscape of the future it seems probable that the 9/11 memorial, which will include a museum and a tower with a 1776-foot tower designed by Studio Daniel Libeskind[17] for the Lower Manhattan Development Corporation, will become a major draw.

The travel history of America also has its literary markers. Mark Twain's *Roughing It* was published in 1872 – an account of Twain's seven-year journey going west from St Louis to Virginia and thence to San Francisco and Hawaii in the hopes of making his fortune – and this raised destination awareness at the time. A more recent equivalent might be Jan Morris's *Coast to Coast* (1956/2002), published for the European market. American travel classics include Jack Kerouac's iconic *On the Road*, which was published in 1957 and still going strong at the time of his death in 2005. John Steinbeck travelled with a poodle and a makeshift camper-van, supposedly to 're-acquaint himself with America', and the numerous works of the American humourist Bill Bryson have left a record of contemporary America and probably account for a sudden surge in interest in walking the Appalachian Trail.[18]

The industrialization of America in the latter part of the nineteenth century created an emergent and wealthy middle class, just as it had done in Europe, although one whose propensity for overseas travel took longer to develop. Greater disposable income from factory work resulted in increased urbanization, and America began once again to become a player on the world stage, defeating the fragile remnants of the Spanish colonial empire in 1898 to pick up Puerto Rico and Guam. Further south, the USA assisted Panama to gain freedom from Columbia in return for the right to complete the Panama Canal and run it as a monopoly link between the Atlantic and Pacific Oceans from the time it opened in 1914, revolutionizing sea transport in the southern hemisphere. In 1900 the railroads dominated travel in North America, with passenger service provided on nearly all 258 000 miles of track in the USA and 18 000 miles in Canada. Fast trains connected major cities, although railroad services dwindled with increased popularity of cars and alternative transport. In 1930 the Pullman service in North America extended to 130 000 miles of railroad, but by 1957 had reduced to only 85 068 miles. The travel experience on the railroads remained much the same throughout the early twentieth century, with departures, movements and arrivals tied to fixed routes and fixed schedules and only accommodation standards varying. The USA also utilized river travel by steamship everywhere from the Mississippi and Ohio Rivers to cruises on the Great Lakes or St Lawrence River. A lingering memory of these great river and lake journeys survives in the Inside Passage of the north-west coast linking the Pacific States, Vancouver and Seattle with Alaska. In the nineteenth and twentieth centuries, steamships served as alternatives to rail travel and cruise ships were floating hotels.

Before 1910 most car manufacturers produced only a few hundred cars a year, which sold at prices that approached several thousand dollars. Even after the advent of mass car production the price of a car remained well beyond the means of American workers, whose annual income averaged only $574 in 1910. Moreover, car up-keep could rise as high as $350 in the first six months of driving, so the ownership of cars in North America was clearly related to status and income – as it was in Europe. However, this was soon to change.[19] Compared with the railroad, touring by car offered freedom of action and closer contact with the destinations and people encountered in the course of a journey. The widespread use of cars had implications for the development of the highway-based tourism infrastructure throughout North America with which we are so familiar today, but in its early days motor travel was hindered by poor road surfaces and obstructions such as farm carts and machinery in rural areas. In 1905 a Michigan law required motorists to slow to ten miles per hour when approached by a horse-drawn vehicle. As car ownership increased so did the demand for better roads, although car driving was still a leisure time activity throughout the 1920s and only in the 1940s was the intercity network of hard-surfaced highways completed. It was not until the 1950s that limited-access freeways began, resulting in modifications to the American landscape – including commercial strips with gas stations, restaurants and (later on) the first motels. Within the USA only 8000 cars were registered in 1900, but more than 23 million by 1930. By 1960 the USA had one automobile for every 2.3 persons, and extensive investment in new highways had begun, with motorists getting organized and lobbying for new hard-surfaced roads to replace the gravel and sand roads that criss-crossed rural areas.

In 1914 the first passenger airline was established in North America, utilizing flying boats to take Florida holidaymakers between Tampa and St Petersburg. This was later followed by trips between New York City and Atlantic City, and tourist trips in the winter between Miami and Nassau, and Key West and Havana. The public thought seaplanes were safer than other aircraft, as there was always the possibility of landing on water if the plane ran into trouble. Pilots rarely flew higher than a few hundred feet above the water, reinforcing passengers' sense of security. Coastal beach resorts were ideal for these first experiments in air travel, since seaplanes did not require expensive runways or airport buildings. Tourists in seaside resorts were a ready market for the novelty of flying, and such trips became another resort attraction. In the 1920s passenger services and federal airmail contracts became interrelated (with passenger revenues supplementary to the money earned from mail carrying), but by the 1930s most commercial flights were taken at night – not just to accommodate the mail but also to provide businessmen with fast intercity connections. At this time we can see the emergence of travel giants that would dominate North American commercial travel in the future, such as the merger of American Transworld and United Airlines. In 1930 TWA introduced the first transcontinental air service. Travellers could fly coast-to-coast in thirty-six hours, with ten stops and an overnight rest in Kansas City; in 1932 night flying was added to reduce the time to twenty-four hours, with the government subsidizing emergency landing fields every twenty miles along the route. The principal benefit of air travel was speed, but the flights were not comfortable – many passengers complained of extreme cold and lack of pressurization in the cabin causing discomfort at high altitude. In addition, early aircraft handled turbulence very badly, but specifications improved rapidly and by 1938 planes had cut flying time across the country to fifteen hours eastbound, utilizing the prevailing westerly winds. New airliners were efficient enough to produce profits from passengers alone, and airports improved rapidly, especially during the Second World War, so that by 1945 more than 650 airfields had been developed to handle large modern planes.

The collapse of the stock market in 1929 started the Great Depression, which saw an estimated 50 per cent of the American workforce unemployed and its propensity to travel thus greatly reduced. American isolationist policy became very evident, but after the Second World War pent-up buying power and increased leisure time resulted in a flood of domestic tourists travelling the North American highways. Highway improvements accelerated the commercialization of roadsides, including the omnipresent commercial strips, and standardized roadside services became the norm. After the war, beach resorts reopened and roadside commerce resumed; American workers also enjoyed shorter working weeks and longer vacation periods, and statistics began to appear that described tourism as a growing industry. By 1963 the Bureau of the Census reported that 43 per cent of all American families took a long vacation trip annually, travelling distances averaging 600 miles. Increasing affluence also led to the purchase of second homes – during the 1960s an estimated 1.7 million households in the USA owned vacation cottages, a pattern that continues to be significant in American domestic tourism today.[20]

Another result of the Second World War was the increased destination awareness, on behalf of Americans, of the vacation possibilities of Asia. America had fought a war in the Pacific against Japan between 1941 (after Pearl Harbour) and 1945, producing a generation of Americans familiar with the south Pacific, resulting in a subsequent boom in honeymoon and leisure travel to Hawaii – shortly to become an essential component of America's pleasure periphery.[21] The many American troops stationed in the UK during the Second World War also gained enhanced destination awareness regarding what living in Europe was actually like, giving young Americans who had never previously travelled abroad some idea of what Europe must be like in peacetime, and young Europeans the chance to see these young, wealthy and handsome young men previously encountered only on the cinema screen. European interest in leisure travel to America can really be said to date from this period. Post-war affluence created an American society with exceptionally high levels of domestic comfort. Cheap cars and cheap gas encouraged domestic travel and the creation of a society more mobile than that of Europe, assisted by rapid investment in road-building (the interstate highway system was begun in the 1950s) and zoning policies encouraging the construction of homes and shopping malls on former farmland surrounding cities – an essential contribution to the modern American landscape.

Domestic travel patterns within North America have also been shaped by the development of its extensive network of Protected Areas, as well as by a number of purpose-built visitor attractions – of which the most significant are undoubtedly the Disney theme parks. Map 6.3 shows the distribution of the USA's ten most heavily visited National Parks, which together welcome a high percentage of the estimated 64.5 million visitors to the USA's National Parks each year.[22] The National Park concept is generally credited to the artist George Catlin, but its development mirrors the history of travel within the continent, and its motivations. On a trip to the Dakotas in 1832, Catlin worried about the impact of America's westward expansion on Indian civilization, wildlife, and wilderness. They might be preserved, he wrote, 'by some great protecting policy of government … in a magnificent park … A nation's park, containing man and beast, in all the wild and freshness of their nature's beauty!'[23] Catlin's vision was partly realized in 1864, when Congress donated Yosemite Valley to California for preservation as a State Park. Eight years later, in 1872, Congress reserved the spectacular Yellowstone country in the Wyoming and Montana territories 'as a public park or pleasuring-ground for the benefit and enjoyment of the people'. Yellowstone remained in the custody of the US Department of the Interior as a National Park – the first in the world to be so designated. Congress followed the Yellowstone precedent with other National Parks in the 1890s and early 1900s, including Sequoia, Yosemite, Mount Rainier, Crater Lake and Glacier. The idealistic impulse to preserve nature was often joined by a more pragmatic desire to promote tourism: western railroads lobbied for many of the early parks and built grand rustic hotels in them to boost their passenger business. The late nineteenth century also saw growing interest in preserving prehistoric Indian ruins and artifacts on the public lands. Congress first moved to protect such a feature, Arizona's Casa Grande Ruin, in 1889. In 1906 it created Mesa Verde National Park, which contains dramatic cliff dwellings, in southwestern Colorado, and passed the Antiquities Act authorizing presidents to set aside 'historic and prehistoric structures, and other objects of historic or scientific interest'

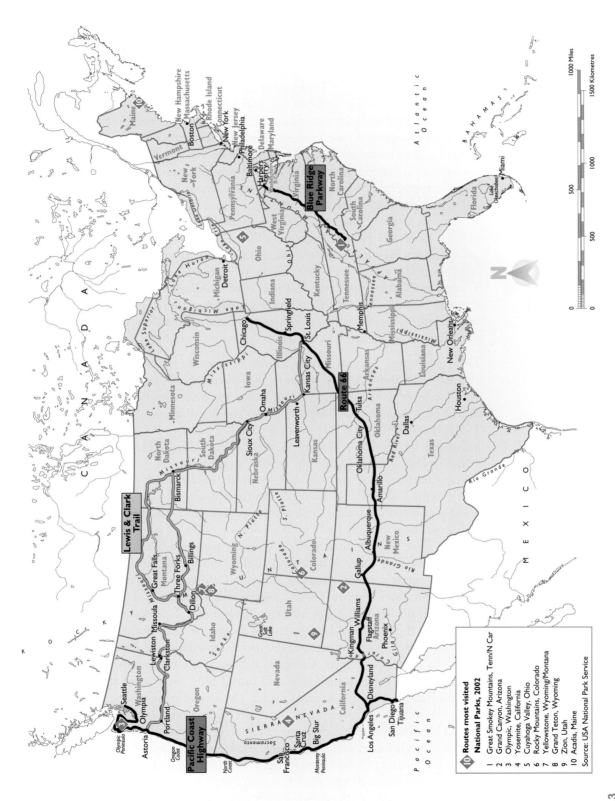

Map 6.3

Routes and Parks 2002

in federal custody as national monuments. Theodore Roosevelt used the act to proclaim eighteen national monuments before he left the presidency. They included not only cultural features like El Morro, New Mexico, site of prehistoric petroglyphs and historic inscriptions, but also natural features like Arizona's Petrified Forest and the Grand Canyon. Congress later converted many of these natural monuments to National Parks.

In 1916, President Woodrow Wilson approved legislation creating the National Park Service within the Interior Department. There was a conviction that more visitors must be attracted and accommodated if the Parks were to flourish. Cars, not permitted in Yellowstone until 1915, would be allowed throughout the system, with accommodation provided in hotel concessions, and museums and other educational activities encouraged for better interpretation. The post-war era brought new pressures on the Parks as the nation's energies were redirected to domestic pursuits, and in December 1951 a ten-year, billion-dollar programme was started to upgrade facilities, staffing and resource management in the Parks. As of 1999 the National Park system comprised 379 areas throughout nearly every state and US possession.

Tourism in North America today

If we look at the distribution of the USA's most popular Parks, we find a close relationship with its most popular tourist destination regions (Map 6.3). Great Smokey Mountains Park in Tennessee/North Carolina welcomes nearly ten million visitors a year, and is close to the major population concentrations of the American east coast. The National Parks of Yosemite, Yellowstone, Rocky Mountains and Grand Teton are all located within the Rocky Mountains central spine of the country, and are all included in the ten most visited National Parks today. Yellowstone National Park, home to half the world's geysers and an enormous variety of wildlife, attracts 300 000 visitors daily, with such extreme popularity having become a threat to the wildlife which it was created to preserve.[24] Grand Canyon in Arizona is near Las Vegas and the popular destinations of the California coast. Las Vegas itself, a onetime remote railroad town, is now one of the country's top destinations. It was once a regular stop for the wagons travelling the Spanish Trail, and home to a Mormon mission, but in 1902 most of the land was sold to a railroad company. The resort on the famous Las Vegas Strip opened in 1941, and Las Vegas developed rapidly in the post-war years – a development accelerated by casino building in the 1960s and a growth spurt in the mid-1980s based on new themed mega resort hotels.[25]

Map 6.1 shows the major tourist regions and up-and-coming areas, although the marked circles are somewhat arbitrary and in practice cover enormous land areas. As leisure tourism and domestic travel developed in the USA, the American West became highly attractive to tourists. This huge land area includes not only the Great Plains but also the foothills of the Rockies, the Sierra Nevada Cascade Mountains, as well as their Pacific slopes. The region epitomized the American frontier experience and was, at the time, an accessible area of outstanding scenic beauty. The south, from Virginia to Louisiana, remained economically depressed and suffered from the effects of the Civil War and reconstruction until after the Second World War, with an economic boom in Texas and Oklahoma as the result of the discovery of oil. After the Second World War New England became a popular tourist destination in the north-east, with its landscape retaining a sense of the past, critical in developing a regional character. In New England tourism as an industry replaced farming, with greatly increased prosperity but associated changes in landscape quality in states such as Maine as a result of seaside development. This relatively intensive development contrasted strongly with a relative absence of tourists visiting the Midwest; the wide open spaces of the prairies were not seen as attractive to visitors, and offered little landscape variety but a high degree of homogeneity in their small towns. The south attracted visitors because it was perceived to have retained a distinctive (and curiously timeless) identity, and even today many visitors feel that the culture and character of the states south of the Mason–Dixon line between Pennsylvania and Maryland are intrinsically different from those of the north. Travellers to the south expected to see plantations of cotton, tobacco, rice and sugar, and to be able to visit the great antebellum houses. Currently fashionable southern destinations, such as Charleston, have invested in their historic properties and created a very successful southern heritage tourism industry as a result. In the post-war period Florida became more attractive to visitors than any other part of the American south, and this is still the case today. Here the land was flat, and its palm trees were seen by tourists from the north as being extremely exotic. Some towns in Florida experienced a real-estate boom after the war and subsequently reinvented themselves in response to changing demand patterns. The 1920s was a time of real-estate boom in Florida. Orlando, for example, was successively a railroad town, a theme park centre and a resource centre for the development of America's space exploration at nearby Cape Canaveral, and today attracts substantial volumes of conference and meetings tourism attracted by its reputation as the theme park capital of America. Orlando is also popular as a centre for golf, with sports becoming a significant travel motivator in the twentieth century. Many of today's domestic and international tourists in America are seeking rather more active vacation experiences than their predecessors might have done two or three generations ago, accounting for the development of entirely new tourist resort areas, such as the ski resorts of the Rockies, and of tourism to far-flung states such as Alaska where wildlife-watching is the main attraction. And yet there is continuity as well, with many Americans seeing the 'Wild West' as a region which epitomizes the things that their country should be – a place of tremendous natural beauty and perceived freedom. Indeed, during the Second World War the West was heavily promoted to domestic travellers as a realistic alternative to travelling in Europe, with the result that Americans began to discover the wonders of regions such as New Mexico and Arizona, previously regarded as peripheral. The Hispanic influences in New Mexico attracted artists and writers, much as the French influence of New Orleans did, with the result that towns such as Santa Fe and Taos became significant artistic and cultural centres.[26]

However, the huge size of the USA makes it difficult to generalize about its tourism development; therefore, in the remainder of this chapter, a few regions have been considered in more detail by way of illustration. Map 6.1 indicates some of the established and some up-and-coming destination regions within contemporary America. Three areas are particularly significant (the eastern seaboard, California/Nevada and Florida), both for domestic and incoming international travel, but within these areas there is a multiplicity of individual destinations and resorts.

The eastern seaboard includes not only the great cities of New York, Philadelphia and Washington DC, but also the area covered by the initial colonies and the popular coastal region of Maine, etc. This region includes the USA's major cities and is also a major tourism-generating area, with shorter flight times from Europe than from elsewhere in the USA. Its urban tourism product is dominated by New York, one of the most exciting cosmopolitan cities in the world, with over 150 museums, 400 art galleries and nearly 20 000 restaurants, plus unlimited shopping, music and theatre. Secondary tourist cities include Philadelphia, one of America's oldest towns, with its traditional attractions including the historic waterfront district, Liberty Bell and Independence Hall now supplemented by the new National Constitution Centre visitor experience based on the signing of the Constitution in 1787. Washington DC is the most significant seat of power in the world, with visitors attracted to the fourteen museums that comprise the Smithsonian Institute, the White House and the Washington Monument. Visitors to Washington DC or Philadelphia come for the culture, and they go to the coast of the eastern seaboard, especially around New England, for the same reason. New England is the hub of North America's colonial heritage attractions, especially within the states of Massachusetts, Maine, New Hampshire Vermont, Connecticut and Rhode Island, with their attractive landscapes of little fishing villages and forest. Cape Cod (Map 6.1) swings out into the Atlantic like a giant arm, and offers excellent beaches as well as access to the exclusive holiday islands of Martha's Vineyard and Nantucket, first colonized in the seventeenth century. Maine, the largest state in the region, has 90 per cent forest cover and 3500 miles of rugged coastline punctuated by white clapboard houses. Nearby Vermont offers some of the best skiing in the country, and Rhode Island claims to be America's first resort. Boston is becoming attractive to Europeans seeking a different urban short-break experience; it is an important financial and educational centre with over sixty universities and colleges, and provides the chance to visit the location of the Boston Tea Party and the John F. Kennedy Library and Museum. Rather more prosaically, many visitors are also drawn to the Bull and Finch bar, which was the inspiration for the TV series *Cheers*!

Florida, the second major destination region, offers a very different kind of product, and for the visitor has become essentially a vast playground, with its perfect climate, spectacular hotels and wide range of attractions. For international visitors the theme parks of Orlando (Walt Disney World, Universal Studies, Sea World, etc.) are a major draw, as are the coastal resorts of Naples, Longboat Key, Marco and Captiva Island on the Gulf of Mexico coast, with large resident populations of Americans who have migrated there from less welcoming climates and high rates of second-home ownership. Some resorts (such as Daytona Beach on the Atlantic coast) appeal primarily to domestic tourists. Others (Miami's South Beach) interest a more cosmopolitan clientele, and the ethnic composition of Miami is now dominated by Hispanic people, especially Cuban-Americans, and immigrants from the Caribbean. Miami acts as a gateway for the Everglades, offering boating and ecotourism, and for the Florida Keys – a string of islands stretching 140 miles southwards into the Gulf of Mexico. The Keys have built a tourism product around diving and fishing on the USA's only offshore coral reef. A fourth resort area is to be found on the so-called Gold Coast around Ft Lauderdale, built around the waterways and including the exclusive resorts of Palm Beach and Boca Raton. The Keys provide another excellent example of the historical development of American tourism. Today's visitor can drive from Key Largo to Key West over 126 miles of the Overseas Highway linking the individual islands, but only became possible after its completion in 1938. Yet Key West, America's southernmost city, is famous for being the home of Ernest Hemingway and (more recently) for its museum, which displays treasures from the Spanish galleon *Atocha*, emphasizing the town's key position at the fringes of the Caribbean. This favourable location and its tropical climate have made it a favourite artistic and recreational destination since the Great Depression. In the 1970s it was often described as the gay capital of North America (a designation contested by San Francisco), but the laid-back tropical atmosphere has now resulted in the city becoming America's largest cruise ship point of call, with the shops of Old Town and Duval Street swamped by thousands of cruise ship passengers. Key Largo became famous after the eponymous 1948 film starring Lauren Bacall and Humphrey Bogart.

Although *the western states*, such as Texas, New Mexico, Colorado, Utah, Wyoming and Arizona (Map 6.3), attract very significant numbers of tourists, the sheer size of the area means that tourist densities tend to be less than in the urban locations of the eastern seaboard or the great coastal resorts of Florida. Texas is the second largest state in the USA, with huge landscapes, the Great Plains and the Rio Grande – famous from a thousand cowboy movies. Dallas was founded in 1839 and became a major railroad junction in the 1870s, although its economy only took off when the East Texas oil field was found in 1930. Its destination image took a dive after the assassination of President Kennedy in 1963, but was somewhat reclaimed in the subsequent decade through the TV series *Dallas*, featuring the fictional oil tycoon JR Ewing. New Mexico has a highly distinctive portfolio of tourism products blending First Nation, Hispanic and European traditions, which include the pioneer legacy of the Santa Fe Trail, the palaeo-Indian site of Chaco Canyon and the artist city of Santa Fe.

Tourism to the diverse environments and landscapes of *the southern Rockies* in Colorado, Nevada, Utah, Wyoming and Arizona is developing fast. Colorado, with 300 days of sunshine per year, offers spectacular ski resorts such as Aspen, Beaver Creek and the 4000 square mile wilderness of Rocky Mountain National Park, which stretches south as far as the Great Sand Dunes in southern Colorado (Map 6.1). Wyoming is home to the now heavily congested Yellowstone National Park and has also preserved many of the historic sites, such as the military outpost at Fort Laramie associated with the Oregon Trail – a natural route through the prairies which carried significant numbers of emigrants in covered wagons as early as 1841. But the playground of the western USA is undoubtedly the desert city of Las Vegas, which (together with southern California) comprises the third major USA destination area, including everything from the watersports of Lake Tahoe to the Getty Museum and Hollywood near Los Angeles, and the vastness of Death Valley. Like Florida, the tourist regions of California are distinct. The northern coastline from the Oregon border via Monterey to San Francisco is visited for the historic Cannery Row and Fisherman's Wharf in Monterey, and the sea otters who live in the kelp forests outside Monterey Bay Aquarium, with the surfing and coastal scenery of Big Sur attracting quite a different kind of tourist. The immigration history of California's west coast is reflected in the ethnic diversity of San Francisco, with the ex-prison island of Alcatraz reflecting quite a different kind of history. The significance of National Parks as drivers of American domestic tourist is seen inland with the popularity of the Sierra Nevada Mountains and Yosemite National Park, but California's current image of laid-back casual sophistication may best be seen in the Napa Valley wineries and expensive resorts such as Palm Springs, on the desert route to Las Vegas. The many attractions within Los Angeles include Hollywood, from the golden age of cinema, and the J. Paul Getty Museum at Malibu, the best resourced museum in the world. California is synonymous with beaches for many tourists, from the exclusive beach resorts of

Malibu (a favoured place for movie-star watching) southwards to the spectacular empty beaches of the Baja peninsula stretching south from San Diego to the Pacific Ocean and Sea of Cortez. The starkly beautiful coastline of Baja now attracts tourists interested in big game fishing, sailing, diving and whale-watching, while the southernmost Los Cabos region at its very tip was once sought after by pirates for its safe harbours but now shelters the Cabo san Lucas underwater nature reserve.[27]

The upper west coast of North America is an increasingly popular tourism destination, with tourism driven by the 'cool' cities of Seattle (home to Microsoft) and Vancouver, the other side of the Canadian border. The natural history of the region is a major tourism driver, especially for landscape-based tourism to the coastal regions and Cascade Mountains of British Columbia, Oregon and Washington State, with a major wildlife sanctuary in Puget Sound and skiing in the Cascades. The 'Inside Passage' through the coastal waters of the north-west coast involves a cruise down the fjords and glaciers of Alaska and British Columbia – generally taken for the scenery but also involving a lot of sites associated with coastal First Nations people, especially on the Queen Charlotte Islands off British Columbia, now a World Heritage site.[28] Alaska itself is an up-and-coming destination, with traditional products such as the opportunity to see the Iditarod dogsled race which finishes at Anchorage being supplemented by increased interest in the wildlife of Alaska. British Colombia is also home to some famous ski resorts, notably Whistler near Vancouver, as are the Canadian Rockies near Calgary (home of the 1988 Winter Olympics). Calgary also promotes its mid-western heritage by staging the world's largest rodeo, and is the jumping-off point for the far older heritage attractions of the fossil remains found in Dinosaur Provincial Park. However, with the exception of the Calgary region of Alberta, Canada's prairie provinces are insignificant in attracting international visitors, being perceived as flat, uninteresting grainlands. The foothills of the Rockies at their interface with the prairies do host a major attraction, Head-Smashed-In-Buffalo-Jump (p. 113), based on the history of the Plains Indians, but apart from that few incoming European tourists could name a single attraction in Alberta, Saskatchewan or Manitoba.

Within Canada it is the sophisticated coastal cities that attract the majority of tourism, with Vancouver in the west balanced by Ottawa and Toronto in the east. Here the wonders of Niagara Falls still attract a substantial honeymoon market (and have done so for the last century), but visitors are now coming to see French Canada, in particular the city of Quebec, the only walled city in North America (Plate 6.3). Quebec was claimed by France barely forty years after Columbus discovered America and is the bastion of French culture in North America, with the cultural city of Montreal (capital of Quebec province) also popular. Canada is also seeing tourism growth to its eastern seaboard, with historic sites in Nova Scotia and Newfoundland (Map 6.1).

Despite this pattern of tourism driven by particular nodes, whether the node is a walled city, a National Park or a contemporary visitor attraction, North America is also a place of tourism routes (Map 6.3). The huge scale of the continent and vast travelling distances have encouraged the development of routes that either commemorate major historical events or link features of historical interest. These vary from the relatively short, such as Skyline Drive, which runs through Shenandoah National Park, to the better-known Blue Ridge Parkway, which stretches for over 200 miles along the Appalachians. In the east the Blue Ridge Parkway links Civil

War sites from Harpers Ferry in West Virginia and Shenandoah National Park in Virginia to Appomattox, where General Lee surrendered and ended the Civil War, through to the Great Smoky Mountains National Park straddling the Kentucky/ Tennessee border. This is the USA's most visited National Park, largely due to its relative proximity to the huge population centres of New York and Washington DC further north on the eastern seaboard. Walkers can travel the 500-mile Appalachian Trail all the way from Maine to Georgia. The enormous size of the USA and the high propensity of its citizens to make domestic trips have ensured that the shape of its domestic travel industry is determined not only by airline routes and resort destination areas and natural resources such as the National Park system, but also by major highways. And those major highways often have some historical significance. Interstate 95, along the eastern seaboard, for example, connects Boston and its revolutionary history with New York, Philadelphia, Baltimore and Washington DC, and goes southwards to Richmond Virginia, which is the gateway to the antebellum south epitomized by the great plantations of Savannah. On the western seaboard, the Pacific Coast highway links Seattle in the Pacific north-west with San Diego, just over the border from Tijuana in Mexico, going through Los Angeles, San Francisco, the surfing beaches of Big Sur and the coast of Oregon (Map 6.3). Route 66, once the main street of America, has only portions of the original road remaining today (the rest has been paralleled or bypassed), but the road links Chicago and St Louis and goes through Missouri and the heartlands of Oklahoma on its way to California (Map 6.3). Route 66 goes through Albuquerque in New Mexico, with its Native American heritage, via Gallup and Flagstaff in Arizona and terminates in Los Angeles. Popular interstates also include I90, which begins in Boston and goes via Niagara Falls, skirting Lake Eyrie and crossing the Dakotas via the Black Hills, Badlands National Park and Yellowstone National Park, and ending in Mt Rainier National Park in Oregon and Seattle. Highway 61 runs north to south along one of America's great spines, and connects some of its musical history in blues, jazz and rock-and-roll music from Minneapolis in the north following the course of the Mississippi River to St Louis and Memphis near the home of Elvis Presley at Gracelands. South of Baton Rouge it passes near the nineteenth century Mississippi River plantations on its way to New Orleans, the birthplace of jazz.

Today, the average American enjoys one of the highest standards of living in the world but retains a distrust of overseas travel and a patriotism manifested in high levels of domestic travel. Distrust has been escalating since the terrorist attack of 9/11, which exposed the average American to the realities of international terrorism for the first time. Although this event interrupted domestic, outbound and inbound tourism, North America has recovered well and is currently experiencing rapid growth in incoming tourism. This is not unconnected to enhanced security, investment in new resorts and attractions (especially in theme parks), the continuing promotion of American National Parks, and the attractive image of American film, music, sport and pop culture. The rest of the world's distrust of American foreign policies is not reflected in their propensity to take holidays in America, but one could argue that the attacks of 9/11 merely reinforced the isolationism that stems from events that took place, and formed a national identity, some 200 years earlier.

CHAPTER 7

South America and the Caribbean: Aztecs to Antarctica

South America has a greater latitudinal range than any other region in this book, although it occupies only 15 per cent of the world's land surface. For tourism purposes this produces an amazing set of environmental differences, from the mountains of the Andes right southwards to the edge of Antarctica. Tourism to Antarctica is considered in this chapter because, although not technically part of South America, tourists visiting seasonally accessible parts of the Antarctic continent usually leave from South American ports in Chile and Argentina. Many South American destinations are relatively late to emerge on the global tourism stage, and the potential of the continent has not yet been fully realized. The Caribbean, however, is firmly established as a holiday destination, with heavy reliance on the USA market and on the developing cruise industry. Central America has seen rapid growth over the last decade, with Mexico and Guatamala becoming firmly established, along with ecotourism in Costa Rica and the rise of Cuba as a new hot destination. All three areas (Map 7.1) share main elements of travel history; initial colonization by Amerindian people from the north, 'discovery' by Columbus and his successors, and a colonial period with South America mainly under Spanish and Portuguese dominance. These were followed by a post-colonial period driving towards independence, marked in South America by struggles to replace military dictatorships with democracy, and protectionism with free trade. A similar pattern can be seen in the Caribbean, although colonial interests were more varied and the picture is complicated by the importation of slaves from West Africa, mainly imported to work in the sugar-cane fields. Before the arrival of Columbus, both Central and South America had seen the rise of major pre-Columbian civilizations, some of which came to occupy enormous territories. Of these the most significant were the Aztecs and the Incas, whose vast empires were dismantled in the fifteenth century by small numbers of incoming Spanish *conquistadores*. The remains of their civilizations are central to the tourism industries of Mexico (Aztecs) and Peru (Incas). The Aztec Empire in Mexico probably included between ten and twelve million people at the time of the Spanish conquest, with the Inca Empire, centred on Peru, having a population of about half that. Although there were some other major population centres it seems probable that, at the time the map of South America was to be shaped by the arrival of the *conquistadores* in the sixteenth century, only about a million people lived in the rest of the continent, divided into thousands of small tribal societies, most of them nomadic and only a few with settled agriculture. At that time travel outside the Inca Empire was local, domestic and on foot. The Spanish conquest of Central and South America included the introduction of the horse, which revolutionized travel in the continent and led to rapid Spanish expansion, the discovery of new mining areas and the foundation of

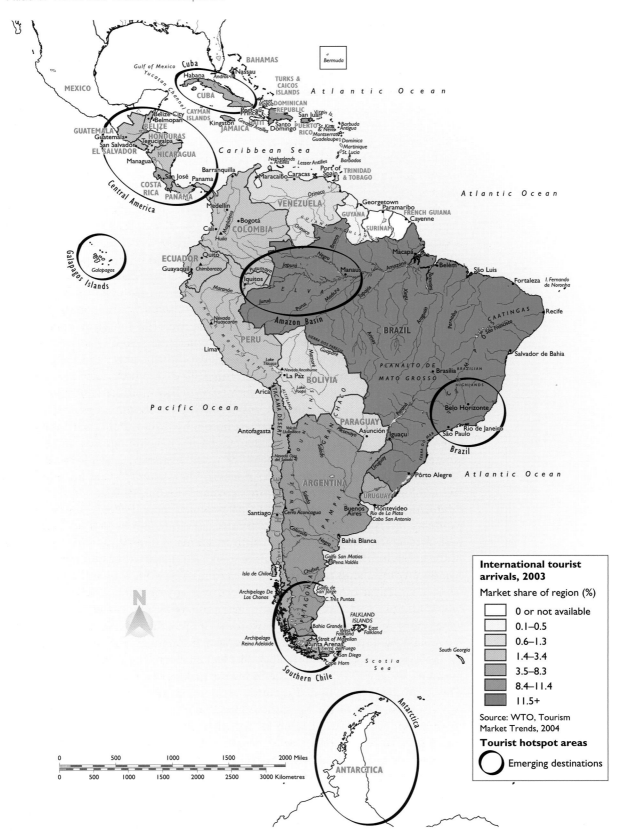

Map 7.1
South America and the Caribbean – international tourist arrivals 2003

Within the map legend:

International tourist arrivals, 2003

Market share of region (%)

	0 or not available
	0.1–0.5
	0.6–1.3
	1.4–3.4
	3.5–8.3
	8.4–11.4
	11.5+

Source: WTO, Tourism
Market Trends, 2004

Tourist hotspot areas

◯ Emerging destinations

Christian Missions. The early coastal trade routes were replaced by the establishment of Spanish foothold ports in the late fifteenth century, followed by formal Spanish colonization over a large part of the continent by the sixteenth century and the export of its wealth via huge galley fleets to Spain. In pre-Columbian times Central and South American travel was dominated by coastal short-haul trade routes circulating luxury goods around the coasts, to be replaced by the long-haul sea travel of incoming colonizers. Outgoing spoils of the empires, including the fabled Spanish treasure ships, were often preyed on by the pirates (buccaneers) of the Caribbean. As the sixteenth and seventeenth centuries progressed new sources of mineral wealth, especially tin and silver, were exported from the continent to Europe and North America, later to be joined by sugar (the main cash export of the Caribbean islands), rubber (from the Amazon Basin) and meat products (from Argentina and Brazil). Land travel in the Andes was always carried out on foot, with the Incas developing and maintaining a spectacular system of roads along the western spine of the continent. These routes are still used as tourist itineraries, such as the walking routes of the Inca Trail and its numerous subsidiaries in the Andes and the *Ruta Maya* (Mayan Trail) in Central America from Honduras to Mexico. But it is the Spanish influence and language that have shaped the culture, language and religion of the vast majority of this region. Spanish influence still remains pervasive in the transport network of the region today, with the Spanish carrier Iberia gaining control of various South American airlines and improving access to other continents from regional hubs served by local domestic feeder airlines. Improvements in the regional airline networks have opened new areas up for tourism. Central and South America are developing new markets in beach and adventure tourism, and (especially) in ecotourism to the Amazon, Costa Rica, Belize and Guatemala.

Central and South America contain some areas which are growing rapidly; however, as with all other regions, development is not uniform (Map 7.1). The region is one of great geographical and historical diversity, but its huge area has meant that different regions have developed at different paces. While the sophisticated Aztec and Inca civilizations exerted religious and political control over vast areas, dominating the territory which is modern Mexico and most of the High Andes, the rest of the continent was sparsely populated by hunter-gather communities whose way of life has remained essentially unchanged for several thousand years, although today it is highly endangered by development in the Amazon Basin. It is, however, possible to highlight both major trends and historical synchronicities. The tourist map of South America would have been very sparse even twenty years ago, but now a new crop of destinations are emerging from the post-colonial world of increasing democracy and stability. The region's current market leaders in tourism terms are Mexico, Brazil and Puerto Rico (the latter having a large VFR market from the USA), but factors that continue to contribute to its uneven development include perceived lack of safety (Colombia), social and political instability (Venezuela), and uncertain climatic events (hurricanes in the Caribbean). There has been a rapid rise in interest of ecotourism, to Central American destinations such as Costa Rica and Belize, the Amazon Basin (including Manu National Park in Peru), the Peninsula Valdés in fashionable Patagonia, Los Llanos in Venezuela, and the islands of the Galapagos off the coast of Ecuador. Contemporary cultural tourism in South America is dominated by interest in the remains of ancient empires, such as the Inca city of Machu Picchu (Plate 7.1) and the Aztec capital of Tenochtitlan (now Mexico City), as well as the continent's colonial past, such as the walled cities of Cartagena in Colombia, Salvador in Brazil and Havana in Cuba.

The Caribbean has a history of genocide, slavery and immigration, and as being a stage for rivalry between world powers. It played a significant role in the colonial struggles of European powers between the sixteenth and nineteenth centuries and became important again in the twentieth century, not least in crises such as the tension between communist Cuba and the USA which remains today. In the early post-war years the Caribbean was a favoured winter beach destination for wealthy Europeans and North Americans, and although some countries (such as Jamaica) have moved into the mass market, bastions of privilege remain – including the Sandy Lane Hotel in Barbados, islands such as Mustique, which was bought by Lord Glenconner in 1956, and Richard Branson's Necker Island, available as an exclusive rental property. Trinidad has become famous for its wildlife tourism and birding, and the Cayman Islands have differentiated into diving tourism and offshore banking, but as a whole the Caribbean region remains a sun and sand destination whose fragility has been evidenced by recent hurricanes.

European interest in the region began in the sixteenth century Golden Age of Exploration. Most early explorers believed that a great southern land, *Terra Australis Incognita*, existed, and some early maps show the great mass joined with the southern tip of Africa, South America, Australia and New Zealand. In 1487 a Portuguese naval voyage, led by Bartolomeu Díaz and Joâo Infante, sailed around the southern tip of Africa and up to Mozambique. This voyage was followed by that of Vasco da Gama in 1497, who sailed south from Europe down the western coast of Africa, around the Cape of Good Hope and north up the eastern coast of Africa until he reached India. These explorations proved that *Terra Australis Incognita* was not part of the continent of Africa, as was previously supposed. Ferdinand Magellan, supported by King Charles I of Spain (who was anxious about Portugal's firm hold on trade to the East Indies), set out from Seville in 1519 to find a new westward route to the Spice Islands or Moluccas (p. 85). After crossing the Atlantic (Map 7.2) he followed the coast of Brazil south, and wintered in southern Patagonia for six months before being blown by a storm into the passage hereafter to be known as the Magellan Strait; thus he found a way into the Pacific (so-called because of its calm waters after the storm). The fleet finally reached Guam, and later the explorers became the first Europeans to see the Philippines. Magellan demonstrated that the Pacific and Atlantic Oceans were linked, and that the Indian Ocean was not landlocked as had been thought. He also established the form and size of South America, and the fact that the Americas were a separate land mass from Asia. His voyage was followed in 1577 by that of an Englishman, Francis Drake, sailing in the *Pelican*, who set out to make a circumnavigation of the globe. While making a deviation through the Straits of Magellan he reported sailing around the south of Tierra del Fuego, and discovered the passage which is now named after him. This proved that the great southern continent was not continuous with Tierra del Fuego either. The end of the seventeenth and most of the eighteenth centuries saw several voyages of exploration south of Tierra del Fuego and many of the sub-Antarctic and southern ocean islands were discovered. The Falklands, South Georgia and Kerguelen Islands were all once thought to be northern projections of the southern land, as were Tasmania and New Zealand, but gradually it was discovered that they were not. However, although these voyages gave sailors and explorers some idea of the shape of the continent and opened a sea route between the south Atlantic and the Pacific, the greatest influence on the cultural development of the region was undoubtedly Columbus, whose voyages between 1492 and 1504 discovered the Bahamas and explored the coasts of Cuba and Hispaniola, Trinidad, Venezuela,

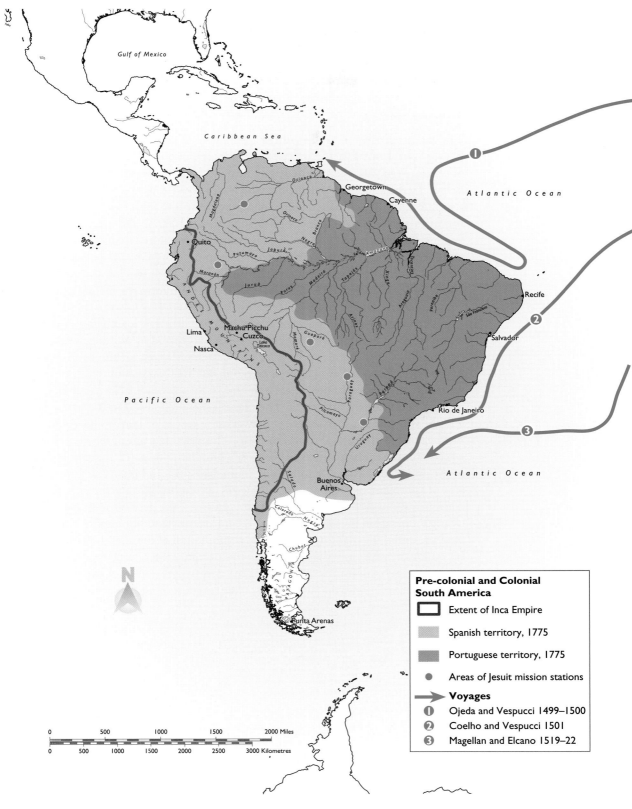

Map 7.2
Pre-colonial and colonial South America

Honduras, Nicaragua and the Isthmus of Panama, thus opening a gateway for the subsequent colonization by Spain which left its mark on the region.

Pre-colonial times

South America

The earliest settlers in South America were related to people who had crossed the Bering Strait from Asia and moved southwards from 50 000 BC onwards. The coast of central Peru was where settled agricultural communities developed most rapidly, helped by the abundant marine life which was boosted by the Humboldt Current. Around 2000 BC climate change made the coast less attractive, so farming communities spread inland, developing sophisticated canal and irrigation systems. From *c.* 900 BC, partly as a result of increased regional trade, new social structures and hierarchies, two important states began to develop: Chavin de Huantar in the Central Andes and Sechin Alta on the north coast, both in what is now Peru. The Nazca culture succeeded the Chavin in southern Peru from the second century BC, with sizeable towns of 5000–10 000 inhabitants and a sophisticated political and commercial network along whose tracks travelled artisans, merchants, government administrators and religious officials. Alpaca hair found in Nazca textiles suggests trading links with highland people. The extreme dryness of the southern desert regions near Pisco in Peru has preserved outstanding Nazca mummies, textiles and ceramics, but the Nazca people are best known for the unique Nazca Lines, now the region's major tourist attraction. The Nazca Lines are located in the Nazca Desert, a high, arid plateau that stretches between the towns of Nazca and Palpa on the *pampa* (a large, flat area of southern Peru). The desolate plain of the Peruvian coast, which comprises the pampas of San José (Jumana), Socos, El Ingenio and others in the province of Nazca, is some 400 kilometres south of Lima. The Lines cover an area of approximately 450 square kilometres, are etched into the desert surface, and comprise about 300 figures made of straight lines; the geometric shapes are most clearly visible from the air. The unique environmental conditions of the Nazca Plain have preserved the markings, due to the combination of the climate (one of the driest on Earth, with only twenty millimetres of rainfall per year) and the flat, stony ground, which minimizes the effect of the wind at ground level and has a lighter-coloured subsoil under the surface crust. With no dust or sand to cover the plain, and little rain or wind to erode it, lines drawn here tend to stay drawn. Even the discovery of the Nazca Lines is related to an event in the history of travel, since they were first spotted when commercial airlines began flying across the Peruvian desert in the 1920s.[1] Passengers reported seeing 'primitive landing strips' on the ground below. Today people sometimes fly in hot-air balloons to view the Nazca Lines, whose meaning is still unclear despite many theories – the most favoured being those of Maria Reiche, a German mathematician and archaeologist who researched the Nazca Lines for most of her long life and believed that they were an astronomical calendar indicating the direction of the rising of important stars and of planetary events like solar solstices.

Nazca contemporaries on the north coast were the militaristic Moche people, who from AD 100–800 built a huge empire with pyramid temples and a sophisticated network of roads and way-stations, which were to be the inspiration for the better-known Inca roads. Moche people developed canal networks, including the La Cumbre Canal, still in use today, but are best known for their naturalistic ceramics giving a vivid idea of Moche daily life. The discovery of a spectacular Moche royal tomb at Sipan[2] in 1987 by Walter Alva demonstrated that the Moche were trading semi-precious stones from Chile and Argentina and seashells from Ecuador as part of a flourishing network of coastal and sea-borne trade. The collapse of the Moche Empire *c.* AD 700 was related to a great drought, with the subsequent rise to power of series of cultures in south Peru, Bolivia and Argentina before the emergence of the Inca dynasty – the largest empire ever known in the Americas[3] – which dominated west and central south America between AD 1200 and 1500. Its maximum extent is shown on Map 7.2, and at its peak, just before the Spanish conquest, the Inca Empire stretched from central Chile northwards to present-day Ecuador and the Colombian border, containing most of Ecuador, Peru, west Bolivia, north Chile and north-west Argentina – some 980 000 square kilometres. Cuzco was established as capital by first Inca ruler, Manco Capac. The vast road system was essential to the Inca Empire's success, transporting goods, linking the highland and coastal provinces with Cuzco, and allowing political and military control to be exerted over those who lived in remote provinces. The Incas built around 12 500 miles of road, with two 'royal roads' which ran parallel to each other; one through the Andes and the other along the coast. Each road was punctuated by distance markers (*topo*) and travelled by the organized system of messengers who carried communications along the road (*chasquis*). In mountainous areas the roads were stepped or zig-zagged, streams were crossed by wooden or stone bridges, and mountain rivers were crossed by terrifying reed-plaited suspension bridges. Inca engineers also built the canals and irrigation works that brought water over long distances and helped to maintain the efficient agricultural economy on which the empire depended. The Incas had a genuine imperial system with a highly trained bureaucracy; all land was state-owned and the ordinary Inca peasant spent nine months of the year working for the state in return for access to state food reserves in times of famine, and provision for sickness and old age. Civil war broke out in the Inca Empire in 1527, following the death of the ruler Huayna Capac, which weakened the empire and was instrumental in the eventual success of the Spanish *conquistadores*. This force of 179 men arrived commanded by Francisco Pizarro,[4] some on horseback – the first time that the horse had been seen in South America. Pizarro defeated a formidable Inca army, executed the Inca rulers Huascar and Atahualpa, who were rival claimants to the throne, and instituted Spanish colonial rule.

Among the many contributions of the Inca to the cultural development of southern America, the most prominent, and most visible today, are their surviving spectacular monuments (of which the best known is Machu Picchu) and their road networks. The 14 291-mile Inca road network was the largest contiguous, prehistoric archaeological structure in the Americas – built over 500 years ago, it connected the various subject peoples of the Inca Empire with a central authority in Cuzco. Even today the route is scattered with ancient Inca sites, many of which are still relatively unexplored by tourists. Machu Picchu (see Box 7.1), the fifteenth century Inca citadel, has become a cornerstone of South American tourism since the American historian, Hiram Bingham, first stubbed his toe on an overgrowth-covered stone slab in 1911. Hiram Bingham was the American historian whose Yale Peruvian expedition actually set out in 1911 in search of the lost city of the Incas, Vilcabamba, which had been established by the Inca ruler Manco when he fled Cuzco after an unsuccessful rising against the Spaniards. Vilcabamba was the centre of the resistance movement for thirty years; even the *conquistadores* were unable to find it, and its location eventually became forgotten. When Bingham found the Machu Picchu ruins on 24 July 1911, heavily overgrown with jungle, their scale was only revealed once the excavations had started. It was a long time before archaeologists finally realized that this was not the mythical city of Vilcabamba, which was eventually found later at the site of Espíritu Pampa. In 1948 Bingham published *The Lost City of the Incas*,[5] thus achieving immortality, and the road leading to Machu Picchu was named the Hiram Bingham Highway in his memory.

**Box 7.1:
Machu Picchu**

Machu Picchu is located on the highest part of the eastern Andes, above the Rio Urubamba and north-west of Cuzco, and was created as a historical sanctuary (santuario histórico) and inscribed on the World Heritage List in 1983. It is thought that it was a royal Inca residence and was perhaps the centre for collecting coca leaves from surrounding plantations.[6] The site eventually fell into ruin, was covered by the encroaching forest and 'lost to science' until its rediscovery in 1911. In the mid-1980s some 180 000 people annually visited the Inca Trail and the ruins, but by the late 1980s this had risen to 300 000, including 7000 on the Inca Trail. Today the site attracts up to 700 000 visitors each year, and in high season (July and August) it is easily possible for 1000 people to be at the site to catch the first rays of the sun at dawn. In recent years, however, concerns have been expressed that Machu Picchu is falling victim to its own success. Despite a sharp rise in the admission price and the abolition of a plan to build a cable railway, it is felt by UNESCO that visitor numbers should be limited to 800 per day, and that they should only be allowed to wear soft shoes. However, it seems unlikely that so severe a set of restrictions will ever be implemented. As a compromise another plan has been submitted to UNESCO to preserve the site, with a bill of US$130 million and a suggested limit of 2500 tourists. Pressure on the Inca Trail is to be relieved by tripling the entry fee and excluding hikers who do not have an authorized Inca Trail guide or who travel in groups of more than fifteen. A limit of 500 people per day will be imposed on the Inca Trail, and visitors will not be able to stay for more than four nights within that portion of the trail which lies within the Machu Picchu sanctuary. Moreover, the trail will be closed for one month each year for maintenance. Visitors will be assigned to specific campsites, and restrictions imposed on fuel and rubbish disposal. As a result of the introduction of most of these measures, visitors must now generally wait for four to five days in Cuzco before getting a place to trek on the Inca Trail. Despite this, Machu Picchu remains the number-one must-see for visitors to South America, although tour operators are searching for a viable, ecologically sound alternative to cope with the huge pressure of numbers. In practice there is no shortage of alternative Inca trails, although they are not as well known. The Choquequirao Trail, fifty miles from the Inca Trail, is being hotly tipped as the next Machu Picchu, and other trekking agencies are publicizing trails in Bolivia and Ecuador, although the lack of existing infrastructure means that it will be some time before the travel industry is able to offer less well-known sites as realistic alternatives to Machu Picchu.

Central America

The Aztecs were warriors from the north who had entered Mexico during the thirteenth century and settled on islands around Lake Texcoco, where in 1325 they founded the town of Tenochtitlan, later to be their capital. Their empire was expanded aggressively from around AD 1427, reaching its peak under the Emperor

Montezuma II (1502–1520), at which time the Aztecs were in control of most of Mexico and were beginning to enter the lands of the Maya people in the Yucatan peninsula (Map 7.3). The Aztec Empire was based on heavy-handed control of subject peoples, demanding tributes of gold, food and sacrificial victims in a pattern of unsustainable consumption to placate warlike and bloodthirsty gods. Archaeologists have estimated that around 50 000 victims a year (mostly captured slaves or people received as tribute) were being sacrificed at the time of the Spanish arrival – one reason why some of the subject peoples welcomed the Spanish as liberators. Hernan Cortés led the *conquistadores* who defeated the Aztec emperor, Montezuma, to bring Mexico under Spanish rule. Equipped with an army of 508 soldiers, 1000 sailors and 16 horses, Cortes burnt his ships on the Mexican coast and marched inland to reach the Aztec capital, Tenochtitlan (site of present-day Mexico City), which the Spanish eventually took by deception. Cortes had been trained as a lawyer and joined Diego Velázquez in the conquest of Cuba, and was sent by Velázquez in 1519 to establish a Spanish colony on the Mexican mainland. The Spaniards took advantage of dissent among the Aztecs, just as the *conquistadores* under Francisco Pizarro were to do against the Incas in Peru a few years later. They soon had thousands of Indian allies and were able to capture the Emperor Montezuma and make him a puppet of Spain, although he was eventually killed in a subsequent uprising.[7] Cortes went on to conquer the whole of the Aztec Empire (Map 7.3), and ruled it between 1523 and 1526. At that time, Tenochtitlan was a city of 200 000 people and the centre of a complex civilization like nothing the incoming *conquistadores* had imagined. One of Cortes' officers, Díaz de Castillo, kept a journal in which he noted that the pyramids and buildings rising from the great crater in Tenochtitlan seemed like an enchanted vision. Two years later the city was a ruin and its people decimated by siege and disease. Cortes notes, in his own book,[8] that the city was as big as Seville or Cordoba in Spain, and was built on a salt lake. He comments on the buildings and seems especially impressed by the marketplaces, whose range of goods demonstrated just how wide the trading links of the Aztec Empire were. Montezuma noted that the Spanish were preoccupied with the precious metals, describing them as 'snatching up the gold they were given like monkeys, swollen with greed'. Thus the great artistic treasures of the Aztec Empire disappeared rapidly, melted down into ingots and shipped off to Spain.

Even before the Spanish treasure ships crossed the Caribbean, the Aztecs had already been trading with the Maya of Yucatan across the Bay of Campeche (Map 7.3) since at least the ninth century. The Maya of the Classic period lived in the dense forests of the Yucatan, where their descendants remain today, and at the time of the Spanish conquest different Maya provinces were in dispute over land rights. The Maya had established extensive coastal trading links for food crops, cacao, silver, jade, feathers and obsidian around the Yucatan peninsula, including a base on the island of Cozumel, now developed as one of Mexico's major tourist destinations. Classic Mayan sites in Yucatan, including the World Heritage sites of Chichen Itza and Uxmal, make this one of modern Mexico's major tourist regions.[9] Campeche, a historic fortified city, has also been declared a World Heritage site, and is near the archaeological zones of Edzna and Calakmul – the latter forming part of the biggest biosphere reserve in the country. Many of the ancient traditions of the Mayas that persist in the region are attracting tourists travelling the *Ruta Maya*, which links many of the major sites. Local Mayan women still wear a traditional blouse called a *huipil*, and some homes are still built with Mayan-style straw-thatched rooftops. There are also the regional *henequen* haciendas, many of which have been converted into

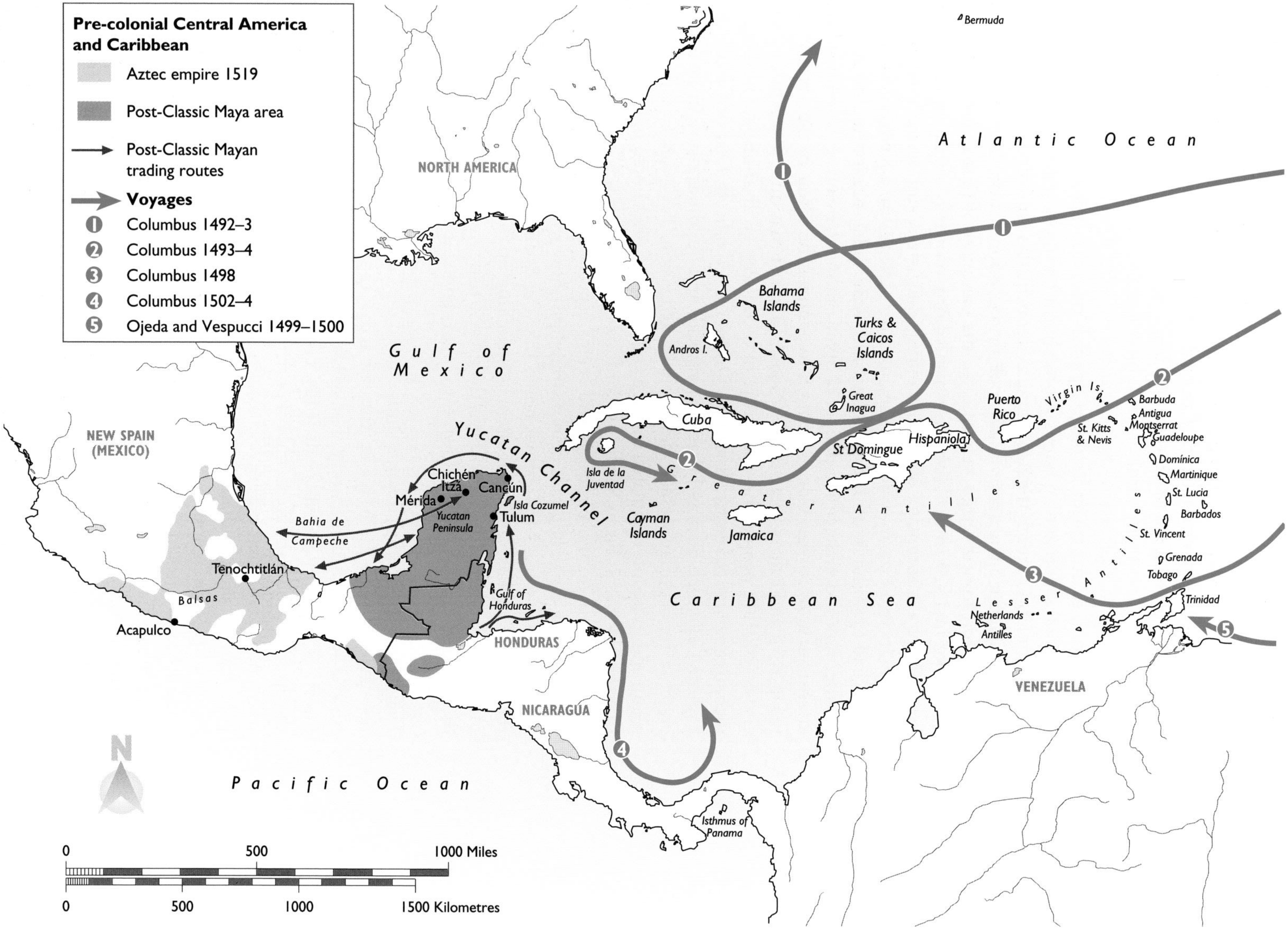

Legend

Pre-colonial Central America and Caribbean

- Aztec empire 1519
- Post-Classic Maya area
- Post-Classic Mayan trading routes

Voyages

1. Columbus 1492–3
2. Columbus 1493–4
3. Columbus 1498
4. Columbus 1502–4
5. Ojeda and Vespucci 1499–1500

Map 7.3

Pre-colonial Central America and Caribbean

exclusive hotels. The greatest draw in the Yucatan peninsula today, though, is the purpose-built beach resort of Cancun, established to balance the tired and aging resort of Acapulco on Mexico's Pacific coast. Nearby is the series of attractions that have been branded as the 'Mayan Riviera', including the protected areas of Xcaret and Xel-Ha. The ancient Mayan port islands of Cozumel and Isla Mujeres have been developed as centres of diving because of their position on the Great Mayan Reef, the second largest reef in the world.

Colonial times

The colonial history of South America really started with Francisco Pizarro's victory over the Incas and his foundation of the city of Lima, capital of today's Peru. Pizarro's arrival in Peru had actually been preceded by Columbus' landfall on the Paria Peninsula in Venezuela on 5 August 1498 and Spanish reconnaissance of the Pacific coast in 1522. The first permanent Spanish settlements were established at Santa Marta (Colombia) in 1525, with the foundation of the walled city of Cartagena in 1533. European seafarers had visited the Rio de la Plata since 1516, followed by Sebastian Cabot and his rival, Diego Garcia, in 1527. An expedition led by Pedro de Mendoza founded Buenos Aires in 1536, meaning that by the middle of the sixteenth century Spanish influence extended over a substantial proportion of southern America.

Pizarro's conquest of the Incas was partially motivated by rumours that had circulated as far as Europe in the 1520s of the wealth and magnificence of the Inca Empire. The victories of Hernan Cortés in Mexico against the equally powerful and magnificent Aztec Empire had shown that such empires were vulnerable and could succumb to superior European arms, armour and indeed diseases. Before Pizarro's successful expedition of 1532 several previous expeditions had been attempted, and in 1528 Pizarro had actually been appointed Governor of Peru in advance by the King of Spain. By the time of Pizarro's eventual advance the Incas were weakened and preoccupied with a struggle over the succession to the throne. The Spaniards entered Cajamarca in 1532, where the successful usurper Atahualpa was based, and faced an army of 30 000 men. The Spanish bewildered the Incas with their horses and guns, with the small 170-man force probably killing anywhere between 7000 and 17 000 Incas and holding Atahualpa to ransom. The real reason for the conquest became immediately apparent when the Spaniards extorted enormous amounts of gold and silver from the Incas for his ransom, then executed him on a pretext. Pizarro himself went on to conquer the Inca capital at Cuzco, and continued plundering the Inca Empire after establishing a puppet emperor, Manco Capac, in Cuzco and founding their new capital city in Lima in 1535.

The *conquistadores* Francisco de Orelanna and Gonzalo Pizarro headed, in the first half of the sixteenth century, an expedition inland from Quito in Ecuador, which led to the first European navigation of the whole of the River Amazon. Pizarro set out from Quito in 1541 in search of 'the land of cinnamon', an expedition also motivated by tales of El Dorado, 'the golden one', which they thought was a city of unimaginable wealth but for which they searched in vain. Pizarro's huge expedition (220 Spaniards, 4000 Indians and a herd of pigs) eventually met up with Orelanna in northern Ecuador, with the pair achieving the first recorded crossing of the South American continent.[10] They eventually followed the course of the Amazon downstream to its tidal basin and thus to the Atlantic – a journey of some

2000 miles. Legends of the journey included attacks by pale-skinned female warriors which the expedition scribe Friar Carvajal likened to the Amazons of Greek legend – hence the name of the river. The expedition was to end with Pizarro eventually finding his way back to Quito, but Orelanna effectively deserting – an episode about which much has been speculated.

The Spanish colonizers established new cities and set about exploiting their new mineral wealth including, in 1545, the hill of silver at Potosi in Bolivia, which was soon to be followed by other mining centres. By the early seventeenth century Potosi was the largest city in the Americas, but over the next 200 years lodes began to deteriorate and silver was found elsewhere. This new industrial activity also generated new transport networks, connected with the development of trade routes to supply the industrial centres and to export the material. Although the Spanish had exported substantial quantities of gold (and a few native artifacts) in the immediate aftermath of the conquest of the Incas, during the subsequent colonial period the emphasis passed towards the export of silver, and Bolivia remained the major global exporter of silver until the twentieth century when the production and export of silver was replaced by that of tin. But Spanish dominance of southern America was not complete. The Portuguese Pedro Alvares Cabral landed in Brazil in 1500, shortly followed by Amerigo Vespucci, and the expansion of Portuguese interests primarily on the eastern seaboard began from that time. The Portuguese established a system of feudal principalities in their territories, eventually replaced by a Viceroyalty to control trade. In Spanish-controlled territories a new colonial bureaucracy was established under the Viceroyalty of Peru, which became the major outlet for the wealth of the Americas. Spain and Portugal eventually signed a treaty in 1494 at Tordesillas, dividing the earth between them at 270 leagues west of Cape Verde, bisecting South America. One result of this is the demarcation between Spanish-speaking countries to the west (such as Peru) and Portuguese-speaking countries in the east (such as Brazil) (Map 7.1). The Spanish and Portuguese architectural legacies of South America are still clearly manifest today, as is a different kind of legacy evidenced in the Christianity which they brought with them and the thousands of churches, cathedrals and mission stations that resulted. Between 1609, when they built their first *reduccion* or mission in the region of Guaira in present-day Brazil, to their final expulsion from Spanish America in 1767, the Jesuits founded at least fifty missions located around the upper reaches of the Rivers Parana, Paraguay and Uruguay (Map 7.2). The missions were efficiently organized and strictly laid out, with the objective of 'civilizing' and converting the indigenous people and effecting a change from a nomadic hunter-gatherer lifestyle to stable (and more profitable) agricultural settlement. The film *The Mission*, starring Robert de Niro, provided a graphic account of the tribulations of the early Jesuit missionaries, who travelled extensively on foot throughout the heartland and often defended local communities against the activities of European slave-traders. The Spanish missions grew both indigenous and European crops successfully, but their increasing economic power made them many enemies, from the Spanish crown to local landowners. Map 7.2 shows the location of some of the missions, the best known of which are San Ignacio Mini in Argentina, Jesus and Trinidad in Paraguay, and Sao Miguel in Brazil.[11] After the forced removal of the Jesuits and the termination of their political power in 1767 many missions fell into disrepair, but they have now become pegs in a resurgent cultural tourism industry, particularly around Iguaçu on the Argentina/Brazil border where the World Heritage listed Iguaçu Falls[12] contributes substantial volumes of incoming international tourism into the area. Better domestic air access has now facilitated visits to the Jesuit Missions near Posadas in Argentina on the Paraguan border, the most impressive of which is San Ignacio Mini, which was founded on its present site in 1696. San Ignacio is now a World Heritage site whose interpretation centre focuses on the lives of the Guarani Indians before the Spanish arrival.

Post-colonial times

The post-colonial history of South America is highly chequered, but essentially involves complex and gradual attempts to gain freedom from Spanish and Portuguese control and to establish democratic independent countries – an objective that has still not been achieved over the whole continent. Major events include the late eighteenth/early nineteenth century independence movement led by Simon Bolivar in the north, which established a new republic of Gran Colombia, including modern Colombia, Venezuela and Ecuador. A second uprising, led by José de San Martin in Argentina and Chile, provided another example of the complex politics of struggle to be free from colonial powers, which were replaced by temporary federalism, succession movements and eventual military uprising, but always accompanied by the gradual weakening of political ties with Europe. Economic ties and trade remained long afterwards, as seen by surviving economic links such as the network of trade from Argentina to Europe in meat and minerals. In the twentieth century this turbulence continued in a series of coups and local wars, as well as the rise to power of figures such as Colonel Juan Perón in Argentina. Guerrilla warfare (such as that involving the Maoist *Sendero Luminosa*, or 'Shining Path') in Peru, civil wars and, later, military dictatorships such as that of General Augusto Pinochet in Chile and the rise of the narcotics trade in Colombia made much of South America a no-go area for international travel until the late 1980s, and sometimes it was not possible even then.

As we have seen, European explorers sought the fabled 'El Dorado' in the Amazon Basin, which they called 'Green Hell', but which as we know today contains amazing biodiversity and 20 per cent of the world's plant and animal species, with many still to be discovered. The Indians of the massive Amazonian plain, a 1300-kilometre wide maze of rivers and tributaries, remained virtually untouched by the incoming Spanish colonists for a century because of the difficulties of travelling within the area. The population concentrations of Brazil are still to be found on the coast; although 56 per cent of Brazil is actually in the Amazon Basin only 8 per cent of its population lives there today, mostly around Belem at the mouth of the Amazon and Manaus at the confluence of the Rio Negro and Rio Solimoes. Manaus is the hub of river transport, ferries, cargo and tourist ships, but has now become a cultural tourism destination in its own right, with visitors motivated by the city's architectural legacy. This dates from the time when Manaus became prosperous as a result of the boom in rubber, exported from the Amazon. After the decline in rubber[13] Manaus became an isolated urban island in the jungle, but it is now growing fast and, since 2001, has been investing in a restoration programme for its historic buildings in the wake of their designation as World Heritage sites. Manaus's famously opulent theatre, the *Teatro Amazonas*, was completed in 1896 at the height of the rubber boom, and its market, the *Mercado*, was built in 1902 using imported wrought iron from Europe and designed by Eiffel as a copy of Les Halles in Paris. The lives of the Amazonian Indians were affected by the rubber boom, but the impact of the subsequent gold rush in Brazil has been much greater. During the 1980s it is estimated that 20 per cent of the Brazilian Yanomamo Indians died from diseases introduced by gold miners, loggers and farmers invading their lands, and the pattern is similar for other tribal groups. Although communications throughout Amazonia have always been dominated by water transport, recent attempts to build roads parallel to the Amazon in the south, including the as yet uncompleted Transamazonica highway,[14] have had huge environmental and social impacts as agricultural settlements and loggers have removed trees, exposing the shallow rainforest soil to erosion. The indiscriminate use of mercury by gold prospectors and large-scale deforestation for hardwoods have caused a severe deterioration in Amazonian biodiversity and had a fast and irreversible impact on the way of life of indigenous Indians living in the Amazon Basin. Some have become tourist attractions, although the main reason for visiting the region today is wildlife-watching. Ships of up to 5000 tonnes can travel up the Amazon as far as Iquitos in Peru, the trip from Belem to Manaus taking five or six days going upriver.

However, tourism to the Amazon region, although growing rapidly, is insignificant in terms of volume compared with tourism to Brazil's beaches. Rio de Janeiro is popularly seen as the most glamorous destination in South America, being famous for its beach culture, carefree atmosphere and carnival. Its travel history started with the Portuguese navigator Gonçalo Coelho, who arrived in what is now Rio on 1 January 1502. After seventy years of conflict between the French and Portuguese, Rio eventually became the capital of Brazil's southern province, and by the eighteenth century it was Brazil's leading city, used as a port to export gold and also for the export/import trade of surrounding agricultural lands. Rio became the seat of the Portuguese viceroy in 1763, and after independence in 1834 it remained the capital of the empire for 125 years. Its attraction for visitors today include the familiar silhouette of Sugar Loaf mountain, the statue of Christ the Redeemer on Corcovado, and the beaches of Copacabana (which are divided into numbered sections, or *postos*, for different market segments). Rio is justly famous for its five-day carnival which starts before Lent, on the Friday before Shrove Tuesday, with exuberant processions and the breaking of the social barriers that still remain in Brazilian society (a colonial legacy). Carnival parades show off Rio's samba schools, and are accompanied by lavish fancy dress balls. But Rio is also famous for its *favelas* or slum neighbourhoods, where its underclass live, and successful attempts have been made to interest overseas visitors in this element of Brazil's heritage despite its reputation for violence and poverty.[15]

Among South America's colonial cities, Salvador de Bahia is perhaps the best known. It is the third largest city in Brazil, and was founded on All Saints Day in 1501 by the navigator Amerigo Vespucci. Salvador de Bahia is a fortified city, built to protect Brazil's colonial interests from threats of French and Dutch invasion. Its *centro historico* is a World Heritage site, with some of the most important examples of colonial architecture in the Americas; it is the subject of a massive restoration programme funded by the Bahian state government and UNESCO. It was the capital of Brazil until 1763 and the most important city in the Portuguese Empire after Lisbon, providing a safe, sheltered harbour along the trade routes of the New World. Its wealth came from sugar cane and tobacco, harvested using slave labour imported from the west coast of Africa. Salvador was the centre of South America's slave trade, and that legacy is still obvious today, since it is easily the most African city in the western hemisphere. The University of Bahia has the only Chair in Yoruba in the Americas, and Salvador has its own religion, Candomble, which is a fusion of African and Brazilian religious practices. The city includes 15 forts, 166 Catholic churches and 1000 Candomble temples, and still remains a major port, though its chief import today is tourists attracted by its cultural richness – including the famous Bahianas, black female foodsellers who still wear traditional eighteenth century costumes. Salvador's history and trading links are exemplified by the Church of Sao Francisco, whose cedarwood carving was completed in 1748 using cedar imported from Lebanon. A string of popular resorts extends south from Salvador on the same coast that the Portuguese made their first landfall, but these are now popular with Brazil's domestic tourists as resort towns for the middle classes of Sao Paolo.

Just as the African heritage of many Bahians attracts visitors, so too do the legacies of other migrations. More recent famous immigrants to Latin America include Butch Cassidy and Sundance Kid, whose legend is responsible for a tourism industry which has grown up around the Bolivian town of Tupiza. Visitors can follow their last days, until the pair were killed by a military patrol after their last bank robbery in 1908. Welsh immigration to Patagonia in the late nineteenth century has also generated a VFR market. Welsh was spoken in Patagonia for four generations following the immigration, but is now dying out. Tourists go to Lake Titicaca in Bolivia, made famous by the explorer Thor Heyerdahl, who publicized its traditional craft of reed boat-making. Craftsmen from the nearby village of Suriqui made reed boats for Heyerdahl's *Ra II*, which he sailed between Morocco and Barbados in 1970 in an attempt to prove that contact between North Africa and North America would have been technically feasible even in the days of relatively primitive shipping.[16]

Despite the fact that South America is steadily opening up new destinations to attract international visitors, it still remains dominated by huge volumes of domestic tourism. Pilgrimage is a significant activity in this Catholic continent, such as the world's longest *Via Crucis* (Way of the Cross) pilgrimage, whose fourteen stops along Ruta 81 in north-east Argentina require pilgrims to walk more than 500 kilometres, and qualifies for the *Guinness Book of Records*. Many festivals and ceremonies which started as local events have now been expanded to attract tourists, such as the annual ceremony in Oruro, Bolivia, which pays homage to the miraculous Virgen del Socavon, patroness of miners. The dances were traditionally performed by Indian miners, but have now become a huge international attraction since the site was included on UNESCO's Heritage of Humanity List in honour of the syncretism of Andean, pre-Columbian tradition and Catholic faith. Inevitably, prices from La Paz triple at the time of the festival, which is accompanied by high hotel rates and now has formal ticketed seating. The same is true of the *Inti Raymi* (Festival of the Sun God) held at Cuzco in Peru, and mentioned by early Spanish chroniclers. This has now been recreated, partly from written accounts and partly from the memories of descendants of the Incas who still practise some of the ceremonies during the year to honour their tutelary gods. Nowadays the ceremony is acted as ritual theatre on the stage of Saqsaywaman Fortress, and uses a written script to which new scenes are sometimes added. Each year special stands are built for the visitors, the numbers of whom can reach about 100 000 on the main day of the festival, with local people watching from vantage points around the complex. However, these numbers are nothing compared to the visitors who come for Rio's famous carnival.

Nor is Rio the only major historic city in South America to develop a significant tourism industry. Having now escaped from a long period of military dictatorship Chile is fast emerging as an international tourism destination, with visitors to its capital, Santiago, able to sample the vineyards of the Maipo Valley and ski in the

Andean foothills. Nearby Valparaiso was first settled in 1542 and became, in the colonial period, a small port serving the coastal trade with Peru. It was raided by pirates (including Sir Francis Drake) at least seven times, and was then developed in the nineteenth century by commercial agents from Europe and North America as their trading base in the southern Pacific, and as a major international banking centre. Valparaiso was a key port for US shipping between the east coast and California during the California Gold Rush, and also for European ships that had rounded Cape Horn, but its significance declined as a result of the development of steamships and the opening of the transcontinental railway in the USA and the Panama Canal in 1914. However, Valparaiso is now being revived as the official cultural capital of Chile, although few of its colonial buildings survived the devastating earthquake of 1906.

New areas recently opened up for ecotourism include the vast wetlands of the Pantanal, which spreads over into Paraguay and Bolivia but is mostly in Brazil. The area is partly flooded in the rainy season, but is a wildlife-watching destination which contrasts sharply with the Amazon Basin because it is grassland, meaning that the wildlife is easier to see than in dense rainforest. The market leader in ecotourism, though, remains the Galapagos Islands, part of Ecuador since 1832. The Galapagos are the peaks of gigantic underwater volcanoes and lie on the Equator nearly 1000 kilometres west of the coast of Ecuador. There are six main islands (San Cristobal, Santa Cruz, Isabela, Floreana, Santiago and Fernadina), twelve smaller islands and a maze of small islets. Isabela, the largest island, has half the total land area, and was home to a convict colony until 1858. Due to their inhospitable nature and lack of water, the Spanish paid the Galapagos Islands little attention, giving them the name 'Las Encantadas' (the bewitched islands) because the strong currents and light winds made them hard to find. Unfortunately European sailors, pirates and buccaneers had more success, and established watering places on Santiago, Floreana and San Cristobal. The first intentional and extended visit to the islands was made in 1683 by an English buccaneer vessel, the Batchelor's Delight, under Captain John Cook; she numbered amongst her crew William Dampier, who was the first to provide the world with an accurate description of the islands and their fauna and flora. As demand for European goods grew, normal trade progressively replaced piracy and those few islands which had supplies of water came to be heavily used by whalers and seal-hunters. Whaling was a highly profitable business in the first half of the nineteenth century, but it caused decimation not only of the whales but also of the giant tortoises, which were used as food by the whalers owing to their ability to survive for long periods without food or water. Ecuador proclaimed its sovereignty over the islands in 1832 and three years later HMS Beagle arrived with Charles Darwin on board. Darwin spent five weeks in the Galapagos, collecting and preserving specimens from four separate islands.[17] He recognized that animals and plants had adapted to the Galapagos conditions and become differentiated not only from their relatives on the mainland but also from those on other islands – a premise that became the basis for his theory of evolution. Without large land mammals, reptiles such as marine iguanas were dominant – as they had been in Earth's very remote past. This started the process of enquiry which led him finally to conclusions published in On the Origin of Species by Means of Natural Selection in 1859. Interest in the wildlife of the Galapagos began from that time. In 1968 the Ecuadorian Government established the Galapagos National Park Service (GNPS). Ten years later the Galapagos were designated as the first World Heritage site, and when the Galapagos Marine Reserve was established in 1998, that too was designated a World Heritage site. They are a Biosphere Reserve, a Whale Sanctuary and a RAM-SAR site, and have recently been designated as one of only two Particularly Sensitive Sea Areas (PSSA) by the International Maritime Authority. In Fernandina, they possess the largest 'near pristine' island in the world. Since the islands were uninhabited when discovered by the Spanish in 1535, the animals seem tame, with little fear of man. The islands' most spectacular species are the giant tortoises, mostly found on Isabela, as well as the iguanas, Galapagos albatross, red- and blue-footed boobies, frigate birds, and 123 species of Darwin's finches, sea lions and fur seals all still being studied at the Darwin Research Station in Academy Bay. Visitors pay National Park tax and theoretically the number of tourists to the islands is controlled to protect the environment, as is visitor behaviour. Tourism infrastructure is still basic and the islands are threatened by current tourism levels and domestic in-migration.[18]

Costa Rica (Map 7.1), an ecotourism success story, is different from the rest of Central America – indeed from the rest of Latin America – both because of its social welfare system and parliamentary democracy and for its ecotourism industry. Costa Rica was the most neglected segment of Spanish colonial Central America, in large part because it was farthest from the colonial governors based in Guatemala. As large-scale colonization began elsewhere, only 330 Spanish colonists had claimed lands in Costa Rica by 1611. This was because it had neither of the two things the Spanish *conquistadores* wanted: mineral wealth (gold and silver), and an abundant Indian population to work their *haciendas*. The absence of minerals and indigenous workers meant that settlers worked their own land, and there was plenty of it to go around for centuries, forming a huge middle class of yeoman farmers. Like Guatemala and El Salvador, Costa Rica was transformed by coffee in the nineteenth century. The coffee industry attracted foreign capital and immigrant merchants, and promoted road and railroad development. In 1871 American engineers built a railroad from the settled central plateau over the rugged mountains to Puerto Limon on the Atlantic. While much of Costa Rica has been stripped of its forests, the country has managed to protect a larger proportion of its land than any other country in the world. In 1970 there came a growing acknowledgement that something unique and lovely was vanishing, and a systematic effort was begun to save what was left of the wilderness. That year, the Costa Ricans formed a National Park system that has won worldwide admiration.[19] Costa Rican law has set aside more than 10 per cent of the country as sanctuary, and an additional 17 per cent is legally set aside as forest reserves, 'buffer zones', wildlife refuges and Indian reserves. Throughout the country, representative sections of all the major habitats and ecosystems are protected within a National Conservation Areas System consisting of more than 186 areas, including 32 National Parks, such as Manuel Antonio, Braulio Carrillo and the high montane Cloud Forest of Monteverde.[20] The National Parks and reserves protect the soil and watersheds and harbour an estimated 75 per cent of all Costa Rica's species of flora and fauna, including species that have all but disappeared in neighbouring countries.

Antarctica

The port of Puntas Arenas, more than 2000 kilometres south of Santiago in Chile and facing the Straits of Magellan, has a wealthy past as a port and wool exporting centre but has now become the tourism centre for Chilean Patagonia, comprising the increasingly popular Torres del Paine and Balmaceda National Parks with their glaciers in southern Patagonia, visited for their wildlife and walking. Puntas Arenas is also one of the main ports for tourist visits to the Antarctic, as is Ushuaia in Argentina, with visitors connecting to either port via a domestic flight from Santiago (Chile) or Buenos Aires (Argentina). Antarctica is fifth in size among the world's continents and is 99 per cent covered by a 14.2 million square kilometre ice sheet. Its isolation from other continents, unpredictable weather and freezing temperatures has prevented any permanent human settlement. While the history of Arctic adventure essentially began with the nineteenth century quest for the North-West Passage and North Pole, the early explorers to Antarctica travelled solely for commercial reasons, with new discoveries being made accidentally. The majority of these early voyages were related to the nineteenth century peak of the whaling and sealing industries. Shore stations were in operation in the Falkland Islands, South Shetland Islands, South Orkney Islands, South Georgia, Iles Kerguélen, Macquarie Island and Campbell Island. Until as late as 1820 no one had even seen the Antarctic mainland, but in the 1890s explorers of various countries began to compete to be the first to reach both the North and the South Poles. In 1901–1904 Captain Robert Falcon Scott was the first person to explore Antarctica extensively by land, in two expeditions (Map 7.4). After Scott died in 1912 during his return from the South Pole, Sir Ernest Shackleton attempted to cross Antarctica from the Weddell Sea to the Ross Sea via the South Pole. Although the expedition failed, because Shackleton did not reach the South Pole, he overcame enormous difficulties to bring all his men safely home after his ship, the *Endurance*, was trapped and crushed by ice in the Weddell Sea. His incredible journey to get help, leaving his men on Elephant Island and setting out in a small boat for an 800-mile trip to the whaling station on South Georgia, the nearest inhabited island (Map 7.4), is one of the great classics of exploration history.[21] During the First World War scientific interest in the Antarctic waned, but the start of tourism to the continent can be placed in the mid-1920s, with occasional visitors being carried on mail ships to whaling stations on South Georgia, the South Shetlands, the South Orkneys and the Falkland Islands. These locations remain the pegs of today's Antarctic cruise industry, a typical route of which is shown on Map 7.4. Regular cruises were established by 1966,[22] and since then it is estimated that more than 45 000 tourists have visited Antarctica, mainly by cruise ship, although numbers could be considerable higher, since this figure does not include expeditions by private and charted yachts. Visitation is concentrated around the historic sites of the Antarctic peninsula, but has now been extended to sub-Antarctic islands such as South Georgia and the Falklands (the latter in particular since the Falklands War generated so much interest). A typical contemporary tour might leave Ushuaia in Argentina for the Falkland Islands, continuing across the Scotia Sea toward South Georgia. Stops are made for wildlife-watching (especially penguins and albatross), and on South Georgia a visit is usually made to Grytviken, once a thriving whaling station, where Sir Ernest Shackleton is buried. Cruises may also take in the South Orkneys, Laurie Island and Elephant Island, scene of the start of Shackleton's great 1916 rescue journey. Return trips often come back via the South Shetlands and Drake Passage, and pass Cape Horn on their way back to Ushuaia.

The 1990s saw a rapid expansion of tourist activity in the Antarctic as a result of improved technology, increased accessibility, media documentaries, changing consumer preferences and the search for new products, but there are many difficulties regarding activity regulation, not unrelated to disputes over sovereignty over both land and ocean. Nowadays, the southern continent is shared between the scientists

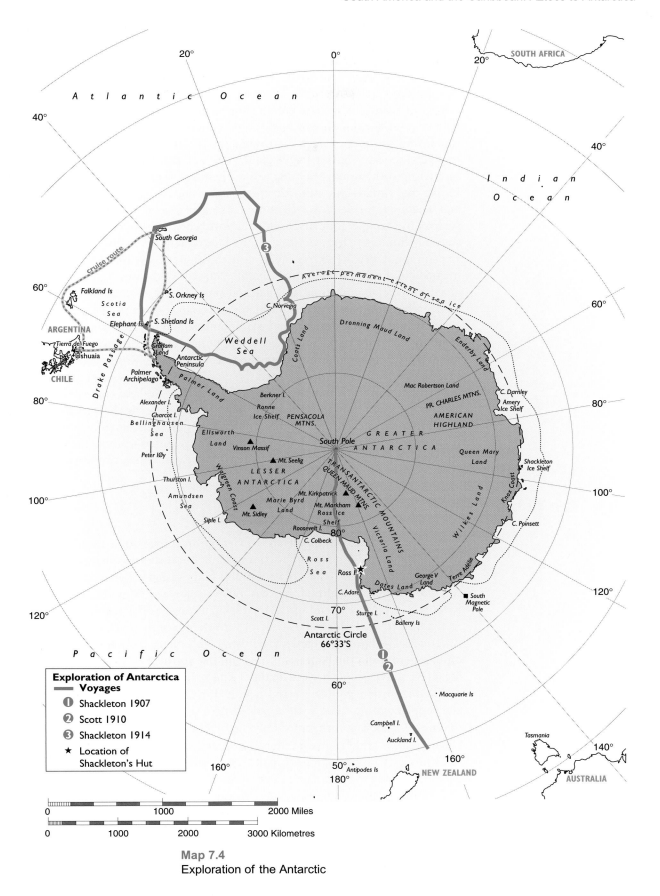

Map 7.4
Exploration of the Antarctic

Legend (from map):

Exploration of Antarctica
Voyages
❶ Shackleton 1907
❷ Scott 1910
❸ Shackleton 1914
★ Location of Shackleton's Hut

of twenty-seven nations who are based there, studying everything from the destruction of the ozone layer to the mating habits of penguins. Future levels of tourism activity in Antarctica depend on interest, cost, accessibility, weather and transport availability, but will certainly include increased cruise ship activity into the Ross Sea and sub-Antarctic islands. There are many concerns about the environmental impact of such activities, including hydrocarbon residues from aircraft fuel, and wildlife disturbance from low flights. Ship-based tourism can result in water pollution from inadequate sewage and waste disposal, and fuel spills. Repeat visits, even by careful tourists, destroy fragile plant cover, and there is the possibility of visitors interfering with current scientific work. There is also great concern about visitors' impact on Antarctica's cultural and historic sites, which include early sealing and whaling settlements as well as the remains of several early exploration bases – such as the famous huts of Shackleton and Scott, already extensively looted by souvenir-hunters.[23] Indeed, Shackleton's hut, built as part of his British Antarctic Expedition of 1907–1909, is so seriously threatened by visitor activity that it was included in the World Monument Fund's 2004 list of the world's 100 most endangered historic, architectural and cultural sites. The hut is one of the few intact wooden buildings on Antarctica which dates from the 'heroic age' of exploration, and was used by Shackleton as an expedition base and research laboratory. It is still standing a century later, complete with thousands of expedition artifacts but both hut and artifacts are in serious need of conservation. The Ministry for Culture and Heritage of New Zealand supported the nomination and has provided core funding assistance to the Antarctic Heritage Trust, a New Zealand charity that seeks to care for the site. This was the first time that a site in Antarctica had been considered so seriously threatened, and is a direct reflection of increased levels of visitor activity. It is estimated that a further US$2.6 million is required to implement the work and conserve Shackleton's hut and its remarkable contents for future generations.

The Caribbean

The oldest evidence of humans in the Caribbean comes from southern Trinidad, where 7000-year-old remains have been found, but early settlement is also claimed for Hispaniola, Cuba, the Lesser Antilles and Antigua. Between 400 BC and AD 400 the first agriculturalists seem to have colonized Trinidad via the Orinoco River in South America and spread rapidly up through the islands of the Caribbean. At the time of the European discovery of the islands of the Caribbean, three major Amerindian indigenous peoples lived there. Columbus made contact with several different groups in the Bahamas, Cuba and the northern coast of Hispaniola, taking a few native people back to Spain.[24] The Spanish, who came looking for gold, enslaved the native population and rapidly drove them to near-extinction, eventually supplementing them with imported African slaves. Although Spain claimed the entire Caribbean, they settled only the larger islands of Hispaniola, Puerto Rico, Cuba, Jamaica and Trinidad. Other European powers, such as the French, Dutch and British, established a presence in the Caribbean after the Spanish Empire declined, partly due to the reduced native population of the area owing to European diseases. The Spanish policy of conquest and settlement in trying to establish a great colonial empire was challenged by the trading activities of the Portuguese, British and Dutch. The islands of the Caribbean were a prime source of sugar for the European market, and as such much sought after. Columbus first made landfall in the 'West Indies' in 1492, and on his second visit in 1493 encountered the Carib Indians who would give the islands their name. The Spanish settlement at Hispaniola began in the same year, to provide a base from which settlers hoped to find gold and also for trade to China (thought to be nearby), and to facilitate the Spanish settlement of central America, which utilized a base on Hispaniola with Cuba functioning as a further base for the conquest of Mexico. Sugar was the most profitable of all trade crops imported into Europe, and from the middle of the seventeenth century until after the end of the eighteenth century the sugar-producing islands of the West Indies were regarded as valuable prizes. Early European knowledge of the Caribbean was patchy; in England it came from the exploits of Sir Francis Drake, who attacked many Spanish ships and forts in the Caribbean – including San Juan harbour in 1595 – and captured the Spanish Silver Train at Nombre de Dios in 1573.[25] The peak of the piracy season in the Caribbean came between 1640 and 1680, although pirates operated outside this time and came into conflict with incoming colonial powers such as the British, who seized Jamaica in 1655, also holding Barbados, St Kitts and Nevis, Antigua, Montserrat and Bermuda. In 1697 the Spanish ceded the western third of Haiti to France, which also gained control of Guadaloupe, Hispaniola, Martinique and Tortuga. The Dutch took over the Netherlands Antilles and Ayuba (then called Dutch West Indies) in the seventeenth century. Even Denmark had a colony here; the Danish ruled first part and then all of the present US Virgin Islands (then known as the Danish West Indies) after 1672, eventually selling sovereignty to the United States, which still administers them. From the late eighteenth century, most islands of the Caribbean were engaged in a struggle to be free from their colonial masters. In Haiti, a slave rebellion led by Toussaint l'Ouverture started the Haitian revolution, establishing Haiti as a free, black republic by 1804. Some Caribbean nations gained independence from European powers in the nineteenth century. Some smaller states are still colonies of European powers today, including commonwealth countries such as Jamaica. Christopher Columbus landed on the island that became known as Cuba on 28 October 1492, during his initial westward voyage, the name 'Cuba' coming from its aboriginal name, Cubascan. Colonization of the island began in 1511, when the Spanish soldier Diego Cuba Velázquez established the town of Baracoa. Velázquez subsequently founded several other settlements, including Santiago de Cuba in 1514 and Havana in 1515. The Spanish transformed Cuba into a supply base for their expeditions to Mexico and Florida. As a result of savage treatment and exploitation the indigenous people became almost extinct by the middle of the sixteenth century, forcing the colonists to depend on imported black slaves for the operation of the mines and plantations. Despite frequent raids by buccaneers and the naval units of rival and enemy powers, the island prospered throughout the sixteenth and seventeenth centuries, largely because the colonists traded illegally with privateers and neighbouring colonies. During the 1830s, however, Spanish rule became increasingly repressive, provoking a widespread movement among the colonists for independence, which was not finally achieved until 1898. US corporate interests had invested heavily in the Cuban economy, acquiring control of many of its resources, especially the sugar-growing industry, and there was widespread dissatisfaction with fraud and corruption in Cuban politics. Various insurrections against conservative control of the republic occurred in August 1906, and the US Government dispatched troops to the island, which remained under US control until 1909. Mounting economic difficulties, caused by the complete US domination of Cuban finance, agriculture and industry, marked the period following the First World War. Fidel Castro became premier after the overthrow of the unpopular Batista regime in 1959 and gradually made changes to laws which affected US sugar interests. A complete break in diplomatic relations occurred in January 1961, and on 17 April that year US-supported and -trained anti-Castro exiles landed an invasion force in the Bay of Pigs in southern Cuba. American–Cuban relations grew still more perilous in 1962, when the United States discovered Soviet-supplied missile installations on the island. Many of Castro's policies alienated Cuba from the rest of Central and South America. Cuba continued to depend heavily on economic aid from the Soviet Union and Soviet-bloc countries, and in 1972 it signed several pacts with the USSR covering financial aid, trade, and deferment of Cuban debt payments. It became a paid-up communist country in 1975, with the relationship with the USA remaining difficult. With the collapse of the USSR in the early 1990s, Soviet-bloc aid and trade subsidies to Cuba were ended and Soviet military forces were gradually withdrawn. Cuba's sugar cane production dropped to a thirty-year low in 1993 and worsened in 1994, precipitating an economic emergency. As the effects of this poor yield filtered down through the population, greater numbers of Cubans attempted to flee the country for economic reasons, creating a refugee crisis that swamped America. This came to an end when the United States agreed to issue 20 000 entry visas each year to Cubans wishing to enter the country. Many Cuban immigrants settled in Miami, the nearest major city to Cuba, which now has a huge Spanish-speaking Cuban-American community who have greatly influenced the cultural life of the state. However, relations between Cuba and the USA remain difficult, with the economic embargo becoming permanent. Cuba is now a poor country, with pockets of prosperity such as Havana, and a developing tourism industry aimed at Europe. America has a history of intervention in Caribbean affairs, including the invasion of Grenada in 1983 and the Cuban Missile crisis, when US ships blockaded Cuba to prevent the Soviet Union deploying nuclear missiles there. The US still maintains military bases in the region, including the notorious Guantanamo Bay in Cuba, where US terrorist prisoners are held.

Today's Caribbean is highly dependent upon the booming cruise market,[26] with individual Caribbean countries investing in their tourism infrastructure and marketing and promoting the diversity of the region and the distinctiveness of the individual islands – a distinctiveness based partly on geographical factors (such as forest in Trinidad or beaches in Jamaica), but also upon their colonial history. Around 25 per cent of all jobs in the Caribbean are dependent upon tourism, and in some islands this is nearer 80 per cent. The geographical proximity of the Caribbean to the generating markets of North America and Europe is also a factor in its success, as are year-round high temperatures, warm coastal waters and archetypal palm-fringed beaches. Multi-centre holidays and cruises allow visitors to sample the different flavours of the islands, and a dozen Caribbean countries now receive more cruise-ship passengers than overnight visitors. However, the industry is fragile and subject to competition, and many countries are trying to diversify their economies away from tourism, just as they previously utilized tourism as a means to diversify economies away from sugar. Cruise passengers in the Caribbean have a wide choice of ships, including some of the largest in the world, taking 4000 passengers. These are a source of major problems at popular cruise-ship ports such as mainland Key West (p. 127) and Nassau in the Bahamas. Control measures include greater levels of environmental regulation and quotas on the number of ships permitted to enter ports each day.

Australia and the Pacific: outback and outriggers

Australia and Oceania occupy 6.3 per cent of the world's land area but are home to only 0.5 per cent of its population. The area is dominated by Australia, with 50 per cent of all international visitors and 80 per cent of all international expenditure. The main characteristic of travel and tourism within the Australia-Pacific (Oceania) region is the extreme remoteness of the area from either Europe or the Americas (the major source markets for incoming international tourism), and the great intraregional distances that must be covered in travelling around (Map 8.1). This is both the region's strength and its weakness, and travel costs, although now falling, are still high. Global problems tend to bypass the Australia-Pacific region, whose economy is driven by Australia – a country over thirty times the size of the UK, but with less than one-third of its population. New Zealand is more European in scale, and Australia and New Zealand together account for 97 per cent of the economy of the region and over 70 per cent of its visitors. The region has experienced steady growth in international visitors since 1997; of the eleven economies within it that report data to the World Bank all but two saw GDP growth rising in 2001, with Australia and New Zealand having the largest rises. Indeed, Australia is one of the world's fifteen largest economies.[1] The region scores highly on the three major issues that dominate international leisure travel at present – cost, safety and the availability of new or exciting experiences – and includes everything from highly cosmopolitan cities such as Sydney to unspoiled Pacific beaches, the emptiness of the outback, the landscapes of New Zealand and the wonders of the Great Barrier Reef. This unspoiled quality is a major selling point; '100 per cent pure' is Tourism New Zealand's current slogan, which could reasonably be applied to all the other countries of the region as well. The region is also regarded as being safe in a way that large parts of the world are not; crime levels are lower than those in most of the countries from which visitors come. With the exception of Fiji, where past tensions seem now to have been eased, the threat of terrorism is minimal, with no internal issues likely to generate serious military or political stress in the future.

The landscapes of both Australia and New Zealand are major attractions for today's visitors, since neither country has an architectural or archaeological legacy which forms the basis of its tourism product. Both countries do, however, attract visitors interested in the traditional culture of their indigenous people (Aborigines and Maori). The region is well served both by international airlines and by cruise ships, but has undeniably seen cutbacks in Asia-Pacific airline services, which has impacted particularly on the Pacific Islands, which are generally not destinations in their own right (in the sense that Australia is) but are often visited by passengers *en route* to some other final destination. As some islands derive up to 80 per cent of their GDP from tourism and are reliant on a fairly small number of visitors and markets, the effects of cuts in even a few scheduled air services can be extremely

International tourist arrivals, 2003

Market share of region (%)

- 0
- 0.1–2.3
- 2.4–10.0
- 10.1–23.2
- 23.3–59.1
- 59.2+

Source: WTO, Tourism Market Trends, 2004

Tourist hotspot areas

- Established
- Emerging

Map 8.1

Australia and the Pacific – international tourist arrivals 2003 worrying. As in other areas of the world within the Australia-Pacific region, budget airlines are being developed, including Virgin Blue and Pacific Blue, linking Australia and New Zealand with Pacific islands such as Fiji and Vanuatu. Many Pacific islands hope this development will be the first of many.

Touring in self-drive cars and (especially) in motorhomes is a favourite way for international visitors to explore both Australia and New Zealand, since both countries have excellent road networks and it is relatively easy to combine air travel between major cities with regional travel by car or van. Australia also has the longest straight stretch of rail track in the world – 470 kilometres between Nurina in Western Australia and Ooldea in South Australia. International visitors to the region tend to stay quite a long time, partly due to the long flights needed to get there and partly to the size of the destination area. Indeed, the average length of stay in Australia is twenty-seven days, but for visitors from countries such as Canada and the UK it is closer to forty. Tourism to the region is not evenly distributed; around 80 per cent of visitors to Australia, for example, do not spend a night away from the key attractions of its six main cities, the 'Gold Coast' and tropical North Queensland (Map 8.2). The dominant urban centre within the region is Sydney, visited by 60 per cent of all travellers. Queensland attracts visitors to the state capital of Brisbane on the Gold Coast. The Great Barrier Reef and the Whitsunday islands continue to grow in popularity, with the north of Australia, especially around Cape Tribulation, currently fashionable. The Northern Territory was made famous by the *Crocodile Dundee* films,[2] and top attractions of the outback include Alice Springs and Uluru (Ayers Rock; p. 159). Within New Zealand, some three-quarters of incoming international visitors go through Auckland, with the fastest growth in the country being seen in house rental and stays at farms and families. Most visitors are attracted by the exceptional scenery, and there is a growth in wilderness walking, especially in the South Island, and in the development of sophisticated luxury-lodge style accommodation and spa tourism in the geothermal sites in the North Island.

The Pacific Islands (Map 8.1) still remain mainly stopover destinations, offering some of the most unspoiled beaches in the world but dispersed over a very wide area. The islands of French Polynesia, for example, are spread over an area of ocean about the size of Western Europe, yet put together their land area would fit comfortably inside a very small American state. Pacific islands are popular stopovers for travellers to the region utilizing the western route (via North America), with Air New Zealand in particular offering several Pacific islands, such as Samoa, Hawaii and the Cook Islands as stopover destinations. The most significant Pacific island destination in tourism terms is Fiji, which has also gained market share of the Australian leisure market as a result of the bombings in Bali, formerly a favourite leisure destination for Australians. French Polynesia gives the tropical taste of France, although in 1999 American visitors exceeded French visitors for the first time. Its economy is one of the most tourism-reliant in the world, and thus one of the most vulnerable, although a development plan backed by France is currently in place to address this. Guam has long been a popular travel destination, particularly for American and Asian markets, and is the site of an important US military base. However, it has seen a decline in visitors from Japan (for whom it was a favoured honeymoon destination, second only to Hawaii), and US military cutbacks have also meant that the island has needed to make a significant investment in its tourism infrastructure. The Northern Mariana Islands are a compact group roughly halfway between Australia and Japan, popular with the American market

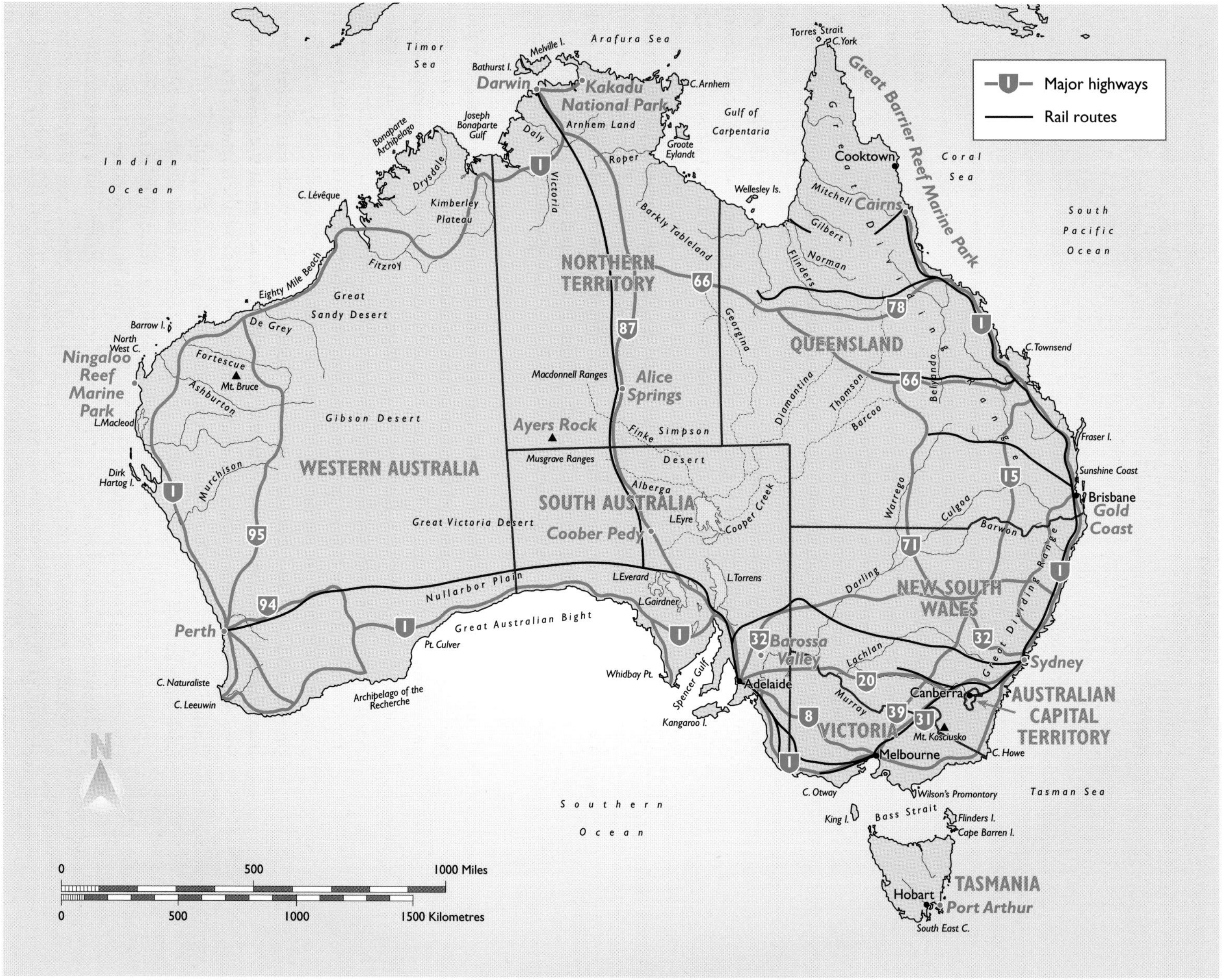

Map 8.2

Australia – highways and railroads

and famous for the diving on the many shipwrecks that date back to the Pacific conflict in the Second World War. All Pacific island states face the challenge of developing sustainable and diverse economies, especially those threatened by rising sea levels. Their markets are affected by the long flights necessary to reach them, at a time when there is much publicity about long-haul hazards such as deep vein thrombosis. Although many islands are significant destinations for diving tourism, the absence of top-quality sea rescue facilities has affected their appeal, as has political problems in Fiji. There is also sporadic unrest on other islands, especially the Solomon Islands, as a result of ethnic conflicts.

Australia

Australia likes to describe itself in superlatives, claiming the world's oldest rainforest (110 million years), the world's best wines and the world's most laid-back people. What *is* certain is that its tourism product is unique and, in contrast with almost any other region of the world, has been influenced less by its history than by its geography. Although history of Australia dates back to the arrival of the ancestors of its first indigenous people at least 250 000 years ago, the continent did not become influenced by European colonialism in the same way that, for example, Africa did. Today's major Australian visitor attractions are more likely to be connected with landscape than culture, with the exception of its capital, Sydney, where visitors come to see the vibrant cosmopolitan city that it has become – not to visit its past as a convict settlement. Sydney is one of Australia's three iconic attractions (the others being the Great Barrier Reef and Uluru/Ayers Rock) which together neatly exemplify the tourism product of the country (Map 8.2). Visitors are also drawn to the great emptiness of the outback in the way that they are drawn to the prairies of North America.

Visitors often tend to underestimate the great travelling distances across Australia, which is linked by a comprehensive network of internal air flights. Flying in Australia is the easiest way to travel, since people who go by train, bus or car are often disappointed by Australia's flat, unchanging scenery. However, Australia's rail system facilitates long-distance travel between the state capitals, not only by the Indian-Pacific railway, but also by the Great South Pacific Express travelling along the east coast, a new luxury train with grand turn-of-the-century décor and timber panelling, which travels the route between Cairns and Brisbane weekly (with a side-trip by aircraft to the Great Barrier Reef). An even newer development is the completion of the railway line which directly bisects Australia and carries the train known as the *Ghan* along a two-day, 1851-mile trip from the southern city of Adelaide to the port of Darwin, on Australia's tropical north coast. The route of the *Ghan* goes through Alice Springs before it joins the 882 miles of recently-inaugurated track completed in early 2005, but the train's name commemorates a far older means of travel. The Afghan camel drivers brought to the country in the nineteenth century to help blaze a trail into the harsh, unexplored vastness of the interior of the continent brought camels with them. Originally camels were the only beasts of burden capable of surviving the hot, dry conditions as the pioneers built a north–south telegraph line. However, in 1929 a railway was built between Adelaide and the central city of Alice Springs, with the last link to Darwin completed in 2005. The camels still remain, and the Australian outback is full of their feral descendants, many of whom have been caught and utilized in Australia's growing camel safari industry.

Bus travel in Australia is also popular, including the economically-priced Greyhound Pioneer network, but long-haul car travel is significantly less popular here than it is in the USA, simply because the driving distances are so great and in peripheral areas the quality of the roads may not be good. Travelling within Australia is often a matter of utilizing a combination of methods of transport, from the newly-emerging budget airlines to 'classic' train journeys such as by the Indian-Pacific train, which makes a three-day train journey across the outback, right across the Nullabor Plain (Map 8.2) from Perth to Sydney. More novel means of transport include the sky-rail gondola accessing the wet tropics rainforest from Cairns, and the numerous boats, ferries and catamarans linking the tourist nodes of the 2000-kilometre long Great Barrier Reef with resorts such as the Whitsunday Islands, Green Island, Lizard Island, Heron Island, etc. Just as in North America, the tourism geography of Australia also tends to be doughnut-shaped, with many major attractions round the east coast, from Kakadu National Park and the Northern Territory down through northern Queensland (with the Barrier Reef offshore) and the beaches of the Gold Coast to Sydney (Map 8.2). In the west tourism has traditionally been centred on Perth, although it now includes famous wildlife-watching sites north of the city, such as Rottenest Island and the Ningaloo Reef 250 kilometres north, with its opportunities to snorkel or dive with manta rays and whale sharks. Central Australia is really dominated by Alice Springs and Uluru (Ayers Rock), and in the south the wine industry of the Barossa Valley, a German-speaking region less than an hour's drive from Adelaide, attracts domestic and international visitors alike. Adelaide itself is known as the 'city of churches', and has a reputation as a sleepy place surrounded by vineyards, with more than a little remaining of the comfortable lifestyle of the 1950s. Like Canterbury in South Island New Zealand, it still has a feel of England about it, and is the only Australian capital that was settled entirely by English free settlers rather than convicts. Many more English people came there at the end of the Second World War, to work in the city's car plants and domestic appliance industries. However, it was earlier immigrants from Germany, in the 1930s, who gave Adelaide's hinterland its reputation for winemaking, bringing with them winemaking skills and establishing wineries. Today more than one-third of all Australian wine comes from areas mostly within an hour's drive from Adelaide, with the Barossa Valley having become the centre of a major wine tourism industry.[3]

Australia's history goes back very much further than this, though. Before the arrival of European settlers, Aboriginal and Torres Strait Islander peoples inhabited most areas of the Australian continent, with hundreds of different cultural traditions and languages that differed on a regional basis, each with complex social systems and traditions that reflected a deep connection with the land and environment. An excellent example of this can be seen at Uluru (see Box 8.1; Plate 8.1).

Box 8.1: Uluru The famous silhouette of Uluru (Ayers Rock) is probably the most recognizable geographical feature in Australia. Uluru is the focus of the sacred landscape of the Uluru-Kata Tjuta National Park, in much the same way that Mt Everest is the centre of the Sagarmartha World Heritage landscape or Mt Sinai is the focus of the Sinai/St Katherine's Monastery region. It is sacred to the Anangu Aboriginal people who have lived there for 30 000 years, but now receives more than 350 000 visitors per year. For the Anangu, Uluru is associated with the travels of ancestral Tjukurpa (dreamtime) beings and is the focus for several dreaming tracks and ceremonial exchange routes. There are many areas of the site that must not be visited by particular types of people. For non-Australians, whose familiarity with Australia may have come as a result of exposure to popular films or wildlife documentaries, a visit to Uluru may be a unique opportunity to encounter Aboriginal art, mythology and culture. Visitors consume the landscape of Uluru in a variety of different ways, including photography, walking round the rock, visiting waterholes, or taking tours by coach, helicopter, balloon, camel or Harley-Davidson motorbike. Not all of these activities are appropriate for a sacred site.[4] The most contentious is climbing the monolith itself – a procedure discouraged but not forbidden by its Anangu custodians. Temporary closure of the climb in 2001 as the result of the death of a tribal elder resulted in increased awareness of Uluru as sacred landscape, a process already facilitated by Anangu-led tours. The visitor experience of Uluru is gradually refocusing from photography to participation, as the visitor is offered new ways of consuming the landscape. Future plans for Uluru include the provision of a greater number and variety of recreational opportunities, primarily walks, which are both non-consumptive and educational. Visitor flows are to be improved to eliminate crowding, and more information and orientation will be provided. The visitor infrastructure is to be relocated away from culturally sensitive places, including the development of new visitor nodes near the climb, and new walks diverting visitors from culturally sensitive locations. The result will permit the visitor to appreciate the totality of its landscape, to consume it appropriately and reflect on its meaning. In political terms, the transition from Ayers Rock to Uluru mirrors the evolving post-colonial relationships between Aboriginal cultural commitments and the white-run tourism industry of Australia.

The first recorded European contact with Australia was in March 1606, when Dutch explorer Willem Janszoon (*c.* 1570–1630) charted the west coast of Cape York Peninsula, Queensland. Later that year, the Spanish explorer Luis Vaez de Torres sailed through the strait separating Australia and Papua New Guinea. Over the next two centuries European explorers and traders continued to chart the coastline of Australia, then known as New Holland. In 1688, William Dampier became the first British explorer to land on the Australian coast. It was not until 1770 that another Englishman, Captain James Cook, aboard the *Endeavour*, extended a scientific voyage to the South Pacific in order to further chart the east coast of Australia and claim it for the British Crown. Britain decided to use its new outpost as a penal colony, and the first fleet of 11 ships, carrying about 1500 people (half of them convicts) arrived in Sydney Harbour on 26 January 1788. It is on this date every year that Australia Day is celebrated.[5] In all, about 160 000 men and women were brought to Australia as convicts from 1788 until penal transportation ended in 1868. Free immigrants began to arrive in the early 1790s, attracted by the newly-established wool industry and also by the discovery of gold in the 1850s, the evidence of which is still seen today at places like Balarat or Kalgoorlie. One result of this was the displacement of Aboriginal people from much of their tribal land. It was not until 1967 that the Australian people voted overwhelmingly in a national referendum to give the federal government the power to pass legislation on the behalf of indigenous Australians, and to include indigenous Australians in future censuses – an action widely seen as a strong affirmation of the Australian people's wish to see its government take direct action to improve the living conditions of Aboriginal and Torres Strait Islander peoples. Today, Australia is one of the most cosmopolitan and dynamic societies in the world. Over 200 languages are spoken, with English the common language. The nation has thriving ethnic media, an international business reputation, an innovative artistic community, diverse religious and cultural activities, and variety in foods, restaurants, fashion and architecture.

A glimpse into Australia's early European history can be seen in 'The Rocks' area of Sydney, the sight of the oldest settlement in the country. Initially a convict settlement, the timber houses lining the rocky ridge gave the area its name. Dockyard buildings formerly lined the water's edge, but in the 1840s a range of more permanent stone buildings grew up, including most of the pubs and shops still standing today, some of which survived clearances when bubonic plague came to Sydney in 1900, causing the government to demolish most of the shanty buildings. Between 1923 and 1932 a large portion of the historic stone cottages in the area were also pulled down to make way for the construction of the Harbour Bridge, but the rest were saved from further demolition by residents' action in the 1970s. The area includes Cadman's Cottage, built in 1816 and the headquarters of the government body that regulated the colony's waterways; it is named after John Cadman, who became the governor and lived there from 1827 to 1846. The small Anglican garrison church was built in 1839; soldiers sat on one side and free settlers sat on the other. Susannah Place is a small terrace of four historic houses, built in 1844, which give visitors a glimpse into the life of working-class families of the period. Australia's most recognizable building, Sydney Opera House, is one of the world's great iconic buildings, and is a working building, a full-scale performing arts complex with five major performance halls. It was built after the New South Wales Government raised the money needed from a public lottery. From the start the design was controversial, and its Danish architect[6] returned home without ever seeing it completed. Initially the budget was assessed at nearly US$6 million, but by the time it was finished in 1973 it had cost US$71.4 million, mostly raised through a series of lotteries, and it has since required almost continual refurbishment, with expensive replacement of hundreds of thousands of the white tiles that make up its distinctive shell.

Australia's recent industrial history is not well known, but does serve as the basis for a number of distinctive visitor attractions. Tourists also come to the outback opal mining town of Coober Pedy (Map 8.2), but today such visits are more to see the eccentric characters for which the town is famous than the remnants of its mines. The first opal was found there in 1915, but it was not until 1970, when the transcontinental railway was completed, that serious opal mining began, with the heat driving the inhabitants of Coober Pedy to construct their town underground. The Desert Caves Hotel is one of the few underground hotels in the world, its rooms dug out using mining machinery and its guests getting the opportunity to fossick through the old mine workings in search of overlooked opals. The more recent history of Australia, and its mining industry in particular, can be seen at Broken Hill in New South Wales, which is reputed to have more public houses per head than anywhere else in the world. It is also home to the 'School of the Air', which transmits its lessons by radio to isolated farming communities that maintain the country's sheep farming legacy all over the outback. The architectural legacy of

Broken Hill includes not only some colonial mansions and heritage homes, but also the famously eccentric Palace Hotel, used in the cult film *The Adventures of Priscilla, Queen of the Desert*.[7] The town of Broome in Western Australia on the Kimberley Coast demonstrates a different set of legacies, with 'traditional' Australian corrugated-iron architecture being found alongside the red pagoda roofs left by the Chinese pearl-divers who settled here. Ballarat was the gold rush city west of Melbourne where a lode was discovered in 1851; within a year 20 000 people had drifted into the area and the Australian gold rush had begun. Its modern visitor attractions include a recreation of the Eureka uprising, one of the most important events in Australia's recent history. After gold was discovered the government devised a system of gold licences, and charged miners a monthly fee even if they came up empty-handed, with corrupt goldfield officials (many of whom were former convicts) diligent in extracting the money. When licence checks intensified in 1850, even though most of the gold was worked out, resentment flared and prospectors began demanding political reforms such as the right to vote in parliamentary elections and secret ballots. The situation exploded when the Eureka's hotel owner murdered a miner but was set free by the government. The hotel was burnt down in revenge, and more than 20 000 prospectors joined together, burned their licences and built a stockade. The rising was put down by troops about a month later, but it forced the government not only to reconsider miners' rights but also to introduce into Victoria, for the first time, the right to vote. Kalgoorlie, in Western Australia, sits on the richest square mile of gold-bearing earth in the world, with today's visitors able to see the enormous opencast goldmine in much the same way that visitors to Kimberley in southern Africa can see the vast crater which resulted from the extraction of diamonds (p. 61). Kaloorlie's pit is 4.5 kilometres long and nearly 300 metres deep and yields an astronomical 1863 ounces of gold a day. Australia's biggest gold producer, its history has been capitalized on by many gold-mining attractions, including a recreated miners' village and the Museum of the Goldfields. Australia is full of the remains of successive waves of immigration. Hahndorf, located just outside Adelaide in South Australia, was founded by a group of Lutheran settlers in the 1830s and is very Germanic in style. Launceston, in Tasmania, is full of Victorian and Georgian architecture and has plenty of remnants of Australia's convict past. The maritime heritage of Australia can also be seen at the heritage port of Fremantle, 19 kilometres from Perth in Western Australia, at the mouth of the Swan River. Fremantle has completed a major restoration of its distinguished but rundown warehouses and derelict Victorian buildings, which today have been converted into an historic district of 150 National Trust buildings, cafés, museums, galleries and pubs next to the still-working port. Fremantle Arts Centre is located in a striking near-Gothic 1850s building which was actually built by the convicts who ended up inside it when it was a maximum security prison. Quite a different legacy can be seen inland at New Norcia Benedictine Monastery, 132 kilometres north of Perth, located in a town full of elegant European architecture and containing a collection of Renaissance art. There is a simple explanation; the town and its surrounding 8000-hectare farm were established in 1846 by Spanish Benedictine missionaries, and today's visitors can see the beautifully frescoed chapels and one of the best religious art collections in Australia.

While one of the first acts of the new Commonwealth Parliament was to pass the Immigration Restriction Act 1901, which restricted immigration to people of primarily European origin, this was dismantled after the Second World War. Today

Australia has a global, non-discriminatory policy, and is home to people from more than 200 countries.

Australia's wildlife (undoubtedly better known than its religious sites) is a major attraction for visitors and can be encountered in a number of managed attractions, such as the famous Lone Pine Koala Centre near Brisbane, which permits koala cuddling (outlawed in many other locations because it is thought to stress the animals). However, most Australian wildlife can easily be seen in the wild, including kangaroos, wallabies, parrots, wombats and Tasmanian Devils.[8] Its wildlife is a major factor in the increased popularity of Western Australia as a tourist destination. Since the 1960s, a pod of bottlenose dolphins has become resident in the shallow waters of Monkey Mia in the Shark Bay World Heritage region of Western Australia (Map 8.2), and they have become so popular that a new resort has been built on the previously deserted shore just to accommodate visitors. But there is still some way to go before the area competes with the most famous wildlife-watching location – the Great Barrier Reef. Marine tourism boomed here in the early 1990s, and the city of Cairns boomed with it; having previously been a small farming town on the north Queensland coast, it is now home to a number of five-star hotels and is the jumping-off point for tours and ferries to the outer reef. Cairns is also near the 110-million-year-old tropical rainforest area around Daintree, part of a World Heritage-listed area[9] that stretches from north of Townsville to beyond Cairns and houses one-half of Australia's animal and plant species. From Cairns the visitor has the option of using the sky-rail forest cable railway, which glides over the rainforest canopy to the mountain village of Kuranda, home to the Aboriginal Cultural Park founded in 1987 and now Australia's major Aboriginal cultural centre. The Daintree rainforest is part of the Wet Tropics World Heritage area that stretches from Cape Tribulation to Townsville (Map 8.2); a dense, lush environment has remained unchanged for over 100 million years, including mangroves, eucalyptus woodlands and tropical rainforest. Here are 65 per cent of Australia's bird species, 60 per cent of its butterfly species and many of its frogs, reptiles, marsupials and orchids. The sky railway is one of Australia's most famous feats of engineering, with gondolas leaving every few seconds from the terminal in northern Cairns for the 7.5-kilometre journey, permitting the visitor to experience the rainforest in quite a different way from the boardwalks at ground level. A far more recent addition to Australia's tourist attractions is Australia Zoo on the Sunshine Coast, famous for Steve and Terry Irwin's collection of dangerous saltwater crocodiles and the TV series based on their activities. The *Crocodile Dundee* films brought these crocodiles to the world's attention and made the 1.7-million-hectare Kakadu National Park in the Northern Territory one of Australia's major tourist attractions, although there are anxieties about its status since the Park is classed as 'threatened' under the World Heritage listing because of uranium mining operations on its boundaries.

Tasmania, often viewed literally as the end of the earth, is somewhere where all these themes can be seen coming together to underpin a relatively recently developed tourism industry. It has been circled in Map 8.1 as an up-and-coming area for its utilization of a magnificently varied natural environment. Distances are more manageable on the island than in the rest in Australia, and the island has a great diversity of habitats. More than 20 per cent of Tasmania has been declared a World Heritage area, and nearly one-third is within some kind of protected area, including fourteen National Parks. Contemporary visitors also come to Tasmania to see the remains of its Aboriginal history in a series of rock paintings and engravings.

Europeans discovered Tasmania or (originally Van Diemans Land) in 1642, when the great seafarer Able Tasman is said to have anchored off its south-west coast, but it was not realized that it was an island until 1798. It soon became a dumping ground for convicts who were often transported for petty crimes committed in their homeland. The brutal system of control is still evident in the ruins at Port Arthur on the Tasman Peninsula and elsewhere. Port Arthur was essentially Australia's version of Devil's Island in French Guyana, and can be paralleled by Alcatraz in the USA and Robben Island (South Africa) for its harshness in so picturesque a setting. From 1832 to 1870 Port Arthur was one of the harshest institutions of its type anywhere in the world, built to house the settlements' most notorious prisoners (often those who had previously escaped into the bush). Nearly 13 000 convicts were held there, of whom more than 2000 died while in prison. Port Arthur is connected to the rest of Tasmania by a narrow strip of land called Eaglehawk Neck, which was guarded by people and rows of dogs, so that only a few convicts ever managed to escape. The Port Arthur historic site contains many of the original nineteenth century buildings, although most were damaged during bush fires in 1877 shortly after the property ceased to be a penal institution. It functions today as one of Australia's major heritage tourism attractions, even offering ghost tours of the area by lantern light. The policy of brutality towards convicts spilt over into persecution of the native Aboriginal population, and the last full-blooded Tasmania Aborigine died in 1876, just fifteen years after the last convict transportation, with all the others having died of disease or having been hunted down and killed.

New Zealand

Tasman himself went on to chart the coastline of New Zealand, giving his name to one of the country's best-known National Parks. New Zealand is famous as a twenty-first century visitor destination for its magnificent scenery, and particularly as a centre for activity tourism, offering everything from bungee jumping to white-water rafting. As a destination, New Zealand's main characteristic is its isolation – even Australia is 1500 kilometres away – but the country has a highly positive global image of being clean and green. New Zealand is never crowded and is very easy to get around, since it has a land area only a little larger than that of Britain. The population is just 3.8 million, over half of whom live in the three largest cities of Auckland, Wellington and Christchurch. Unlike Australia, distance is not a problem for the incoming international visitor, and in rural New Zealand it is possible to travel miles through farmland and hardly see anybody. New Zealand has a unique ecosystem in which birds adapted to fill the role normally held by mammals, but the balance changed around 1200 years ago with the arrival of the first Polynesian navigators, who made this the last major land mass to be settled by humans. New Zealand was called 'Aotearoa' ('the land of the long white cloud') by the first Maori, and they proceeded radically to alter its fragile ecosystem, making the giant ostrich-sized moa extinct. A precarious ecological balance had been achieved before the arrival of white Europeans, predominantly of British origin. In the 1840 the Treaty of Waitangi effectively ceded New Zealand the British Crown, while guaranteeing some Maori rights over the land plus traditional gathering and fishing rights. As time wore on increasing numbers of settlers demanded to buy ever larger parcels of land, resulting in the eventual subjugation of the Maori and their way of doing things.

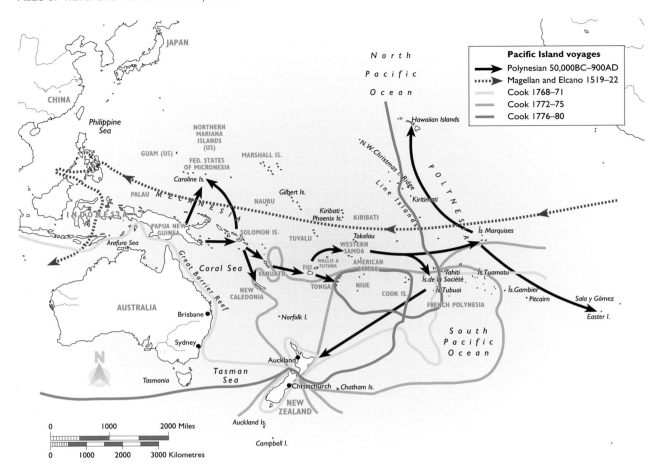

Map 8.3
Pacific island voyages

The New Zealand of today is something of a hybrid between Presbyterian Anglican values and Maori generosity and hospitality. It also (famously) still has more than forty sheep to every one human inhabitant (although this figure is less than 50 per cent of the 1980s figure), emphasizing the country's traditional agricultural economy, although this is now being substantially boosted by tourism (Map 8.3). Within New Zealand key destinations include Queenstown (adventure and outdoor tourism) and Rotorua (hot springs and spas), but many international visitors travel widely within what is still a small country. Easily the most significant stimulator of recent tourism has been the use of many different New Zealand landscapes in the filming of *Lord of the Rings* (Wellington airport even has a sign reading 'Welcome to Middle Earth').[10] New Zealand is promoted for its beach destinations such as the Coromandel Peninsula, the wineries of the Marlborough region and the sea-kayaking of the Able Tasman National Park, as well as for outdoor sports in the Southern Alps and whale-watching off Kaikoura. New Zealand's most historic village is what was the small hillside settlement of Russell in the Bay of Islands, which in the 1830s was a swashbuckling town full of drunken sailors – although all this changed when it was colonized by missionaries, eventually becoming the largest settlement in the country in 1840. Rotorua is New Zealand's major tourist destination, and one of the most concentrated and accessible geothermal areas in the world, with twenty-metre geysers and mineral pools in a barren landscape. It was this thermal activity that attracted Maori people to settle around Lake Rotorua, utilizing the hottest pools for cooking, and building houses on the hot ground to drive away the winter chill. Under European influence Rotorua was set up as a spa town on land leased from the Maori in the late nineteenth century, and eventually included a government sanatorium complex which has now evolved into a large resort where many hotels offer private hot pools. By the early years of the twentieth century Rotorua was already New Zealand's premier tourist town, and this is evident in its government gardens and bowling greens, which could easily be in Harrogate or Bath. The Maori village of Whakarewarewa, south of Rotorua, was founded in pre-European times; today's visitors can still see steam-box cooking and visit the Maori cultural centre. New Zealand's highly developed network of National Parks owes much to a Maori chief of the late nineteenth century, who recognized that the only chance his people had of keeping their sacred lands intact was to donate them to the nation on the condition that they could not be settled or spoiled. This 1887 gift formed the core of the country's first major protected area, the Tongariro National Park, a cultural landscape designated as a World Heritage site in 1991 and now famous for the opportunities it offers for fishing, skiing and walking, as well as for its Maori sacred sites.[11] Able Tasman National Park, named after the seventeenth century explorer, is a stunningly beautiful area with an international reputation for walking and sea-kayaking. Maori sites in the area date from the 1500s, with seasonal encampments along the coast pre-dating the arrival of European explorers in 1642, when Tasman anchored his two ships in Golden Bay. He lost four crew men in a skirmish with the Maori, but achieved considerable personal fame.

Quite a different kind of national heritage is evidenced in Christchurch, on the South Island, an outpost of Anglicanism named after an Oxford College and with the feel of a traditional English university town. It came into being as a result of a programmed policy of colonization by the Canterbury Socialist Society, formed in 1849 by members of Christ Church College, Oxford, with the Archbishop of Canterbury at its head. The aim was to create a new Jerusalem in New Zealand for a middle-class Anglican community. The Association's ideals had a profound effect on the cultural identity of the city, evident in its elegant Victorian Gothic architecture and gridiron street plans.

The Pacific Islands

The Pacific Ocean extends from the Arctic to the Antarctic regions between North and South America on the east and Asia and Australia on the west, bisected by the International Date Line. It is connected with the Arctic Ocean by the Bering Strait; with the Atlantic Ocean by the Drake Passage, the Straits of Magellan and the Panama Canal; and with the Indian Ocean by passages in the Malay Archipelago. In all, the Pacific covers nearly one-third of the world's land surface – an area larger than all the Earth's land combined – but the thousands of islands in the Pacific have a total area of less than 1.3 million square kilometres, the bulk of which is in New Guinea, New Zealand and Hawaii. Seventeen independent states are located in the Pacific: Australia, Fiji, Japan, Kiribati, the Marshall Islands, Micronesia, Nauru, New Zealand, Palau, Papua New Guinea, the Philippines, Samoa, the Solomon

Islands, the Republic of China (Taiwan), Tonga, Tuvalu and Vanuatu. Eleven of these nations have achieved full independence since 1960. The Northern Mariana Islands are self-governing, with external affairs handled by the United States, and the Cook Islands and Niue are in similar relationships with New Zealand. Also within the Pacific are the US state of Hawaii and several island territories and possessions of Australia, Chile (such as Easter Island), Ecuador (including the Galapagos, p. 146), France, Japan, New Zealand, the United Kingdom and the United States.

The French explorer D'Urville divided the Pacific along racial and cultural grounds into three major subdivisions. Melanesia (the Greek for 'black islands') included New Guinea, the Solomon Islands, New Caledonia and Fiji. Micronesia ('small islands') encompasses many of the small islands north-east of New Guinea and the Solomons, and Polynesia ('many islands') includes the huge triangle of islands bounded by Hawaii, Easter Island and New Zealand. However, these geographical divisions are artificial, and in practice each island is different and has reached a different level of development for tourism. Rising sea levels as a result of global warming will cause flooding and coastal erosion in many Pacific countries, especially on low-lying coral atolls, and although high island countries, such as those in Melanesia, will be able to relocate their population (even at enormous cost), those living in countries composed only of atolls and low-lying islands such as Tuvalu will have no choice but to emigrate entirely to other countries, with the extinction of their unique cultures. The Government of Tuvalu is so concerned about overpopulation and rising sea levels that it has already purchased land in Fiji (the island of Kioa) and resettled some of its population, and is looking for more land. Some of the larger Melanesian nations, such as Vanuatu, New Caledonia and Fiji, have relatively strong economic positions because they are rich in mineral resources, agriculture and fisheries, while others, such as Tuvalu, are heavily reliant upon tourism, subsistence agriculture and fishing. More than one million visitors go to the South Pacific Islands each year, especially from the USA, Australia, Korea, New Zealand and France, with the most popular destinations being Fiji and French Polynesia. Over 20 per cent of jobs in Fiji are generated by tourism, although there are concerns about its environmental effects and social stresses. It has been estimated that about 15 per cent of Pacific Islanders live in other countries around the Pacific Rim, creating much business and leisure travel traffic between the Pacific Islands and developed nations. Many Pacific island emigrants living in the USA, New Zealand and Australia send a proportion of their earnings back home, and have also created a Pacific VRF market.

The Pacific Islands of the south and west were populated by Asian migrants who crossed long distances of open sea in primitive boats (Map 8.3). European travellers, including Marco Polo, had reported an ocean off Asia, and in the late fifteenth century trading ships had sailed around Africa to the western rim of the Pacific. However, recognition of the Pacific as distinct from the Atlantic Ocean dates from Balboa's sighting of its eastern shore in 1513. Magellan's crossing of the Philippines (1520–1521) initiated a series of explorations, including those of Drake, Tasman, Dampier, Cook, Bering and Vancouver, which by the end of the eighteenth century had disclosed the coastline and the major islands. In the sixteenth century, supremacy in the Pacific area was shared by Spain and Portugal. The English and the Dutch established footholds in the seventeenth century, France and Russia in the eighteenth century, and Germany, Japan and the United

States in the nineteenth century. Sealers and whalers sailed the Pacific from the late eighteenth century, and Yankee clippers entered Pacific trade in the early nineteenth century.

The first migrant people (known as Papuans) to reach the Pacific Islands arrived in New Guinea from South-East Asia via Indonesia.[12] They shared an ancestry with Australia's first Aboriginal people and moved slowly south and east, reaching the north Solomon Islands about 25 000 years ago, and gradually developing the maritime skills and technology necessary to cross increasingly wide stretches of open ocean. The wider stretch of ocean from the Solomons to Vanuatu was crossed in about 1500 BC by an Austronesian culture known as the Lapita. The culture we now know as Polynesian was derived from this, but developed in Fiji, Tonga and Samoa. The Lapita Polynesians of Tonga and Samoa eventually developed more advanced ocean vessels and the skills to cross longer ocean stretches to the east, in the direction of the Society Islands and the Marquesas (Map 8.3), reaching modern French Polynesia around 200 BC. From there the canoes travelled south-west around Tonga and the southern Cook Islands, south-east to Rapa Nui, north to Hawaii and south-west to New Zealand in a most remarkable feat of ocean sailing. Even the furthest islands of the Pacific were colonized by 200 BC, 1200 years before the Vikings crossed the Atlantic. The Melanesian people of New Guinea and the Solomons had regular ocean trade routes, and all Pacific nations travelled between the islands. Some traditional stories also indicate exploratory journeys into Antarctic waters. Ancient Pacific Islanders made voyages motivated by war, trade and colonization; in search of resources; and from curiosity and pride; the best were the Tongans (known as 'the Vikings of the Pacific'), who ruled Samoa and Fiji and raided over an ocean nearly 3000 kilometres across. Polynesian ocean-going canoes were giant vessels that accommodated hundreds of men and were sometimes 25 metres long carrying outriggers, one or more masts and sails, and capable of speeds greater than those of James Cook's first ships. They could travel 150–250 kilometres per day, so that trips of 5000 kilometres could be achieved without needing more provisions than could be carried on board. Initial exploratory journeys would often follow the migratory flights of birds. When a new land was discovered the route was remembered and communicated, together with complex navigational information including which stars to follow, wind directions, currents and the flight of land birds. Many European explorers were unable to believe that a Stone-Age culture without a written language or the use of the compass could have accomplished such amazing feats of navigation, but the evidence of a systematic migration from island to island is supported by linguistic, genetic, anthropological and archaeological studies, together with computer modelling of wind and currents. Archaeological sites do exist throughout the islands. Most take the visible form of ancient stone foundations upon which religious meeting places were built (the temples and houses were built from wood and coconut fronds, and have since eroded with time). Highlights include the sunken city of Nan Madol on Pohnpei Island in Micronesia, the Pumulei Stone mound on Savaii Island in Samoa (the largest known ancient structure in Polynesia), the Trilithon and ancient city of Lahapa on Tongatapu Island in Tonga, the To'aga archaeological site on Ofu Island in American Samoa with its spiritual significance, the tiki and paepae of Meiaute on Ua Huka Island in the Marquesas, and the Mailekini Heiau and City of Refuge Historic Park on the Big Island of Hawaii. However, the most famous site of all is still under the control of Chile – the *moai* of Rapa Nui (Easter Island; see Box 8.2, Plate 8.2).

Box 8.2:
Rapa Nui
(Easter Island)

Rapa Nui (Easter Island) is most famous for the gigantic stone statues whose abundance and distinctiveness has generated many theories about how and when they were made and moved. The island became well-known in the West as a result of the theories of Thor Heyerdahl, who suggested that it had been colonized from South America. The bleak island and its statues became the focus of a tourism industry (which grew dramatically after the 1970s) based entirely upon its heritage. Tourism now supports virtually the entire population.[13] Comprehensive archaeological work has provided extensive documentation about the pre-history of the island, from colonization by Polynesians around AD 400. Of the island land mass, 70 per cent is included in a National Park, designated as a World Heritage cultural landscape in 1996. However, tourism on the island is at the mercy of the Chilean national airline Lan Chile, which has a monopoly over incoming air routes. Easter Island is the most distant inhabited point in the world, being 3700 kilometres from mainland Chile and more than 4000 kilometres from Tahiti. Its early Polynesians settlers called the island 'O te hunua' (navel of the world), and the first European to see it was the Dutch explorer, Jacob Roggeveen, in 1720 on Easter Day. He described the island as a wasteland of barren rock and grass without a single tree over three metres high, yet it once supported lush tropical forest and a large population. The few remaining islanders that he saw had no native animals larger than insects, and the island is remarkable today for an almost complete absence of wildlife (apart from a few seabirds). The land, language and people are all referred to as Rapa Nui. Its strange *moai* stand on raised rectangular platforms (*ahu*), and there are also the remains of ancient houses and burial cairns, and artifacts including unidentified tablets that may be written in a Polynesian language, *rongorongo*. The large numbers of statues in what is today a bleak and inhospitable landscape have led to theories about the society that created them. Heyerdahl suggested they were made by Peruvians travelling from South America on the basis of similarities in the stonework and his own voyage which replaced a journey from South America to Polynesians. But his theory now has few supporters, and attempts are being made to make visitors aware of the island's Polynesian heritage. The Rapa Nui language is a Polynesian dialect related to Marquesan. The peak of statue construction took place around AD 1215, by which time the population was as high as 10 000 – far exceeding the resource capacity of the small island's ecosystem. Scarce resources and the destruction of lush palm forests, both by agriculture and by cutting timber to transport more than 1000 statues, probably plunged a thriving complex society into decline. The statues are seen on the island in varying stages of completion, the largest being up to eleven metres high and weighing eighty-two tonnes. Modern archaeological evidence suggests that even the largest statue could have been completed by around twenty carvers within a year. Forest clearance was well underway by AD 800, and the final palm trees became extinct around 1400, at the same time the statue carving stopped. The subsequent history of the island included cultural decline into a very small remnant population, sheep-farming, annexation by Chile, and the construction of a large runway by NASA as an emergency landing strip for the Space Shuttle. Easter Island remains the major heritage tourism destination of the Pacific, with over 10 000 tourists per year.

Just as the Pacific Islanders had done before them, European explorers came into the Pacific in search of gold and spices. Some were driven by the pervasive myth of *Terra australis*, the great southern continent which had, since the time of Ptolemy, been predicted to exist in the southern hemisphere, to balance the Earth's northern continents. Its absence was only realized after the voyages of Magellan, who became the first person to circumnavigate the globe, having previously visited the Philippines from the other direction. A series of Spanish Dutch and French expeditions followed those of Magellan, during the late sixteenth and early seventeenth centuries, which discovered Tonga, Bora Bora and the Society Islands in 1722. As we have already seen, Able Tasman charted Tasmania and the east coast of New Zealand in 1642, and then sailed on to make contact with the islands of Tonga and Fiji. The most famous and successful figure in the history of early Pacific exploration is Captain James Cook,[14] who made three voyages, in 1768–1771, 1772–1775 and 1776–1780 (Map 8.3). Within these expeditions he charted New Zealand, New Caledonia and the Pacific coast of Australia, landed on Tahiti, Tonga and the Cook Islands, and finally charted and landed on Hawaii, where he met his death. Another famous navigator (for a less elevated purpose) was the infamous Captain Bligh, whose crew on the *HMS Bounty* mutinied, casting him adrift in Tongan waters in a small wooden boat which he managed to sail to Fiji and, eventually, to the nearest European settlement at Dutch Timor, some 5000 miles away.[15]

The first missionary outposts in the Pacific were established by the London Missionary Society in 1797 on Tahiti Island, the Marquesas Islands and Tonga. In the 1820s the Bible was translated into Tahitian, and its people travelled the Pacific to spread the gospel, with enormous success. By the mid-1800s, whaling, sandalwood trade, beache-de-mer and 'blackbirding' (recruitment of indigenous people to sailing ships against their will) were making merchants rich. European outposts were being established, and the gradual demolition of the numerous traditional Pacific cultures was begun. European trade routes into the Pacific date from the late eighteenth century, peaking in the mid-nineteenth century, by which time Europeans trading with China had been impressed by the Chinese use of fragrant sandalwood for ornamental carving in cabinet-making as well as for burning as incense.[16] As a result of this, by the 1820s traders had stripped the sandalwood forests of Hawaii and forests on the islands to the south-west, including Fiji, the Solomons and New Caledonia, but the trade was soon to become unsustainable. Island after island was stripped out, and the trade finished around the 1860s with the removal of the last accessible stands of timber. By the late nineteenth century cheap labour was being sought for mines and plantations, and Pacific Islanders were recruited for Australia from Fiji, New Caledonia and Samoa – sometimes voluntarily, but often being tricked into boarding ships or sometimes herded at gunpoint, a practice known as 'blackbirding'.[17] People were taken as slaves from many islands in the Southern Pacific until the end of the nineteenth century, when the trade was abolished as a result of lobbying by missionaries.

Fletcher Christian, who had evicted Captain Bligh from the *Bounty*, was to discover Tonga and the southern Cook Islands in 1789. The French explorer Louis Antoine de Bougainville discovered Tahiti and claimed it for France in 1768, going on to discover Samoa and Australia's Great Barrier Reef. His accounts of the South Pacific sparked massive interest in Europe, and created the myth of a southern paradise of palm-fringed beaches, blue water and friendly tropical maidens – an image still heavily used in tourism promotion today.[18] Explorers returned to

Europe with traditional artifacts and stories of South Sea Islands in the late eighteenth century, painting a picture of an earthly paradise uncorrupted by the modern world. This motivated many artists and writers to visit, including Paul Gaugin, W. Somerset Maugham and Robert Louis Stevenson. A legacy of quite a different kind that was brought back to Europe was tattooing. The word comes from the Polynesian *tatau*, and until the eighteenth century full-body tattoos were common throughout many of the South Pacific Islands. Although this practice was discouraged by missionary activity, it did pass to British officers and crewmen returning from Pacific voyages in the late eighteenth and early nineteenth centuries, and even Sir Joseph Banks had tattoos done in Tahiti – as did the *Bounty* mutineers. European seamen often acquired tattoos, a fashion copied furtively by nineteenth century European aristocracy and which has now become widespread.[19]

Colonial takeovers in the South Pacific were gradual, with the French annexing French Polynesian in the 1840s and New Caledonia in 1853. Britain ended up as the largest of all the Pacific empires after being forced by various lobby groups to assume responsibility for islands, including Fiji and the Southern Solomons, up until 1906, although several islands were later offloaded onto New Zealand. The Pacific was a major arena of conflict during the Second World War, when Japan extended its activities south and south-west from its Micronesian possessions until 1942, when it was turned back at the Battle of the Coral Sea and in the North Pacific at the Battle of Midway. From 1944 the USA pushed the Japanese back island by island, eventually right back to Japan, with the war in the Pacific ending in 1945 after the dropping of atomic bombs on Hiroshima and Nagasaki in southern Japan. Many Pacific islands suffered greatly under Japanese occupation, but one positive legacy of the Pacific war was a huge improvement in roads and other infrastructure on many islands. The war ended traditional colonialism in the Pacific, and the relative equality between white and black USA soldiers prompted islanders to question why they were still subservient to the British and the French. From Western Samoa in 1962 through to Vanuatu in 1980, most of the Pacific Islands states gained independence or partial independence from the former colonial rulers, and at the end of the twentieth century only a handful of South Pacific territories were still in the hands of the USA, France, Chile and New Zealand.

Today's Pacific island tourism product still centres on beach tourism.[20] However, diving tourism is particularly important in Tahiti and French Polynesia, as well as in Fiji and the Solomon Islands (where Guadalcanal Island has many shipwrecks from the Second World War battle, resting close to the shore). Fiji is one of the most influential of the Pacific nations and, despite recent political upheaval, has a strong tourist infrastructure.[21] The Fiji Archipelago includes about 300 islands, of which only about one-third are inhabited, and has a damp tropical climate which has produced luxuriant vegetation. Sugar was the mainstay of the economy for most of the twentieth century, together with tourism helped by the fact that the archipelago is a popular stopover between North America and Australia or New Zealand and is accessible to young people on round-the-world air tickets. New Caledonia still has a decidedly French feel and is located in the south-west of the Pacific, surrounded by the world's second-largest coral reef. It has been a bastion of French culture since 1853 and is now an official 'special territorial entity' within the French Republic, whose inhabitants are currently French citizens. Tourists visit the tiny Pitcairn Island because of its fame as the home of the *Bounty* mutineers in 1790, when they were looking for a remote hideaway to help escape British naval justice. Pitcairn Island is one of the last remnants of the British Empire, though the viability of the population is now in jeopardy following multiple criminal charges against nine male islanders in the child sex trials of 2003.[22]

In the northern Pacific islands tourism is dominated by Hawaii, first settled by Polynesians from the Marquesas sometime between AD 200 and 600. Captain Cook visited them in 1778, and named them the Sandwich Islands after the First Lord of the Admiralty, the 4th Earl of Sandwich, John Montagu. Until the 1890s the kingdom of Hawaii was independent and had been recognized by the United States, Great Britain, France and Germany, with exchange of ambassadors, but Hawaii is now the USA's fiftieth state, with the highest standard of living in the north Pacific (with the exception of Japan). Hawaii's isolation from the world has created a unique and thriving natural environment with stunning and diverse scenery, from tropical rainforests to active volcanoes. Its component islands are very different. More than four million visitors go to Oahu each year for the beaches and shopping malls of Waikiki, as well as to see Pearl Harbour and (increasingly) for golf.[23] The Big Island is by far the largest island in the far south of the group, with a population of only 140 000, but receives over a million tourists each year, principally attracted by the stunning tropical scenery, diving and game fishing. Maui, by contrast, is a glamorous beach destination, with lots of large international hotels and condominium complexes, although the historic whaling port of Lahaina does give some feel for the history of the island, which is famous today as one of the world's major whale-watching destinations. Kauai, the garden island, is much quieter than Maui, with equally good beaches. Molokai and Lanai have a far less developed tourist infrastructure.

Just as Hawaii predominates in tourism in the northern Pacific, Fiji dominates in the south-west, with more than 300 islands visited by 400 000 tourists a year, and a highly developed tourist infrastructure. Europeans 'discovered' the Fiji Islands in 1643, but it was not until after the mutiny on the *Bounty* in 1789 that contact with the people was made. Over the next 100 years, trade and wars occurred and friendships were made between rival Europeans and rival Fijian tribes. The British brought colonial rule and introduced Indian labourers to the new sugar plantations, but Fiji regained its independence by mutual consent in 1970. Fiji is generally reckoned to be one of the world's best destinations for a beach holiday, with a highly-developed dive-tourism industry profiting from excellent water visibility (often more than fifty metres) and high water temperatures of 26–29°C. Western Samoa, officially known as Independent Samoa, also attracts beach tourists, but is far less developed than Fiji, with the town of Apia and considerable authentic Polynesian culture as well. Neighbouring American Samoa, just 100 kilometres to the south-east, shares an identical culture and language, but was taken over by America in 1899 and remains a US territory. Although its traditional culture and lifestyle have been eroded on the outside, the people are still very much Polynesians at heart and the island has some significant archaeological sites. The Tonga Islands form the only South Pacific country not colonized by Europeans, and remain the only monarchy in the region. Tonga once ruled much of its neighbouring islands, wielding enormous power throughout Polynesia. Tourism to the Cook Islands (a collection of fifteen small islands in the heart of the Polynesian South Pacific) is developing rapidly, especially around the main high island of Rarotonga and the lagoon island of Aitutaki.[24] The Cook Islands are a self-governing dependency of New Zealand, with their own parliament. The Tahiti Islands, known officially as French Polynesia, comprise thirty-five islands and eighty-three atolls in the eastern South Pacific, and were made famous by the mutiny of the *Bounty*, and the paintings of Paul Gauguin. Neighbouring Moorea includes the famous lagoon of Bora Bora, with its picturesque setting and picture-postcard white palm-fringed beaches. The remote Marquesas Islands in the north and Astral Islands in the south are both rich in culture and archaeological sights, and offer splendid and dramatic coastal scenery. Micronesia includes thousands of tiny islands and many dependent and independent states in the North Pacific, and is visited mainly for scuba-diving. Guam is perhaps the best known of the islands and certainly the most visited, with a particular appeal to American and Japanese visitors. New arrivals on the tourism scene include the Northern Marianas, taking in Tinian and Saipan (Map 8.3), which are becoming significant diving tourism destinations. The Solomon Islands are an amazing collection of almost 1000 islands lying to the south of Papua New Guinea. Over half of the islands remain uninhabited, and many are in secluded groups far from the main centre of Guadalcana. The Solomon Islands boast some of the most spectacular scuba-diving reefs in the world, and are renowned for an abundance of soft corals and wreck-diving. The tourist infrastructure is very limited, making exploring the many islands both time-consuming and challenging. Yet in the Solomon Islands we can see the major factors that have shaped tourism in the Pacific: the influence of distance, the legacy of the early Polynesians, the period when the resources of the island's sandalwood forests were being plundered, a time of British control, and subsequent independence – and today, a significant dive-tourism industry whose mainstay is wrecks, especially those in Guadalcanal, which have resulted from the war in the Pacific. Once again the economy of the islands is dependent upon its marine resources, and they achieved independence from British rule in 1978. But since then internal disputes over land ownership between 'indigenous' islanders and 'immigrants' resulted in economic difficulties which its government tried to reverse by indiscriminate logging, a policy which has since ceased, although a level of internal unrest still continues. The Solomon Islands' main industrial prospect lies in their mostly undeveloped mineral resources, especially gold, but the tourism industry now attracts around US$15 million per year, although it is affected by worries over security.

Notes

Chapter 1: Setting the scene

1 Crouch, G. I. and Ritchie, J. R. B. (1999), Tourism, competitiveness, and societal prosperity, *Journal of Business Research*, **44**, 137–152; Fessenmaier, D. and Uysal, M. (1990), The tourism system: levels of economic and human behavior, *in* J. B. and L. M. Caneday (eds), *Tourism and Leisure: Dynamics and Diversity*, National Recreation and Park Association, Alexandria, VA, pp. 27–35; Gunn, C. A. (1994), *Tourism Planning* (3rd edn), Taylor & Francis; Heath, E. and Wall, G. (1992), *Marketing Tourism Destinations: A Strategic Planning Approach*, John Wiley & Sons, Inc.

2 Driscoll, A., Lawson, R. and Niven, B. (1994), Measuring tourists' destination perceptions, *Annals of Tourism Research*, **21(3)**, 499–511; Leiper, N. (1990), Tourist attraction system, *Annals of Tourism Research*, **17**, 367–384; Lew, A. A. (1994), A framework of tourist attraction research, *in* J. R. B. Ritchie and M. R. Goeldner, *Travel, Tourism and Hospitality Research* (2nd edn), pp. 291–297; Ross, G. F. (1994), *The Psychology of Tourism*, Hospitality Press; Uysal, M. (1998), The determinants of tourism demand: a theoretical perspective, *in* D. Ioannides and K. G. Debbage (eds), *The Economic Geography of the Tourist Industry*, Routledge, pp. 79–98.

3 There are several atlases which present a general overview of world history, data from many of which have been used in this book. They include: *Atlas of World History* (2005), Dorling Kindersley; *The Times Compact History of the World* (2005); *Atlas of World History* (2002), Oxford University Press; *Penguin Atlas of World History* (2004), Penguin Press; McEvedy, C. and Woodcock, J. (2002), *New Penguin Atlas of Ancient History*, Penguin; *Atlas of World History* (2005), Collins.

4 Pausanias wrote his *Guidebook of Greece* between AD 160 and 180, and it is the only guidebook to survive from the classical world.

5 Ryan, C., Page, S. and Aicken, M. (eds) (2004), *Taking Tourism to the Limits; Issues, Concepts and Managerial Perspectives*.

6 Herodotus's *History of the Persian Wars* was something new, making him the world's first travel writer and historian. He seems to have spent most of his life abroad, exploring the Greek and Persian world, and made a number of individual journeys, although he is best known for his travels in Egypt *c.* 450 BC.

7 Some time in the third century BC a scholar who probably lived in Alexandria devised a list of the 'Seven Wonders of the World', itemizing what his contemporaries would consider to be major man-made visitor attractions. Most were already ancient. The list included the Pyramids, the Hanging Gardens at Babylon, the Statue of Zeus at Olympia, the Temple of Artemis at Ephesus, the Mausoleum, the Colossus of Rhodes and the Lighthouse at Alexandria.

8 The modern World Heritage List includes all the major natural and cultural sites which have been put forward for designation, and is updated annually.

9 Shackley, M. (2001), The legend of Robin Hood: myth, inauthenticity, and tourism development in Nottingham, England, *in* V. L. Smith and M. Brent (eds), *Hosts and Guests Revisited; Tourism Issues of the 21st Century*, Brent Cognizant Communications Corporation, pp. 315–323.

10 Casson, L. (1974), *Travel in the Ancient World*, George Allen & Unwin.

11　The film *Gone with the Wind* was made in 1939, based on the novel by Margaret Mitchell.

12　The film version of J. R. R. Tolkein's *Lord of the Rings* trilogy emerged between 2001 and 2003, was directed by Peter Jackson, and is famous for its special effects and magnificent New Zealand landscapes. The original books were published in 1954, but have been re-issued in many different formats and were recently voted 'Book of the Century'.

13　'Soft adventure' is often defined as adventure travel which retains an element of comfort and control. An example might be a guided visit to a National Park in the developing world, as opposed to a serious expedition involving some hardship and discomfort.

14　Casson, L. (1974), *Travel in the Ancient World*, George Allen & Unwin.

15　Casson, L. (1959), *The Ancient Mariners*, Allen & Unwin; Leeman, W. (1968), Seagoing commerce in the late 3rd millennium BC, *Journal of the Economic and Social History of the Orient*, pp. 215–216.

16　Burkart, A. J. and Medlik, S. (1974), *Tourism; Past, Present and Future*, Heinemann.

17　The Great Exhibition can reasonably be said to have marked the beginning of the era of managed visitor attractions.

18　For the expedition of Harkhuf, see Casson, L. (1974), *Travel in the Ancient World*, George Allen & Unwin, pp. 28–29.

19　Allen, B. (2002), *The Faber Book of Exploration*, Faber.

20　Cohen, E. (1988), Authenticity and commodization in tourism, *Annals of Tourism Research*, **15**, 371–386; Fawcett, C. and Cormack, P. (2001), Guarding authenticity at literary tourism sites, *Annals of Tourism Research*, **28**, 686–704; MacCannell, D. (1973), Staged authenticity; arrangements of social space in tourist settings, *American Journal of Sociology*, **79(3)**, 589–603; Selwyn, T. (ed.) (1996), *The Tourist Image; Myths and Myth Making in Tourism*, John Wiley & Sons, Inc.

21　Urry, J. (1990), *The Tourist Gaze; Leisure and Travel in Contemporary Societies*, Sage; Urry, J. (1995), *Consuming Places*, Routledge.

22　Burkart, A. J. and Medlik, S. (1974), *Tourism; Past, Present and Future*, Heinemann.

23　Casson, L. (1959), *The Ancient Mariners*, Allen & Unwin; Leeman, W. (1968), Seagoing commerce in the late 3rd millennium BC, *Journal of the Economic and Social History of the Orient*, pp. 215–216.

24　Oppenheim, A. (1954), The seafaring merchants of Ur, *Journal of the American Oriental Society*, **74**, 6–17.

25　Yoyotte, J. (1960), Les pelerinnages dans l'Egypte ancienne, *in Les Pelerinnages, Sources Orientales*, Vol. 3. Gardiner, A. (1961), *Egypt of the Pharaohs*, Oxford University Press.

26　Lucas, A. and Harris, J. (1962), *Ancient Egyptian Materials and Industries*.

27　James, G. H. (2001), *Howard Carter – The Path to Tutankhamun*, Tauris Parke; Reeves, N. and Taylor, J. H. (1992), *Howard Carter: Before Tutankhamun*, British Museum Press; *The Search for Tutankhamun*, from the Griffith Institute website, includes Howard Carter's records of the five seasons of excavations, financed by Lord Carnarvon, in the Valley of the Kings between 1915 and 1922.

28　Littauer, M. and Crouvel, J. (1979), *Wheeled Vehicles and Ridden Animals in the Ancient Near East*, Leiden University Press.

29　Evans, A. (1921–35), *The Palace of Minos at Knossos*.

30 Levi, A. and Levi, M. (1967), *Intineraria picta*, Contributo alto Studo della Tabula Peutingeriana, Rome.

31 'mcadam' was developed by J. L. McAdam in the early 1980s to create a strong free-draining road surface. It consisted of creating three layers of hand-broken aggregates laid on a sloped base with side ditches for drainage. The top layer was of finer stone, and all were compacted with a heavy roller to lock the stones together. However, after the invention of the motor car the roads became dusty, a problem eventually solved by spraying them with tar to create 'tarmac'. Even though tarmac roads are now rare the name remains as a generic term for a made-up road.

32 Marco Polo (1254–1324) is probably the most famous European traveller on the Silk Road. He travelled through Asia for twenty-four years, and became a confidant of Kublai Khan (1214–1294). His account *The Description of the World* or *The Travels of Marco Polo* became one of the most popular books in medieval Europe, but was known as *Il Milione* (The Million Lies) because few believed that his stories were true.

33 The Dissolution of the Monasteries was ordered by Henry VIII in 1538, with the aim of breaking the power of the Church and redistributing its wealth. The smaller and less powerful houses were the first to have their property confiscated – a process partly motivated by greed, since much of the wealth was retained by the king. Some monastic buildings were sold to wealthy gentry for use as country estates, while others became sources of cheap building materials for local people. The Dissolution also resulted in the removal of both a support system for travellers and the provision of many health and religious services for local communities.

34 The Protestant work ethic is a biblically based teaching on the necessity of hard work as a means to achieve the good of society, attain eventual salvation and atone for original sin. It was promulgated by post-Reformation Protestant theologians such as John Calvin.

35 A turnpike is a road that has a gate or barrier preventing access until a toll has been paid. In England most turnpikes were developed in the eighteenth century and eventually controlled 35 000 miles (56 000 km) of road. Money raised by the turnpike system allowed improved roads, which helped the development of passenger coaches and a national postal service. The turnpike idea is still used today to charge for popular motorway-type roads in America and Europe.

36 Turner, J. (1996), *An Historical Geography of Recreation and Tourism in the Western World 1540–1940*, John Wiley & Sons, Inc.

37 Page, S. (2003), *Tourism Management*, Butterworth-Heinemann.

38 Page, S. J. (1999) *Transport and Tourism*, Pearson Education.

39 Burkart, A. J. and Medlik, S. (1974), *Tourism; Past, Present and Future*, Heinemann.

40 Page, S. (1994), *Transport for Tourism*.

41 Ward, C. and Hardy, D. (1986), *Goodnight Campers; The History of the British Holiday Camp*, Mansell.

42 The French Riviera contains the resorts of Menton, Monaco, Nice, Antibes and Cannes along the mediterranean coast of France. It became fashionable in the late nineteenth and early twentieth centuries, and was particularly popular with the British upper classes for its mild winter climate. Today, it is regarded as one of the most luxurious, expensive and sophisticated areas in the world.

43 *Luxury Hotels; Europe* (2006), TeNeues Publishing; Bonet, L. (2005), *Cool Hotels; Asia/Pacific*, TeNeues Publishing; Ypma, H. (2004), *Hip Hotels; Beach*, Thames and Hudson.

44 Butler, R. W. (1980) The concept of a tourist area lifecycle of evolution and implications for management of resources, *Canadian Geographer*, **24(1)**, 5–12; Plog, S. (1973), Why destination areas rise and fall in popularity, *Cornell Hotel and Restaurant Administration Quarterly*, **14(3)**, 13–16.

45 Page, S. (2003), *Tourism Management*, Butterworth-Heinemann.

46 http://www.spacetourismcoeity.org; http://www.spacefuture.com/tourism; http://www.virgingalactic.com.

47 http://www.spacetourismcoeity.org; http://www.spacefuture.com/tourism; http://www.virgingalactic.com.

48 The Voyager Holodeck, at http://www.startrek.com/startrek/view/series/VOY/

Chapter 2: Middle East and North Africa: ancient empires

1 World Tourism Organization (2005), *Tourism Market Trends 2004 – Africa*, WTO.

2 http://www.datadubai.com

3 Narmer, first pharoah of the 1st Dynasty, is credited with the unification of Upper and Lower Egypt.

4 Herodotus's *History of the Persian Wars* was something new, making him the world's first travel writer and historian. He seems to have spent most of his life abroad, exploring the Greek and Persian world, and made a number of individual journeys, although he is best known for his travels in Egypt *c.* 450 BC.

5 Casson, L. (1974), *Travel in the Ancient World*, George Allen & Unwin, p. 32.

6 Pliny the Elder, writing in the second half of the first century BC. His *Natural History* was the first known book (in thirty-seven sections) in the form of an encyclopaedia.

7 Napoleon's invasion of Egypt brought its ancient civilization to the attention of the western world, and was instrumental in laying the groundwork for modern Egyptology.

8 Williamson, A. (1998), *The Golden age of Travel*, Thomas Cook Publishing.

9 Beirman, D. (2003), *Restoring Tourism Destinations in Crisis; A Strategic Marketing Approach*, CABI Publishing.

10 The removal and reconstruction of the two great temples of Abu Simbel (of Rameses II and his wife Nefertari) was necessary when they were threatened by submersion in Lake Nasser, due to the construction of the High Dam. The Egyptian Government secured the support of UNESCO and launched a salvage operation, which took place between 1964 and 1968. During this operation, the two temples were dismantled and raised over 60 metres up the sandstone cliff to be reassembled, in exactly the same relationship, where they had been built more than 3000 years before.

11 James, G. H. (2001), *Howard Carter – The Path to Tutankhamun*, Tauris Parke; Reeves, N. and Taylor, J. H. (1992), *Howard Carter: Before Tutankhamun*, British Museum Press; *The Search for Tutankhamun*, from the Griffith Institute website, includes Howard Carter's records of the five seasons of excavations, financed by Lord Carnarvon, in the Valley of the Kings between 1915 and 1922.

Tutankhamun (or Tutankhamen) was an eighteenth dynasty New Kingdom boy pharoah who ruled from 1334 to 1325 BC. His is the only pharoah's tomb to be discovered (relatively) intact, by Howard Carter, in 1922.

12 There any many academic concerns about the environmental impact of tourists visiting the Tombs in the Valley of the Kings and Valley of the Queens near Luxor. Take, for example, the tomb of Nefertari, wife of Rameses II (see McDonald, J. (1996), *House of Eternity : The Tomb of Nefertari (Culture and Conservation)*, Reed Business Information Inc). Nefertari's tomb has only been open to the public since 1995, although it was found in 1904. It is widely considered to be one of the most beautiful Egyptian tombs, mainly because of its wall paintings, which were conserved between 1986 and 1992 by a partnership of the Egyptian Antiquities Organization and the Getty Conservation Institute. Despite restricting public access, damage to the paintings caused the tomb to be closed to the public again in 2003.

13 Farnie, D. A. (1969), *East and West of Suez: The Suez Canal in History, 1854–1956*.

14 Much of southern Sinai is now enclosed in a system of Protected Areas/National Parks, but is under increasing visitor pressure because of the rapid expansion of tourism to new coastal resorts, especially Sharm el Sheikh.

15 Shackley, M. (1999), A golden calf in sacred space? The future of St Katherine's Monastery, Mount Sinai (Egypt). *International Journal of Heritage Studies*, **4**, 123–134.

16 The annual *haj* (pilgrimage) to Mukkah (Mecca) in Saudi Arabia attracts more than two million Muslim visitors per year, and has generated an entire tourism infrastructure along with many problems with crowding, security and accommodation.

17 T. E. Lawrence's *Seven Pillars of Wisdom* (1928) tells of the campaign of the Arabs against the Turks in the Middle East during the First World War. The film *Lawrence of Arabia*, starring Peter O'Toole, was released in 1962 to universal acclaim.

18 Shackley, M. (2006), Frankincense and myrrh today, *in* D. Peacock and D. Williams (eds), *Food for the Gods; New Light on the Ancient Incense Trade*, Oxbow Books, Chapter 8.

19 Burkart, A. J. and Medlik, S. (1974), *Tourism; Past, Present and Future*, Heinemann.

20 Shackley, M. (2002), The frankincense route – a proposed cultural itinerary for the Middle East, *in* M. Truscott and S. J. Brazil (eds), *Historic Environment*, Australian UNESCO, pp. 356–373.

21 Thesiger, W. (1959), *Arabian Sands*, Longmans.

22 Kings 10, 1–13.

23 Matthew 1, 13–15.

24 Ezekiel, Ch. 26–27.

25 St Anthony was born in the Upper Egypt town of Coma near Heracleopolis in the year AD 251. He became a hermit and, along with St Pachomius, is widely regarded as the ancestor of the Christian monastic tradition which originated in Egypt. He is buried beneath one of the ancient churches (St Antony) of the Coptic monastery (Deir Mar Antonios); together with its neighbour St Paul's, these are the oldest inhabited monasteries in Egypt. Today the monastery is virtually a self-contained village, with gardens, a mill, a bakery and five churches.

26 Casson, L. (1974), *Travel in the Ancient World*, George Allen & Unwin, p. 32.

27 Piggott op. cit.

28 Lane Fox, R. (1994), *Alexander the Great*, Penguin.

29 Thesiger, W. (1969), *The Marsh Arabs*, Longmans; Maitland, A. (2005), *Wilfred Thesiger: The Life of the Great Explorer*, Harper Press.

30 Casson, L. (1971), *Ships and Seamanship in the Ancient World*, Princeton.

31 Quataert, D. (2005), *The Ottoman Empire, 1700–1922 (New Approaches to European History 5)*, Cambridge University Press.

32 Shackley, M. (1998), Visitors to the world's oldest cities – Aleppo and Damascus (Syria), *in* D. Tyler, M. Robertson and Y. Guerrier (eds), *Managing Tourism in Cities*, John Wiley & Sons, Inc., pp. 183–197.

33 Shackley, M. (2004), Managing the Cedars of Lebanon: botanical gardens or living forests? *Current Issues in Tourism*, **7(4&5)**, 97–106 (Special Issue): *The Politics of World Heritage: Thirty Years on from the World Heritage*.

34 Homer, *The Iliad* (trans. Robert Fagles), Penguin Classics, 1990.

35 In 1870, a German entrepreneur called Heinrich Schliemann set out, with *Iliad* in hand, to discover the ancient city of Troy and validate the story of Homer. Schliemann began excavating at the Turkish site of Hissarlik in 1870. By 1873, he had unearthed a sequence of cities. There, in 1873, he discovered what he thought was Homer's Troy, Ilium, although this was found later to be incorrect.

36 The 2004 Hollywood film *Troy* starred Brad Pitt as Achilles, and gave writing credits to Homer.

37 The implementation of the 2010 tourism strategy is provided for in the agreement signed by the Moroccan Government and the national tourism federation in 2001, and is targeted to attract ten million tourists to Morocco in 2010. The project is behind schedule due to poor coordination in the various projects, and a delay in the restructuring plan of the tourism ministry and the national tourism office (ONMPT). Rural and mountain tourism has made the most progress.

38 Films recently shot in Morocco include Mel Gibson's *The Passion of the Christ* and *Gladiator*, starring Russell Crowe.

Chapter 3: Africa: slavery and safari

1 Boniface, S. and Cooper, S. (2005), *Worldwide Destinations; The Geography of Travel and Tourism*, Elsevier.

2 Herodotus's *History of the Persian Wars* was something new, making him the world's first travel writer and historian. He seems to have spent most of his life abroad, exploring the Greek and Persian world, and made a number of individual journeys, although he is best known for his travels in Egypt *c.* 450 BC.

3 Casson, L. (1974), *Travel in the Ancient World*, George Allen & Unwin.

4 Pliny the Elder, writing in the second half of the first century BC. His *Natural History* was the first known book (in thirty-seven sections) in the form of an encyclopaedia.

5 See 1.6.

6 Ibn Battuta, *Travels in Asia and Africa 1325–1354*; Macintosh-Smith, T. (2002), *Travels with a Tangerine; A Journey in the Footsteps of Ibn Battuta*, Picador.

7 Maalouf, A. and Sluglett, P. (1990), *Leo Africanus*, New Amsterdam Books.

8. Caillie, R., *Travels Through Central Africa to Timbuctoo 1830*.

9 http://www.whs.com

10 http://charlesdefoucauld.com

11 http://www.whs.com

12 Park, M. (1799), *Travels into the Interior of Africa*.

13 Allen, B. (2002), *The Faber Book of Exploration*, Faber.

14 *The Three Voyages of Vasco da Gama and His Viceroyalty*, trans. H. E. J. Stanley, 1869.

15 http://www.africanhistory

16 Dieke, P. (2003), Tourism in Africa's economic development: policy implications, *Management Decision*, **41(3)**, 287–295.

17 http://www.ghanatourism.gov

18 Haley, A. (1980), *Roots*, Dell Books.

19 http://www.unesco.org/slave

20 http://www.africaculture.dk/gambia/concern

21 Kingsley, M. (1897), *Travels in West Africa*.

22 Lloyd, A. (1900), *In Dwarf Land and Cannibal Country*.

23 Turnbull, C. (1984), *The Forest People*, Isis Books.

24 Greenfield, J. and Magnusson, M. (1996), *The Return of Cultural Treasures*, Cambridge University Press.

25 Durrell, G. (1958), *The Bafut Beagles*, Hart-Davis.

26 Novelli, M. and Humavindu (2005), Wildlife tourism – wildlife vs local gain:trophy hunting in Namibia, *in* M. Novelli (ed.), *Niche Tourism*, Elsevier, pp. 171–183.

27 http://www.mountaingorillas.org

28 Bruce, J. (1790), *Travels to the Source of the Nile*.

29 Livingstone, D. (1857), *Missionary Travels and Researches in South Africa*.

30 Stanley, H. M. (1878), *Through the Dark Continent*.

31 Cooper, F. (2005), *Colonialism in Question: Theory, Knowledge, History*, University of California Press.

32 Huxley, E. (2000), *The Flame Trees of Thika; Memories of an African Childhood*, Penguin.

33 The 'Happy Valley set' was the popular name for expatriate white (mainly English) settlers in Kenya during the 1940s who became notorious for their debauchery.

34 The film *Out of Africa* (1985), which starred Robert Redford and Meryl Streep, was based on the book by Karen Blixen/Isaac Dinesen (Penguin, 2004).

35 Boniface, S. and Cooper, S. (2005), *Worldwide Destinations; The Geography of Travel and Tourism*, Elsevier.

36 Deike, P. (2000), *The Political Economy of Tourism Development in Africa*, Cognizant Communications.

37 http://www.responsibletravel.com

38 Gamble, W. P. (1989), *Tourism and Development in Africa*, Murray.

39 http://www.southafricatravel-net

40 Shackley, M. (2002), Potential futures for Robben Island; shrine, museum or theme park? *International Journal of Heritage Studies*, **7(4)**, 355–365.

41 McBride, A. (1996), *The Zulu Wars*, Osprey.

42 Rider Haggard, H. (1998), *She*, and *King Solomon's Mines*, Penguin Paperback editions.

43 http://www.ccafrica.com

44 Shackley, M. (1998), Tourism and the management of cultural resources in the Pays Dogon, Mali, *International Journal of Heritage Studies*, **3(1)**, 17–27.

Chapter 4: Asia: culture and colonialism

1 Moenjo Daro (Mound of the Dead) was discovered in 1922 on the West Bank of the River Indus. It was the centre of one of the earliest and the most developed urban civilizations of ancient world, which lasted until the middle of the second millennium BC. Moenjo Daro itself was excavated by Sir Mortimer Wheeler.

2 There are five main accounts of the life of Alexander the Great, by Arrian, Curtius, Plutarch, Diodorus and Justin. The most reliable is generally thought to be that of Arrian, who used material from Alexander's generals Ptolemy and Nearchus. *Historiae Alexandri Magni*, by the Roman historian Quintus Curtius Rufus, was written much later.

3 The twenty Hindu and Jain temples at Khajuraho were built between AD 950 and 1050, and are especially famous for their sculptures.

4 Airey, D. and Shackley, M. (1999), Bukhara (Uzbekistan), a former oasis town on the Silk Road, *in* M. Shackley (ed.), *Visitor Management; Case Studies from World Heritage Sites*, Butterworth Heinemann, pp. 10–25.

5 The Taj Mahal on the banks of the Yamuna River in Agra, north India, is probably the most recognizable building in the world. It was built as a tomb for Mumtaz Mahal, the wife of the Mughal Emperor Shah Jahan. Work began in 1633, and involved 20 000 workers for 17 years.

6 The East India Company dominated trade and commercial affairs between India and Great Britain from the early eighteenth century. In 1717, the Company received a royal dictate from the Mughal Emperor exempting the Company from the payment of custom duties, and a victory by Sir Robert Clive at the Battle of Plassey in 1757 established it as a military as well as a commercial power.

7 http://www.hcilondon.net

8 Collins, L. and Lapierre, D. (1997), *Freedom at Midnight*, HarperCollins.

9 The Khyber Pass is the most important pass connecting Pakistan with Afghanistan, and has been an important trade and invasion route throughout history. It was the route taken by Alexander the Great.

10 The film *A Passage to India*, based on the book by E. M. Forster, was released in 1984 and directed by David Lean.

11 The Kumbh Mela in India is the largest religious gathering in the world and occurs four times every twelve years, once at each of four potential locations. Each twelve-year cycle includes the Maha (great) Kumbha Mela at Prayag, attended by millions of people, making it the largest pilgrimage gathering in the world. In 2001 the Kumbh Mela was the final festival of twelve cycles – the conclusion of a giant 144-year cycle,

making it 'Maha' Kumbh Mela – the Great Festival. It drew an estimated seventy million people over forty-four days, making this the largest single gathering of humanity in recorded history.

12 Project Tiger was formed in 1972 and launched on 1 April 1973 at Corbett National Park. Its aims were to ensure maintenance of a viable population of tigers in India for scientific, economic, aesthetic, cultural and ecological reasons, and to preserve areas of such biological importance as a national heritage for the benefit, education and enjoyment of the people. Project Tiger initially established nine reserves, across different ecosystems. These were devoted specifically to saving the tiger and eliminating those factors which were contributing to its decline, including habitat destruction and poaching. However, lack of funding in many of the reserves (including Ranthambore) means that poaching tigers has continued, with the result that some of the Project Tigers reserves probably now contain no tigers.

13 Trekking to Ladakh, and its capital Leh, has been increasing in popularity over the past fifteen years. The Zanskar valley is famous for its beauty.

14 The polymath Sir Richard Burton (1821–1890) travelled widely in Asia and Africa and spoke twenty-nine languages. He was a controversial figure in his day. An early work was *Goa and the Blue Mountains* (1851).

15 Eric Newby's *A Short Walk in the Hindu Kush* (published in 1981 by Picador) attained cult status, especially because of the author's account of a meeting with Wilfrid Thesiger.

16 The giant Buddha statues of Bamiyan were destroyed by Afghanistan's Taliban in 2001 because they were thought to be 'offensive to Islam'. Museums and governments around the world had hoped to save the two Buddhas, the earliest of which was thought to have been carved into the sandstone cliffs of Bamiyan in the third century AD. At 53 metres (175 feet) and 36 metres (120 feet), the statues were the tallest standing Buddhas in the world.

17 Marco Polo (1254–1324) is probably the most famous European traveller on the Silk Road. He travelled through Asia for twenty-four years, and became a confidant of Kublai Khan (1214–1294). His account *The Description of the World* or *The Travels of Marco Polo* became one of the most popular books in medieval Europe, but was known as *Il Milione* (The Million Lies) because few believed that his stories were true.

18 www.world-tourism.org/projects/silkroad/silkroad

19 http://www.world-tourism.org/projects/silkroad/silkroad.html

20 *Narratives of the Embassy of Ruy Gonzales de Clavijo to the Court of Timur at Samarkhand*, trans. Clements Markham, 1859.

21 Przhevalsky, N. (1876), *Mongolia, The Tangut country and The Solitudes of Northern Tibet: Being the Narrative of Three Years Travel in Eastern High Asia*.

22 Hedin, S. (1926), *My Life as an Explorer*; Stein, M. A. (1912), *Ruins of Desert Cathay*.

23 Hopkirk, P. (1994), *The Great Game, The Struggle for Empire in Central Asia*, Longitude Books.

24 Mattheissen, P. (1978), *The Snow Leopard*, Penguin. This was written about an expedition to the Dolpo region of Nepal, now a developing trekking destination.

25 Shackley, M. (1993), The land of Lo Nepal/Tibet; the first 8 months of tourism, *Tourism Management*, **15(10)**, 17–26; Shackley, M. (1995), Lo revisited; the next 18 months, *Tourism Management*, **16(2)**, 78–81.

26 Hilton, J. (1988), *Lost Horizon*, Pocket Books. This book coined the idea of a mythical Shangri-La.

27 See www.kipling.org.uk

28 Needham, J. (1965), *Science and Civilization in China* (four volumes), Cambridge University Press.

29 Boniface, S. and Cooper, S. (2005), *Worldwide Destinations; The Geography of Travel and Tourism*, Elsevier.

30 http://www.world-tourism.org/regional/south_asia/states/japan/japan.htm

31 It seems likely that bird 'flu (avian influenza) is going to adversely affect travel to Asia in 2006–2007.

32 The scholar Claudius Ptolemaeus (Ptolemy), living in Alexandria, Egypt, created a series of maps around AD 150, some of which were saved by Arabian scholars and were rediscovered and reprinted in Europe in the fifteenth century. Ptolomy's maps show large parts of Europe, the Mediterranean Sea with Northern Africa, and large parts of Asia with great accuracy.

33 Mouhot, H. (1864), *Travels in the Central Parts of Indo-China*.

34 The film *Lara Croft: Tomb Raider* was released in 2001, and partly shot at Angkor Wat.

35 Sir Thomas Stamford Bingley Raffles founded Singapore. He was appointed Lieutenant Governor of Java in 1811, and promoted to Governor of Sumatra soon afterwards during the period in which Britain took administrative control of the Dutch colonies. During his governorship, Raffles stopped the slave trade, led an expedition to rediscover and restore the Borobudur temple, and rationalized the land-holding systems in the territories under his control.

36 http://www.thirdworldtraveler.com/Responsible_Travel/Burma_goornotgo.html

37 Severin, T. (2000), *The Spice Islands Voyage: The Quest for Alfred Wallace, the Man Who Shared Darwin's Discovery of Evolution*, Carroll & Graf Publishers.

38 William Somerset Maugham was a playright and novelist whose short stories often deal with the lives of British colonialists in the Far East. The most significant are *Rain, Footprints in the Jungle* and *The Outstation*. See also Morgan, T. (1980), *Somerset Maugham* (Jonathan Cape).

39 The film *Bridge on the River Kwai* was made in 1957, directed by David Lean and based on the real story of Allied prisoners of war forced by the Japanese to build the 258-mile Death Railway.

40 Smith, V. (1977), *Hosts and Guests; The Anthropology of Tourism*, University of Pennsylvania Press.

41 Yuill, S. M. (2003) *Dark Tourism: Understanding Visitor Motivation at Sites of Death and Disaster*, Texas A & M University.

42 The Vietnam War has generated many films, of which *The Deer Hunter* (1978) is usually thought to be the best.

Chapter 5: Europe: change and continuity

1 See Casson, L. (1974), *Travel in the Ancient World*, George Allen & Unwin.

2 http://www.europarl.org.uk/EU/textonly/txhistory.htm

3   Strabo, the Greek historian and geographer, is mostly remembered for his seventeen-volume work *Geographika*.

4   Julius Caesar, *De bello Gallico* (the Gallic Wars).

5   Riley-Smith, J. (2001), *The Oxford Illustrated History of the Crusades*, Oxford University Press.

6   Sumption, J. (2003), *The Age of Pilgrimage: The Medieval Journey to God*, HiddenSpring.

7   Elm, S. (1989), Perceptions of Jerusalem pilgrimage as reflected in two early sources on female pilgrimage (3rd and 4th centuries AD), *Studia Patristica*, **20**, 219–223; Holum, K. G. (1990), Hadrian and St. Helena: imperial travel and the origins of Christian Holy Land pilgrimage, *in* R. Ousterhout (ed.), *The Blessings of Pilgrimage*, Urbana; Hunt, E. D. (1982), *Holy Land Pilgrimage in the Later Roman Empire A.D. 312–460*, Clarendon Press.

8   Raju, A. (2003), *The Way of St James*, Cicerone Books.

9   Kendrick, T. (2004), *A History of the Vikings*, Dover Publications; Graham-Campbell, J. (2001), *Viking World*, Frances Lincoln Publishers.

10 Fletcher, R. (2004), *Moorish Spain*, Weidenfeld & Nicholson.

11 Steves, R. (2004), *Spain and Portugal 2004*, Avalon Travel Publishing, pp. 204–205.

12 The Age of Enlightenment refers to the eighteenth-century period characterized by the writings of philosophers such as Voltaire, Rousseau and Hume, attacking the existing institutions of both Church and State. At the same time there was a rise in interest in physical sciences and in empirical philosophy.

13 Hudson, S. (1999), *Snow Business: A Study of the International Ski Industry*, Thomson Learning.

14 http://www.unep.org/Documents.Multilingual/Default.asp?DocumentID=363& ArticleID=4313&l=en

15 The political economist and philosopher Adam Smith wrote *Inquiry into the Nature and Causes of the Wealth of Nations*, which examined the historical development of industry and commerce in Europe.

16 http://www.gapyeardirectory.co.uk/

17 Raleigh International is a charity (founded in 1984) committed to the personal growth and development of young people from all nationalities and backgrounds. Its overseas and UK programmes are designed to help young people develop skills and self-confidence in challenging environments beyond the classroom and workplace (http://www.raleighinternational.org/)

20 Williamson, A. (1998), *The Golden age of Travel*, Thomas Cook Publishing.

21 See Note 1.16.

22 *Murder on the Orient Express* (Hercule Poirot Mysteries), by Agatha Christie, was filmed in 1974 with an all-star cast.

23 Richmond, S. and Vorhees, M. (2002), *Trans-Siberian Railway*, Lonely Planet.

24 Laws, E. (1997), *Managing Package Holidays*, Thomson Learning.

25 Wood, C. (2004), *The Complete Guide to Budget Airline Destinations*, Aurum Press.

26 http://whc.unesco.org/

27 Martin, S. (2005), *Every Pilgrim's Guide to Lourdes*, Canterbury Press.

28 Bruges, see http://whc.unesco.org/

29 Holt, T. and Holt, V. (1999), *Major and Mrs. Holt's Battlefield Guide to Normandy Landing Beaches*, Pen and Sword Books Ltd; Lloyd, D. W. (1998), *Battlefield Tourism: Pilgrimage and the Commemoration of the Great War in Britain, Australia and Canada, 1919–1939*, Berg Publishers.

30 Taylor, A. J. (1986), *The Welsh Castles of Edward I*, Hambledon Continuum.

31 http://www.sustrans.co.uk

32 D'Arms, J. (1970) *Romans on the Bay of Naples*, Cambridge University Press.

33 The 'sassi' houses of Matera were added to the World Heritage List in 1993.

Chapter 6: North America: expansion and revolution

1 http://www.world-tourism.org/newsroom/Releases/2006/january/06_01_24.htm

2 Dulles, F. R. (1965), *America Learns to Play: A History of Recreation*, Appleton Century Crofts; Swarbrooke, J. (2002), *The Development and Management of Visitor Attractions* (2nd edn), Elsevier.

3 Ekirch, A. (1963), *Man and Nature in America*, University of Nebraska Press.

4 http://www.head-smashed-in.com/

5 *The Voyage of Saint Brendan (Navigatio sancti brendani abbatis)*, trans. J O'Meara, 1976; Severin, T. (1982), *The Brendan Voyage*, McGraw-Hill.

6 Kendrick, T. (2004), *A History of the Vikings*, Dover Publications; Graham-Campbell, J. (2001), *Viking World*, Frances Lincoln Publishers.

7 http://www.fitzgeraldsociety.org/ http://www.hamptons.com/

8 With more than 500 restored and reconstructed buildings spread across 301 acres of land, and a staff of 3500 archaeologists, researchers, historians and historical interpreters, Colonial Williamsburg is one of the world's leading historical reconstructions, visited by four million people each year (http://www.history.org/)

9 Brown, D. (1970), *Bury My Heart at Wounded Knee: An Indian History of the American West*, Owl Books. Beginning with the Long Walk of the Navajos in 1860 and ending thirty years later with the massacre of Sioux men, women and children at Wounded Knee in South Dakota, the book tells how the American Indians lost their land and lives to a dynamically expanding white society.

10 http://www.nativecasinos.com/

11 The American War of Independence was fought primarily between Great Britain and revolutionaries within the thirteen British colonies in North America. Boatner, M. M. III (1966, rev. 1974), *Encyclopedia of the American Revolution*, McKay.

12 George Washington was the first president of the USA, 1789–1797.

13 http://www.usgs.gov/features/lewisandclark.html

14 Rothman, H. K. (1989), *Preserving Different Pasts: The American National Monuments*, University of Illinois Press; Runte, A. (1997), *National Parks: The American Experience*

(3rd edn), University of Nebraska Press; Sutton, H. (1980), *Travelers; The American Tourist from Stagecoach to Space Shuttle*, William Morrow & Co.

15 Farmer, A. (2002), *The American Civil War 1861–65*, Hodder Murray.

16 The Statue of Liberty was reopened in August 2004, having been closed for security reasons since the terrorist attacks of 11 September 2001 (http://www.statueofliberty. org/).

17 http://www.renewnyc.com/News/mediaresources.asp

18 Mackintosh, B. (1991), *The National Parks: Shaping the System*, Washington: National Park Service.

19 Agg, T. R. (1920), *American Rural Highways*, McGraw Hill.

20 Belasco, W. (1970), *Americans on the Road: From Autocamp to Motel 1910–1945*, MIT Press.

21 Boniface, B. and Cooper, C. (2005) *Worldwide Destinations Casebook*, Elsevier, pp. 224–232; Farrell, B. H. (1982), *Hawaii; The Legend that Sells*, University of Hawaii Press.

22 Hertzog, G. B. Jr (1988), *Battling for the National Parks*, Moyer Bell; Jakle, J. (1985), *The Tourist; Travels in 20th Century North America*, University of Nebraska Press.

23 Sellars, R. W. (1997), *Preserving Nature in the National Parks: A History*, Yale University Press.

24 Rettie, D. F. (1995), *Our National Park System: Caring for America's Greatest Natural and Historic Treasures*, University of Illinois Press.

25 http://www. lvol.com

26 http://www.aspentimes.com/

27 Located in the central part of the peninsula of Baja California, the sanctuary contains some exceptionally interesting ecosystems. The coastal lagoons of Ojo de Liebre and San Ignacio are important reproduction and wintering sites for the grey whale, harbour seal, California sea lion, northern elephant-seal and blue whale. The lagoons are also home to four species of the endangered marine turtle. The Whale Sanctuary of El Vizcaino was added to the World Heritage list in 1993.

28 Shackley, M. (1998), Ninstints (Canadana). A deserted Haida village in Gwaii Hanaas National Park Reserve, Queen Charlotte Islands, in Shackley, M. (ed.), *Visitor Management*, pp. 182–193.

Chapter 7: South America and the Caribbean: Aztecs to Antarctica

1 The Lines and Geoglyphs of Nasca and Pampas de Jumana are located in the arid Peruvian coastal plain, some 400 kilometres south of Lima, and cover about 450 square kilometres. They were scratched on the surface of the ground between 500 BC and AD 500 and depict living creatures, stylized plants and imaginary beings, as well as geometric figures several kilometres long. http://www.htw-dresden.de/~nazca/Englisch/index.html

2 Bawden, G. (1997), *The Moche*, Blackwell Publishers; Kirkpatrick, S. (1992), *Lords of Sipan: A True Story of Pre-Inca Tombs, Archaeology, and Crime*, William Morrow & Co.

3 Hemming, J. (2004), *Conquest of the Incas*, Pan.

4 D'Altroy, T. (2003), *The Incas*, Blackwell Publishing.

5 Bingham, H. (2003), *Lost City of the Incas*, Weidenfeld & Nicholson. First published in the 1950s, this is a classic account of the discovery in 1911 of the lost city of Machu Picchu.

6 Danbury, R. (1999), *The Inca Trail: Cuzco & Machu Picchu*, Trailblazer Publications.

7 *Letters from Mexico*, trans. Hernan Cortes, Yale University Press, 2001.

8 Diaz del Castillo, B., *The Conquest of New Spain*, trans. J. M. Cohen, Penguin Classics; Pohol, J. and Hook, A. (2005), *Aztecs and Conquistadores: The Spanish Invasion and the Collapse of the Aztec Empire*, Osprey.

9 http://www.larutamayaonline.com/

10 Wood, M. (2002), *Conquistadors*, University of California Press.

11 Jesuit Missions of the Guaranis – San Ignacio Mini, Santa Ana, Nuestra Señora de Loreto and Santa Maria Mayor (Argentina), and the Ruins of Sao Miguel das Missoes (Brazil) – are inscribed on the World Heritage List (1983) on behalf of Argentina and Brazil. They are the impressive remains of five Jesuit missions, built in the land of the Guaranis during the seventeenth and eighteenth centuries. Each is characterized by a specific layout and a different state of conservation.

12 Iguacu National Park has one of the world's largest and most impressive waterfalls, extending over some 2700 metres. It is home to many rare and endangered species.

13 http://www.manausonline.com

14 The construction of the Transamazonia highway across Brazil started in 1970, but it is still unfinished. Many have grave concerns about its effect on the natural environment and indigenous people.

15 http://www.alternativetour.portais.net/Default.aspx?tabid=4426

16 Heyerdahl, T. (1993), *The Ra Expeditions*, Flamingo.

17 Darwin, C. (1997), *The Voyage of the 'Beagle'*, Wordsworth Editions Ltd.

18 Boniface, S. and Cooper, S. (2005), *Worldwide Destinations; The Geography of Travel and Tourism*, Elsevier, pp. 31–41.

19 Beletsky, L., Barrett, P. and Beadle, D. (2004), *Costa Rica*, Interlink Books.

20 http://www.monteverdecostarica.info/

21 Armstrong, J. (2000), *Shipwreck at the Bottom of the World: The Extraordinary True Story of Shackleton and the Endurance*, Alfred A. Knopf; Fiennes, R. (2005), *Race to the Pole: Tragedy, Heroism, and Scott's Antarctic Quest*, Hyperion Books; Shackleton, E. (1999), *South: The Endurance Expedition*, Penguin Books Ltd.

22 Bauer, T. G. (2001), *Tourism in the Antarctic: Opportunities, Constraints, and Future Prospects*, Haworth Press Inc.

23 http://news.bbc.co.uk/1/hi/sci/tech/1695897.stm

24 Rogozinski, J. (1994), *A Brief History of the Caribbean: From the Arawak and the Carib to the Present*, Plume.

25 Cummins, J. (1997), *Francis Drake: Lives of a Hero*, Palgrave Macmillan.

26 Higgins, T. (1989), *The Perfect Failure: Kennedy, Eisenhower, and the C.I.A. at the Bay of Pigs*, Norton & Co.

Chapter 8: Australia and the Pacific: outback and outriggers

1   Hall, C. M. (1994), *Tourism in the Pacific Rim*, Longmans; Harrison, D. (2003), *Pacific Island Tourism*, CABI.

2   http://www.deh.gov.au/parks/kakadu/

3   The Barossa Valley, thirty kilometres long by fourteen kilometres wide, is one of Australia's major wine-producing areas, with forty-five wineries producing about a quarter of Australia's total vintage. The region was settled by Silesian migrants who farmed the valley from the 1840s, along with British migrants and their descendants who grazed the adjacent hill country.

4   Shackley, M. (2004), Tourist consumption of sacred landscapes; space, time and vision, *Tourism Recreation Research*, **29(1)**, 273–280.

5   Macintyre, S. (2004), *A Concise History of Australia*, Cambridge University Press.

6   Sydney Opera House, opened in 1973, was designed by the Danish architect Jorn Utzon, and is one of the most recognizable images of the modern world.

7   The film *The Adventures of Priscilla, Queen of the Desert* was released in 1994.

8   Newsome, D., Dowling, R. K. and Moore, S. A. (2005), *Wildlife Tourism*, Channel View Publications.

9   The Daintree Rainforest, north of Cairns in tropical far north Queensland, is home to the largest range of plants and animals on Earth; all are found within an area spanning approximately 1200 square kilometres (http://www.daintreerainforest.com/).

10 The film version of J. R. R. Tolkein's *Lord of the Rings* trilogy emerged between 2001 and 2003, was directed by Peter Jackson, and is famous for its special effects and magnificent New Zealand landscapes. The original books were published in 1954, but have been re-issued in many different formats and were recently voted 'Book of the Century'.

11 Tongariro is New Zealand's oldest National Park and a dual natural/cultural World Heritage site which recognizes the park's important Maori cultural and spiritual associations as well as its outstanding volcanic features (http://www.doc.govt.nz/Explore/001~National-Parks/Tongariro-National-Park/index.asp).

12 Lewis, D. (1994), *We, the Navigators: Ancient Art of Landfinding in the Pacific*, University of Hawaii Press.

13 Shackley, M. (1998), Cultural tourism and world heritage designation on Easter Island, *in* C. Stevenson and G. Lee (eds), *Easter Island in its Pacific Context*, Occasional Papers Series 4, Easter Island Foundation, pp. 178–193.

14 Cook, J. (1771), *Observations made during a Voyage round the World on Physical Geography, Natural History and Ethnic Philosophy*.

15 Bligh, W. (reissued 2003), *The Mutiny on Board H.M.S. Bounty: The Captain's Account of the Mutiny and His 3,600 Mile Voyage in an Open Boat*, Narrative Press.

16 http://www.american.edu/TED/sandalwd.htm endangered sandalwood tree.

17   Forcible removal of Pacific islanders from their homes was known as 'blackbirding', and was a form of enforced slavery.

18   Oliver, D. (1973), *Bougainville: A Personal History*, Melbourne University Press.

19   Durfee, D. (2001), *Tattoo*, St Martin's Press.

20   Boniface, B. and Cooper, C. (2005) *Worldwide Destinations Casebook*, Elsevier, pp. 224–232; Farrell, B. H. (1982), *Hawaii; The Legend that Sells*, University of Hawaii Press.

21   See www.fijifrb.gov.fy

22   Four men convicted of multiple sex offences on the remote British colony of Pitcairn received jail sentences of between two and six years in 2004.

23   There is increasing concern about the cultural and environmental impact of golf course construction in Hawaii, as it entails clearing vegetation, cutting forests and creating artificial landscapes.

24   Berry, O. *Rarotonga and the Cook Islands*, Lonely Planet Publications.